Use of Plant Introductions in Cultivar Development
Part 2

Proceedings of a symposium sponsored by Division C-1 of the Crop Science Society of America in San Antonio, Texas, 23 Oct. 1990.

Editors
H. L. Shands and L. E. Weisner

Organizing Committee
H. L. Shands

Editor-in-Chief CSSA
P. S. Baenziger

Managing Editor
S. H. Mickelson

CSSA Special Publication Number 20

Crop Science Society of America, Inc.
Madison, Wisconsin, USA
1992

Cover Design: Patricia Scullion

Copyright © 1992 by the Crop Science Society of America, Inc.

ALL RIGHTS RESERVED UNDER THE U.S. COPYRIGHT ACT OF 1976 (P.L. 94-553)

Any and all uses beyond the limitations of the "fair use" provision of the law require written permission from the publisher(s) and/or the author(s); not applicable to contributions prepared by officers or employees of the U.S. Government as part of their official duties.

Crop Science Society of America, Inc.
677 South Segoe Road, Madison, WI 53711, USA

Library of Congress Cataloging-in-Publication Data
(Revised for vol. 2)

Use of plant introductions in cultivar development.

(CSSA special publication ; no. 17, 20)
Pt. 1, symposium held in Las Vegas, Nev., 19 Oct. 1989; pt. 2, held in San Antonio, Texas, 23 Oct. 1990.
Includes bibliographical references.
1. Plant introduction—United States—Congresses. 2. Plant breeding—United States—Congresses. 3. Crop improvement—United States—Congresses. 4. Crops—Germplasm resources—Congresses. 5. Plant varieties—United States—Congresses. I. Shands, H.L. (Henry L.). II. Wiesner, Loren E. III. Crop Science Society of America. Division C-1. IV. Series.
SB108.U5U83   1991   631.5'23   90-23887

ISBN 0-89118-528-3 (v. 1)
ISBN 0-89118-534-8 (v. 2)

Printed in the United States of America.

CONTENTS

Foreword vii
Preface ix
Contributors xi
Conversion Factors for SI and non-SI Units xiii

1 Use of Plant Introductions to Develop U.S. Bean Cultivars
    M. J. Silbernagel and R. M. Hannan 1

2 Use of Plant Introductions to Develop New Industrial Crop Cultivars
    A. E. Thompson, D. A. Dierig, and G. A. White 9

3 Use of Introduced Germplasm in Cool-Season Food Legume Cultivar Development
    F. J. Muehlbauer 51

4 Use of Plant Introductions in Peanut Improvement
    T. G. Isleib and J. C. Wynne 77

5 Use of Plant Introductions to Improve Populations and Hybrids of Sugarbeet
    R. T. Lewellen 117

6 Use of Plant Introductions in Sugarcane Cultivar Development
    J. D. Miller and P. Y. P. Tai 137

7 Introduced Germplasm Use in Sunflower Inbred and Hybrid Development
    J. F. Miller, G. J. Seiler, and C. C. Jan 151

FOREWORD

North America is home to only a few of our major food, feed, and fiber crops. The centers of origin or diversity of most crops important to U.S. agriculture occur on other continents, in countries whose geopolitical ideologies may contrast distinctly with those of our nation. The crops underpinning the U.S. agricultural sector are continually at risk from insects, diseases, and physical stress. The stability of the U.S. food system would be compromised without new sources of resistance to pests and stress, which would be a detriment to domestic consumers and our export customers abroad. Plant introductions, often discovered and collected by plant explorers in the remote and desolate primary and secondary centers of origin of major crops, are a principle lifeline of new genes for pest and stress resistance. Additionally, plant introductions are sources of new genes for nutritional quality, carbohydrate and oil content, fiber characteristics, and adaptation. This volume, the second of a two-part series, chronicles the importance of plant introductions to cultivar development of U.S. crops. In publishing this volume, we commemorate the members of the world community of crop scientists who have devoted their careers to collecting and maintaining plant introductions for the betterment of humankind.

Gary H. Heichel, *president*
Crop Science Society of America

PREFACE

Use of Plant Introductions in Cultivar Development, Part 1 presented review articles on barley, cotton, forage grasses, forage legumes, oat, rice, sorghum, soybean, and wheat from a symposium held during the annual meeting of the Crop Science Society of America in October 1989. A second symposium which was held at the CSSA annual meeting at San Antonio, TX in October 1990 included reviews on other crops of importance to U.S. agriculture: bean, food legumes, new crops, peanut, sugarbeet, sugarcane, and sunflower.

The second symposium was to hear and this publication to contain a paper on safflower by retired University of California oil crops breeder, Paul F. Knowles. His fight for life ended before either could occur. His plant collecting and use of plant introductions in transforming the wild, thorny *Carthamus* plant into a high-quality, productive species is without parallel and his contribution must be recognized as a true success story. This volume is dedicated to his memory with sincere recognition.

Along with the CSSA officers supporting this undertaking to recognize and document the use and value of plant introductions in American agriculture, the name of the Past President, V. L. Lechtenberg, must be added. This publication has been possible because of his support.

The timing of these two CSSA publications coincides with three significant events. First, the provisional C-8 Division on Crop Germplasm has been activated and held its first symposium in Denver, CO in October 1991. Second, the construction of the expanded seed storage and research facilities at the National Seed Storage Laboratory at Fort Collins, CO has been funded and is scheduled for completion in 1992. Third, the 1990 Farm Bill contained authorizing legislation for a National Genetic Resources Program modelled after the National Plant Germplasm System. The stalwart support by the membership and officers of the Crop Science Society of America should be recognized as having been instrumental in bringing about these advancements for plant genetic resources.

While words in the international fora continue to speak of national sovereignty in controlling access to plant genetic resources and difficulties continue on the availability front, CSSA plant germplasm scientists are participating in and contributing to international programs and projects with many developing nations. It is scientist-to-scientist interaction that builds trust and understanding between those in developing and developed nations. The proposed Fourth FAO International Technical Conference on Plant Genetic Resources for late 1993 or early 1994 will address the global needs for plant genetic resources by scientists. Hopefully, that conference will bring about a recognition of the resources at risk, the needs, and the required efforts to conserve and protect the genetic resources. Plant germplasm scientists need to bring all their efforts to bear to present the best science to the world.

Henry L. Shands, *co-editor*
USDA-ARS
Beltsville, Maryland

Loren E. Wiesner, *co-editor*
USDA-ARS
Colorado State University
Ft. Collins, Colorado

CONTRIBUTORS

D. A. Dierig	Research Geneticist, USDA-ARS, U.S. Water Conservation Laboratory, 4331 E. Broadway, Phoenix, AZ 85040
R. M. Hannan	Research Horticulturist, USDA-ARS, Plant Introduction, Washington State University, Pullman, WA 99164
T. G. Isleib	Associate Professor of Crop Science, Department of Crop Science, North Carolina State University, Raleigh, NC 27695-7629
C. C. Jan	Research Geneticist, USDA-ARS, Northern Crop Science Laboratory, Fargo, ND 58105
R. T. Lewellen	Research Geneticist, USDA-ARS, U.S. Agricultural Research Station, 1636 E. Alisal Street, Salinas, CA 93905
J. D. Miller	USDA-ARS, Sugarcane Field Station, Star Route Box 8, Canal Point, FL 33438
J. F. Miller	Research Geneticist, USDA-ARS, Northern Crop Science Laboratory, Fargo, ND 58105
F. J. Muehlbauer	Research Geneticist, USDA-ARS, Washington State University, Pullman, WA 99164-6421
G. J. Seiler	Research Botanist, USDA-ARS, Northern Crop Science Laboratory, Fargo, ND 58105
H. L. Shands	National Program Leader for Germplasm, USDA-ARS-NPS, Bldg. 005, BARC-West, Beltsville, MD 20705
M. J. Silbernagel	Research Plant Pathologist, USDA-ARS, IAREC, Prosser, WA 99350-9687
P. Y. P. Tai	USDA-ARS, Sugarcane Field Station, Star Route Box 8, Canal Point, FL 33438
A. E. Thompson	Research Geneticist, USDA-ARS, U.S. Water Conservation Laboratory, 4331 E. Broadway, Phoenix, AZ 85840
G. A. White	Agronomist and Plant Introduction Officer, USDA-ARS, Germplasm Services Laboratory, Bldg. 001, BARC-West, Beltsville, MD 20705
L. E. Wiesner	Research Leader, USDA-ARS, National Seed Storage Laboratory, Colorado State University, Ft. Collins, CO 80523
J. C. Wynne	Professor and Head of Crop Science, Department of Crop Science, North Carolina State University, Raleigh, NC 27695-7620

Conversion Factors for SI and non-SI Units

Conversion Factors for SI and non-SI Units

To convert Column 1 into Column 2, multiply by	Column 1 SI Unit	Column 2 non-SI Unit	To convert Column 2 into Column 1, multiply by
Length			
0.621	kilometer, km (10^3 m)	mile, mi	1.609
1.094	meter, m	yard, yd	0.914
3.28	meter, m	foot, ft	0.304
1.0	micrometer, μm (10^{-6} m)	micron, μ	1.0
3.94×10^{-2}	millimeter, mm (10^{-3} m)	inch, in	25.4
10	nanometer, nm (10^{-9} m)	Angstrom, Å	0.1
Area			
2.47	hectare, ha	acre	0.405
247	square kilometer, km^2 (10^3 m)^2	acre	4.05×10^{-3}
0.386	square kilometer, km^2 (10^3 m)^2	square mile, mi^2	2.590
2.47×10^{-4}	square meter, m^2	acre	4.05×10^3
10.76	square meter, m^2	square foot, ft^2	9.29×10^{-2}
1.55×10^{-3}	square millimeter, mm^2 (10^{-3} m)^2	square inch, in^2	645
Volume			
9.73×10^{-3}	cubic meter, m^3	acre-inch	102.8
35.3	cubic meter, m^3	cubic foot, ft^3	2.83×10^{-2}
6.10×10^4	cubic meter, m^3	cubic inch, in^3	1.64×10^{-5}
2.84×10^{-2}	liter, L (10^{-3} m^3)	bushel, bu	35.24
1.057	liter, L (10^{-3} m^3)	quart (liquid), qt	0.946
3.53×10^{-2}	liter, L (10^{-3} m^3)	cubic foot, ft^3	28.3
0.265	liter, L (10^{-3} m^3)	gallon	3.78
33.78	liter, L (10^{-3} m^3)	ounce (fluid), oz	2.96×10^{-2}
2.11	liter, L (10^{-3} m^3)	pint (fluid), pt	0.473

CONVERSION FACTORS FOR SI AND NON-SI UNITS

Mass

To convert Column 1 into Column 2, multiply by	Column 1 SI Unit	Column 2 non-SI Unit	To convert Column 2 into Column 1, multiply by
2.20×10^{-3}	gram, g (10^{-3} kg)	pound, lb	454
3.52×10^{-2}	gram, g (10^{-3} kg)	ounce (avdp), oz	28.4
2.205	kilogram, kg	pound, lb	0.454
0.01	kilogram, kg	quintal (metric), q	100
1.10×10^{-3}	kilogram, kg	ton (2000 lb), ton	907
1.102	megagram, Mg (tonne)	ton (U.S.), ton	0.907
1.102	tonne, t	ton (U.S.), ton	0.907

Yield and Rate

0.893	kilogram per hectare, kg ha^{-1}	pound per acre, lb acre^{-1}	1.12
7.77×10^{-2}	kilogram per cubic meter, kg m^{-3}	pound per bushel, bu^{-1}	12.87
1.49×10^{-2}	kilogram per hectare, kg ha^{-1}	bushel per acre, 60 lb	67.19
1.59×10^{-2}	kilogram per hectare, kg ha^{-1}	bushel per acre, 56 lb	62.71
1.86×10^{-2}	kilogram per hectare, kg ha^{-1}	bushel per acre, 48 lb	53.75
0.107	liter per hectare, L ha^{-1}	gallon per acre	9.35
893	tonnes per hectare, t ha^{-1}	pound per acre, lb acre^{-1}	1.12×10^{-3}
893	megagram per hectare, Mg ha^{-1}	pound per acre, lb acre^{-1}	1.12×10^{-3}
0.446	megagram per hectare, Mg ha^{-1}	ton (2000 lb) per acre, ton acre^{-1}	2.24
2.24	meter per second, m s^{-1}	mile per hour	0.447

Specific Surface

10	square meter per kilogram, m^2 kg^{-1}	square centimeter per gram, cm^2 g^{-1}	0.1
1000	square meter per kilogram, m^2 kg^{-1}	square millimeter per gram, mm^2 g^{-1}	0.001

Pressure

9.90	megapascal, MPa (10^6 Pa)	atmosphere	0.101
10	megapascal, MPa (10^6 Pa)	bar	0.1
1.00	megagram per cubic meter, Mg m^{-3}	gram per cubic centimeter, g cm^{-3}	1.00
2.09×10^{-2}	pascal, Pa	pound per square foot, lb ft^{-2}	47.9
1.45×10^{-4}	pascal, Pa	pound per square inch, lb in^{-2}	6.90×10^3

(continued on next page)

Conversion Factors for SI and non-SI Units

To convert Column 1 into Column 2, multiply by	Column 1 SI Unit	Column 2 non-SI Unit	To convert Column 2 into Column 1, multiply by
Temperature			
1.00 (K − 273)	Kelvin, K	Celsius, °C	1.00 (°C + 273)
(9/5 °C) + 32	Celsius, °C	Fahrenheit, °F	5/9 (°F − 32)
Energy, Work, Quantity of Heat			
9.52×10^{-4}	joule, J	British thermal unit, Btu	1.05×10^{3}
0.239	joule, J	calorie, cal	4.19
10^{7}	joule, J	erg	10^{-7}
0.735	joule, J	foot-pound	1.36
2.387×10^{-5}	joule per square meter, J m^{-2}	calorie per square centimeter (langley)	4.19×10^{4}
10^{5}	newton, N	dyne	10^{-5}
1.43×10^{-3}	watt per square meter, W m^{-2}	calorie per square centimeter minute (irradiance), cal cm^{-2} min^{-1}	698
Transpiration and Photosynthesis			
3.60×10^{-2}	milligram per square meter second, mg m^{-2} s^{-1}	gram per square decimeter hour, g dm^{-2} h^{-1}	27.8
5.56×10^{-3}	milligram (H$_2$O) per square meter second, mg m^{-2} s^{-1}	micromole (H$_2$O) per square centimeter second, μmol cm^{-2} s^{-1}	180
10^{-4}	milligram per square meter second, mg m^{-2} s^{-1}	milligram per square centimeter second, mg cm^{-2} s^{-1}	10^{4}
35.97	milligram per square meter second, mg m^{-2} s^{-1}	milligram per square decimeter hour, mg dm^{-2} h^{-1}	2.78×10^{-2}
Plane Angle			
57.3	radian, rad	degrees (angle), °	1.75×10^{-2}

CONVERSION FACTORS FOR SI AND NON-SI UNITS

Electrical Conductivity, Electricity, and Magnetism

To convert Column 1 into Column 2, multiply by	Column 1 SI Unit	Column 2 non-SI Unit	To convert Column 2 into Column 1, multiply by
10	siemen per meter, S m^{-1}	millimho per centimeter, mmho cm^{-1}	0.1
10^4	tesla, T	gauss, G	10^{-4}

Water Measurement

9.73 × 10^{-3}	cubic meter, m^3	acre-inches, acre-in	102.8
9.81 × 10^{-3}	cubic meter per hour, m^3 h^{-1}	cubic feet per second, ft^3 s^{-1}	101.9
4.40	cubic meter per hour, m^3 h^{-1}	U.S. gallons per minute, gal min^{-1}	0.227
8.11	hectare-meters, ha-m	acre-feet, acre-ft	0.123
97.28	hectare-meters, ha-m	acre-inches, acre-in	1.03 × 10^{-2}
8.1 × 10^{-2}	hectare-centimeters, ha-cm	acre-feet, acre-ft	12.33

Concentrations

1	centimole per kilogram, cmol kg^{-1} (ion exchange capacity)	milliequivalents per 100 grams, meq 100 g^{-1}	1
0.1	gram per kilogram, g kg^{-1}	percent, %	10
1	milligram per kilogram, mg kg^{-1}	parts per million, ppm	1

Radioactivity

2.7 × 10^{-11}	becquerel, Bq	curie, Ci	3.7 × 10^{10}
2.7 × 10^{-2}	becquerel per kilogram, Bq kg^{-1}	picocurie per gram, pCi g^{-1}	37
100	gray, Gy (absorbed dose)	rad, rd	0.01
100	sievert, Sv (equivalent dose)	rem (roentgen equivalent man)	0.01

Plant Nutrient Conversion

	Elemental	Oxide	
2.29	P	P$_2$O$_5$	0.437
1.20	K	K$_2$O	0.830
1.39	Ca	CaO	0.715
1.66	Mg	MgO	0.602

1 Use of Plant Introductions to Develop U.S. Bean Cultivars

M. J. Silbernagel

USDA-ARS
Washington State University-Irrigated Agric. Res. and Ext. Ctr.
Prosser, Washington

R. M. Hannan

USDA-ARS, Washington State University
Pullman, Washington

Common bean (*Phaseolus vulgaris* L.) is one of the world's most important food legumes, especially in developing countries where it is often a primary source of dietary protein. Annual world dry bean production is more than 8.5 Tg (million tonne), of which the USA produces about 1.0 Tg. More than 40%, or 311 000 t yr^{-1}, of the U.S. production is exported, the rest is consumed domestically at the rate of about 2.5 kg capita^{-1} (Pachico, 1989).

Dry beans in the USA are planted on approximately 607 000 ha, and average yields range from 1400 kg ha^{-1} under midwestern rainfed conditions to about 2500 kg ha^{-1} under northwestern irrigated conditions. Dry beans have a farmgate value of between $350 and $700 million depending on the season and availability of export markets (Kelly, 1990).

Snap beans for processing in the USA are planted on approximately 89 000 ha, and are valued at $110 million annually. The fresh-market crop is planted on about 32 000 ha, with an estimated annual value of $80 million (Kelly, 1990).

Unlike soybean [*Glycine max* (L.) Merr.], wheat (*Triticum aestivum* L.), and corn (*Zea mays* L.), which have enjoyed steadily increasing yields over the past 30 yr, bean yields have been relatively static for several decades. Although many reasons have been postulated for the failure of bean to break the so-called "yield barrier," one of the most frequently suspected causes is lack of adequate genetic diversity in the background of commercial cultivars (Silbernagel & Hannan, 1988). For about 30 yr, U.S. bean breeders have used a relatively narrow germplasm base (Zaumeyer, 1972).

Lack of genetic diversity also can be a factor in the vulnerability of crops to diseases, insects, or environmental stresses. Public concern about the dangers of genetic vulnerability in our commercial crops peaked in the early

---

Copyright © 1992 Crop Science Society of America, 677 S. Segoe Rd., Madison, WI 53711, USA. *Use of Plant Introductions in Cultivar Development, Part 2,* CSSA Special Publication no. 20.

1970s as a result of a corn disease epidemic that swept the U.S. Corn Belt. Since then, most breeders and research directors have promoted the merits of broadening the genetic base of crops. Increasing genetic diversity of a crop is desirable for several reasons, in addition to avoiding disastrous crop losses. In the case of common bean, genetic diversity also may be the key to increasing (and stabilizing) the yield potential of the crop (Silbernagel & Hannan, 1988).

The passage of the 1970 Plant Variety Protection Act (PVPA) was expected to stimulate efforts to broaden the genetic base of commercial bean cultivars. Since legal plant variety protection is based on novelty or uniqueness, it was thought that some of this uniqueness might be derived from exotic germplasms.

The need for genetic diversity and the enactment of PVPA have not stimulated the utilization of the *Phaseolus* collection of more than 11 000 accessions, which is maintained by the USDA-ARS Western Regional Plant Introduction Station located at Washington State Univ., Pullman.

Scientific literature over the past 20 yr involving introduced bean germplasm (Silbernagel & Hannan, 1988) indicates that extensive contributions have been made by the academic community concerning characteristics thought to be useful in new commercial cultivars. However, of approximately 200 commercial bean cultivars that have been grown in the USA, only about 50 (which includes nine Canadian navy cultivars grown for seed in the USA) trace their parentage to exotic germplasm; most of these cultivars were released during the past 10 yr. Most successful commercial cultivars are from crosses among commercial cultivars. This trend is changing slowly because of the tremendous output of time and effort required to bridge the gap between new academic information (and germplasn) and commercial production of a new cultivar.

Advancement for scientists in the public sector is based primarily on publishing original research data, so most researchers only describe a new discovery. Subsequent breeding work (if any) to transfer a potentially useful character is then usually done by public breeders who release improved germplasm, sometimes, or finished cultivars. This process may take 7 to 15 yr, although the increasing availability of winter nurseries in Puerto Rico or Mexico is shortening this development period. Private breeders cannot afford the time and resources required to work with wild germplasm, so they hybridize the public germplasm releases with new characters to commercial cultivars. Then they need another 10± yr before they can incorporate the new character into cultivars that are agronomically and horticulturally superior to become commercial cultivars.

Recently, public breeding programs have been relegated to a lower priority status, and positions focused on breeding, especially cultivar development, have been dropped. The gap between the identification of useful characters in exotic germplasm and the transfer of these potentially useful characters to cultivars has widened. It is economically prohibitive for private companies to commit the time and expense on cultivar development incorporating exotic germplasm in such a minor crop as common bean, and there is no longer much career incentive for public scientists to perform this work. Therefore, the gap ever widens.

COMMERCIAL CULTIVARS WITH EXOTIC GERMPLASM PARENTAGE

Significant contributions have been made, however using exotic germplasm to overcome important regional disease problems. Based on extensive reviews by McClean and Myers (1990) and Silbernagel and Hannan (1988), a summary of characteristics and exotic germplasm sources that were used to develop some of the currently available commercial cultivars are shown in Table 1-1. Coyne and colleagues, Univ. of Nebraska, have produced a series of Great Northern cultivars with common bacterial blight [*Xanthomonas phaseoli* (Erw. Smith) Dowson] resistance from *Phaseolus acutifolius* (tepary) and bacterial wilt [*Corynebacterium flaccumfaciens* ssp. *flaccumfaciens* (Hedges) Dows.] resistance from PI 165078 (Coyne & Schuster, 1983). Burke, USDA-ARS, Prosser, WA (1990, personal communication), developed a series of pink, pinto, and small red dry bean with resistance to root rot [*Fusarium solani* f. sp. *phaseoli* (Burkholder) Snyder & Hans] from PI 203958. Kelly and Adams (1990, personal communications), Michigan State Univ., have released some upright, indeterminate navy, black, and pinto cultivars whose pedigrees include tropical germplasm (Jamapa = PI 268110 and NEP-2 = PI 372353); and Sandsted (1990, personal communications), Cornell Univ., has released some upright Black Turtle types with tropical parentage obtained through the International Center for Tropical Agriculture (CIAT) in Cali, Colombia. The upright habit, for which NEP-2 and other tropical beans were used extensively, is particularly well adapted to planting higher population densities in narrow rows, which may lead to consistent yield gains. Upright cultivars also make direct mechanical harvest feasible in more areas, resulting in better seed quality.

Considerable use has been made of the *Are* gene found in a Venezuelan line, Cornell 49-242 (PI 326418), which conditions resistance to six races of anthracnose [*Colletotrichum lindemuthianum* (Sacc. & Magn.) Scrib.] (Mastenbrook, 1960). Several navy bean cultivars used primarily in Canada and many European snap bean have *Are* gene resistance. Since anthracnose is controlled in the USA primarily with a clean seed program, where breeder and foundation seed is produced in the semiarid western states, there has been no great urgency to incorporate genetic resistance to anthracnose. Many seed bean crops produced in the USA for export to Canada and Europe, however, may carry the *Are* gene resistance.

Halo blight [*Pseudomonas syringae* pv. *phaseolicola* (Burkholder)] (Young et al., 1978) resistance from PI 150414, first described in Wisconsin (Patel & Walker, 1966) has not been used as extensively in the USA as in Europe for the same reasons stated above in regard to anthracnose resistance. Until recently, most U.S. seed companies chose to rely upon clean seed production in the western states rather than develop genetically resistant cul-

Table 1-1. Commercial bean cultivars with genetic characteristics derived from introduced germplasm.

Type and cultivar	Characteristic†	Origin of characteristic	Release
Black			
Blackhawk	Uprt, anthrac. res.	C49–242 (PI 326418)	1989
Black Magic	Uprt	Nep-2 (PI 372353)	1982
Domino	Uprt	Nep-2 (PI 372353)	1982
Midnight	Uprt	CIAT	1982
UI–906	Uprt, *F. sol* res.	PI 209621	1989
Small White Navy			
Agri-I	Anthrac, res.	PI326418	1987
Aurora	Uprt, anthrac. res.	PI 326418	1973
Bunsi/ExRico 23	Uprt, white mold	CIAT	1983/84?
C-20	Uprt, rust res.	Jamapa (PI 268110), Nep-2	1984
Centralia	Anthrac. res.	ExRico 23 BC6ARE, PI 326418	1988
Crestwood	Anthrac. res.	ExRico 23 BC6ARE, PI 326418	1985
Dresden	Anthrac. res.	PI 326418	1986
Harrofleet	Anthrac. res.	PI 326418	1984
Harrokent	Anthrac. res.	PI 326418	1984
Laker	Uprt	ICA-Pijao, Nep-2	1984
Mayflower	Uprt	Nep-2, Arroyo Loro	1988
OAC Rico	Uprt, anthrac. res.	ExRico 23, PI 326418	1984
OAC Seaforth	Uprt, anthrac. res.	PI 326418	1983
Sanilac BC6-Are	Anthrac res.	PI 326418	1983
Sanitas	Anthrac. res.	PI 326418	?
Sm White UI-76	Multiple pods	PI 282057	1976
Swan Valley	Uprt	Nep-2	1984/85?
Pinto			
Holberg	*F. solani* res.	PI 203958	1982
Nodak	*F. solani* res.	PI 203958	1984
NW-590	*F. solani* res.	PI 203958	1980
Othello	*F. solani* res.	PI 203958	1986
Pindak	*F. solani* res.	PI 203958	1981
Sierra	Uprt, rust res.	CIAT, Nep 2	1989
UI 196-2	*F. solani* res.	PI 203958	1989
Great Northern			
Emerson	BW res.	PI 165078	1971
GN 1	CB res.	*P. acutifolius*	1956
Harris	CB res.	Valley	1980
Jules	CB res.	GN 1 sel 27	1969
Star	CB, BW res.	GN 1 sel 27, PI 165078	1976
Starlight	CB, white seed, rust	GN 1 sel 27, Bulgarian white	1990
Tara	CB res.	GN 1 sel 27	1969
Valley	CB res.	GN 1 sel 27	1974
Pink			
Gloria	*F. solani* res.	PI 203958	1974
Roza	*F. solani* res.	PI 203958	1974
Victor	*F. solani* res.	PI 203958	1983
Viva	*F. solani* res.	PI 203958	1974
Small Red			
Big Bend	*F. solani* res.	Liberino	1966

(continued on next page)

Table 1-1. Continued.

Type and cultivar	Characteristic†	Origin of characteristic	Release
NW-59	*F. solani* res.	PI 203958	1980
NW-63	*F. solani* res.	PI 203958	1980
Rufus	*F. solani* res.	PI 203958	1974
Red Kidney			
Kardinal	*F. solani* res.	PI 203958	1986
UI 722	BCMV res.	PI 226856	1989
Yellow Eye			
ARE-Stuben	Anthrac res.	PI 326418	1987
Snap Bean			
Acclaim	HB res.	PI 150414	1988
Applause	HB res.	PI 150414	1987
Brigadeer	HB, anthrac res.	PI 150414, PI 326418	1988
Crest	HB res.	PI 150414	1991
Crusader/Century	HB, anthrac. res.	PI 150414, PI 326418	1988
Envey	Brown spot res.	Wisc 713938	1991
Espada	HB, anthrac. res.	PI 150414, PI 326418	1991
Flo	Anthrac. res.	PI 326418	1982
FM 343	Brown spot res.	Wisc 713938	1991
Goldmine	HB res.	PI 150414	1991
Labrador	Anthrac. res.	PI 326418	1986
Stiletto	Rust tol.	Redlands Greenleaf C	1986
Tess	Anthrac. res.	PI 326418	1987

† Only primary characteristic for which introduced germplasm source was used. Abbreviations: Uprt = upright habit, res. = resistance, BW = bacterial wilt, CB = common blight, HB = halo blight, anthrac. = anthracnose, tol. = tolerance.
Part of the information in this table was taken from McClean and Myers (1990).

tivars. Genes for disease resistance are now being incorporated into the older cultivars (seven in the last 4 yr), rather than relying solely on clean seed production.

CURRENT ACTIVITIES

The recessive *bc*-3 gene in breeding line IVT 7214, found by Drijfhout (1978) in PI 181954, confers resistance to all known strains of bean common mosaic virus (BCMV). It has been used extensively in Europe where the unprotected dominant I gene confers resistance (Ali, 1950) that is subject to severe lethal systemic necrosis when infection occurs by certain new strains of BCMV. These temperature insensitive, necrosis-inducing strains of BCMV have recently been found in the USA and Canada (Provvidenti, 1984; Kelly et al., 1983; Myers et al., 1990; Hampton et al., 1983; Tu, 1986). Many breeders are actively trying to incorporate the *bc*-3 gene (as well as recessive *bc*-2^2 gene) into U.S. cultivars.

Stavely, USDA-ARS, Beltsville, MD (1990, personal communications), has released a series of 26 snap bean and four dry bean germplasm lines with multiple gene resistance to all available races of the bean rust fungus

Uromyces appendiculatus (Pers.) Unger var. *appendiculatus* [syn. *U. phaseoli* (Reben) Wint.]. Most lines obtained resistance genes from sources introduced from Mexico (Mex 309 and Mex 235) and Guatemala (Compuesto Negro Chimaltenango). More recent sources of multiple rust resistances include PI's 151385, 151388, 151395, and 181996. Some of these germplasm releases may result in commercial cultivars through selection. However, some breeders are using these germplasm lines as parental to develop proprietary cultivars. Freytag et al. (1985) also released two rust-resistant navy lines in Puerto Rico that were developed from introduced germplasm.

Steadman and Coyne, Univ. of Nebraska, Lincoln, and Beaver, Univ. of Puerto Rico, Mayaguez, are working on nonrace specific rust resistance resulting from long dense pubescence (Mmbaga & Steadman, 1990). This form of apparently "horizontal" resistance was found in Pomadour bean landraces from the Dominican Republic and is being transferred to U.S. cultivars as part of a Collaborative Research Support Program (CRSP) between UN-UPR-Honduras and the Dominican Republic. Bliss et al. (1989) used a Brazilian black bean 'Rio Tibagi' as a source of higher rates of biological N_2 fixation. This characteristic is being used by numerous breeders.

Nine bean CRSP projects between U.S. land grant universities and developing county programs in the tropics are supported by USAID Title XII legislation. These programs are generating a flood of new scientific information with an array of useful new genetic characteristics from introduced germplasm, which should generate many improved cultivars for the USA in the coming decades.

As an example, a very upright, strong-stemmed, indeterminate breeding line, A-55, from CIAT in Cali, Colombia, was found by Silbernagel (Washington State Univ./Tanzanian CRSP) to be more resistant to root rots incited by *Fusarium solani* f. sp. *phaseoli, Pythium ultimum* Trow, *Aphanomyces euteiches* Drechs. f. sp. *phaseoli* (Pfender & Hagedorn), and *Fusarium oxysporum* Schlecht. f. sp. *phaseoli* Kendrick & Snyder than any current U.S. cultivars. The upright habit will be useful in developing direct harvestable dry bean cultivars, since most U.S. cultivars have a sprawling, decumbent vine habit. A-55 also is resistant to BCMV and has tolerance to white mold [*Sclerotinia sclerotiorum* (Lib.) de Bary] and tolerance to curly top virus.

Dickson, New York State Agric. Exp. Stn., Geneva (1990, personal communications), has produced a series of germplasm releases with resistance to root rots, white mold, and grey mold (*Botrytis cinerea* Pers. ex Fries). These characteristics are being incorporated into many public and private breeding programs.

FUTURE PROSPECTS

It is evident that public breeding programs (USDA-Nebraska-Michigan-New York) with responsibilities to produce commercially acceptable germplasm or cultivars for specific regional needs have been the primary users of exotic bean germplasm. Public breeders in other states like North Dakota, Idaho, Colorado, and California are also now using many of the same sources of introduced germplasm. Recently, many private companies also are using these releases if they are close to commercial type and contribute characters of economic significance. Many public programs have traditionally had strong support from local grower organizations. Ironically, these are the public programs currently suffering serious reductions in institutional support. Conventional breeding programs are currently out of favor while laboratory-oriented genetic engineering projects are more strongly supported (Kalton et al., 1989). Molecular level genetic research can provide "man-made" genes that may be patentable. Whereas, natural genes found in a public repository are not. Serious assessment is needed to determine what is available in natural genetic stocks and whether natural or man-made genes are better suited to solve each specific problem. Is the Plant Introduction bean collection destined to become a museum, or can ways be found to continue to explore this collection for the characteristics needed to keep our future commercial bean cultivars competitive nationally and internationally?

The linkages and networking among various segments of public organizations and the private sector in bean research are excellent (i.e., the *Phaseolus* Crop Advisory Committee, the USDA-ARS Germplasm Research Information Network (GRIN), CIAT, Bean CRSP Programs, and the W-150 Project, "Genetic Improvement of Beans (*Phaseolus vulgaris* L.) for Yield, Pest Resistance, and Food Value," which is sponsored by the Western State Experiment Station Director's Assoc.). These groups all meet at the biannual meetings of the Bean Improvement Cooperative (BIC), for the informal exchange of information and germplasm. The BIC meetings provide a forum for extensive communication with all aspects of the private bean sector (breeding, research, seed production, processing, and marketing).

What is needed now is a new overall approach to integrated collaborative team research that formally links the public and private sectors in a yet more mutually beneficial way. This would ensure the public generation of new scientific information, as well as accelerate the production of commercially successful cultivars derived from exotic germplasm sources. Private funding support for public sector research might be more forthcoming if the private sector could obtain marketing rights to public cultivars and the royalties could then provide needed support for ongoing public research. If this concept of joint ventures between public universities and the electronics industries works well in the Silicon Valley, scientists and administrators should consider a similar joint planning and funding approach to bean improvement research.

Such an activity might be coordinated through the Association of the State Agricultural Experiment Station Directors, perhaps in collaboration with the National Board for Plant Genetics Resources (NBPGR). In the April 1990 issue of the USDA publication *Agricultural Research*, Director R.D. Plowman, Administrator of the Agricultural Research Service, cites the need for the enhancement of technology transfer from public agencies like ARS, through the use of Cooperative Research and Development Agreements. So it appears the stage is being set for a new era of public-private collaboration that will help keep the U.S. bean industry viable and internationally competitive.

REFERENCES

Ali, M.A. 1950. Genetics of resistance to the common bean (bean virus 1) in the bean (*Phaseolus vulgaris* L.). Phytopathology 40:69-79.

Bliss, F.A., P.A.A. Pereira, R.S. Araujo, R.A. Henson, K.A. Kmiecik, J.R. McFerson, M.G. Teixeira, and C.C. DaSilva. 1989. Registration of five high nitrogen fixing common bean germplasm lines. Crop Sci. 29:240-241.

Coyne, D.P., and M.L. Schuster. 1983. Genetics of and breeding for resistance to bacterial pathogens in vegetable crops. HortScience 18(1):30-36.

Drijfhout, E. 1978. Genetic interaction between *Phaseolus vulgaris* and bean common mosaic virus with implications for strain identification and breeding for resistance. Centre for Agricultural Publishing and Documentation, Wageningen, Netherlands.

Freytag, G.F., J.D. Kelly, M.W. Adams, J. Lopez Rosa, J. Beaver, and R. Echavez Badel. 1985. Registration of two navy bean germplasm lines L226-10 and L227-1. Crop Sci. 25:714.

Hampton, R.O., M.J. Silbernagel, and D.W. Burke. 1983. Bean common mosaic virus strains associated with bean mosaic epidemics in the northwestern United States. Plant Dis. 67:658-661.

Kalton, R.R., P.A. Richardson, and N.M. Frey. 1989. Inputs in private sector plant breeding and biotechnology research programs in the United States. Diversity 50(4):22-25.

Kelly, J.D. 1990. Phaseolus Crop Advisory Committee Report—1989 Update. Bean Improv. Coop. 33:xi-xxiv.

Kelly, J.D., A.W. Saettler, and M. Morales. 1983. New necrotic strain of bean common mosaic virus in Michigan. Bean Improv. Coop. 26:49-50.

Mastenbrook, C. 1960. A breeding programme for resistance to Anthracnose in dry shell haricot beans, based on a new gene. Euphytica 9:177-184.

McClean, P., and J.R. Myers. 1990. Pedigrees of dry bean cultivars, lines, and PIs. Bean Improv. Coop. 33:xxv-xxx.

Mmbaga, M.T., and J.R. Steadman. 1990. Adult plant rust resistance and leaf pubescence on dry beans. Bean Improv. Coop. 33:61-62.

Myers, J.R., R.L. Forster, M.J. Silbernagel, and G.I. Mink. 1990. The 1989 bean common mosaic virus epidemic in Idaho. Bean Improv. Coop. 33:169-170.

Pachico, D. 1989. Trends in world common bean production. p. 1-8. *In* H.F. Schwartz and M.A. Pastor-Coralles (ed.) Bean production problems in the tropics. 2nd ed. Centro Int. de Agric. Trop. (CIAT), Cali, Colombia.

Patel, P.N., and J.C. Walker. 1966. Inheritance of tolerance to halo blight in bean. Phytopathology 56:681-682.

Plowman, R.D. 1990. Technology transfer makes business sense. Agric. Res. 38(4):2.

Provvidenti, R. 1984. Local epidemic of NL-8 strain of bean common mosaic virus in bean fields of western New York. Plant Dis. 68:1092-1094.

Silbernagel, M.J., and R.M. Hannan. 1988. Utilization of genetic resources in the development of commercial bean cultivars in the U.S.A. p. 561-596. *In* P. Gepts (ed.) Genetic resources of Phaseolus beans. Kluwer Academic Publ., Boston.

Tu, J.C. 1986. Occurrence of a necrotic (NL-8) strain of bean common mosaic virus in Ontario, Canada. Plant Dis. 70:694 (Abstr.).

Young, J.M., D.W. Dye, J.F. Bradbury, G.G. Panagopoulos, and C.F. Robbs. 1978. A proposed nomenclature and classification for plant pathogenic bacteria. N.Z.J. Agric. Res. 21:153-177.

Zaumeyer, W.J. 1972. Dry beans and snap beans. p. 224. *In* Genetic vulnerability of major crops. Nat. Acad. of Sci., Washington, DC.

2 Use of Plant Introductions To Develop New Industrial Crop Cultivars

A. E. Thompson and D. A. Dierig
USDA-ARS
Phoenix, Arizona

G. A. White
USDA-ARS
Beltsville, Maryland

Diverse germplasm for evaluation, enhancement, and utilization in the development of new industrial crop cultivars is absolutely necessary, perhaps to even a greater extent than with traditional crops. Industrial crops provide a wide array of renewable resources for natural rubber, oils with unique fatty acids, lubricants, fuels, alcohols, waxes, resins, gums, plastics, paints, adhesives, coatings, fibers, newsprint and other papers, essential oils, flavors, fragrances, cosmetics, biologically active materials, and pharmaceuticals.

Much has been written recently on the process of developing new crops and the obvious potential for and merits of new or alternative crop development. Knowles et al. (1984) provide the best available publication that thoroughly discusses the needs, procedures, strategies, constraints, and options for developing new crops. Two excellent reports by Theisen et al. (1978) and Knox and Theisen (1981) provided useful information and developed methodology to evaluate the Production-Marketing (including processing)-Consumption System (PMC), which is basic to successful new crop development.

In 1984, former Secretary of Agriculture John Block set in motion a significant activity by forming a New Farm and Forest Products Task Force. The Task Force brought together representatives from industry, government, and academia, and produced an excellent report (Sampson, 1987). Prominent among the conclusions was the idea that developing new crops to meet real market needs, particularly industrial uses, offered truly significant opportunities. A new crop is one that provides the producer an alternative. Thompson (1988b), in reference to developing strategies for alternative crop development, discussed alternative crop opportunities and constraints on de-

---

Copyright © 1992 Crop Science Society of America, 677 S. Segoe Rd., Madison, WI 53711, USA. *Use of Plant Introductions in Cultivar Development, Part 2*, CSSA Special Publication no. 20.

velopmental efforts. Thompson (1985, 1988b, 1990a) graphically presented a generalized system for new crop research and development, which is closely related to, and a natural extension of the plant germplasm research and development system.

The U.S. Department of Agriculture, Cooperative State Research Service, Special Projects and Program Systems (USDA-CSRS-SPPS) Office of Agricultural Materials (formerly Office of Critical Materials) provides major focus and coordination for industrial new crops development. This office, the objectives and activity of which were well described by Wheaton (1984, 1990), has its roots in the Native Latex Commercialization Act of 1978. At about the same time, the National Academy of Science (NAS) (1975) published an excellent report that called attention to an array of underexploited tropical plants with promising economic value. Many of these plants have potential as industrial raw material sources as well as for food production. The new FY 1990 Farm Bill has for the first time included provisions for authorizing and funding research, development, and commercialization of agricultural industrial products (Subtitle G. "Alternative Agricultural Research and Commercialization"). This authorization should have a significant, positive impact on developing new industrial crop cultivars.

Many candidate species have been evaluated for domestication as new industrial crops with varying degrees of success. Those that have received major attention are guayule (*Parthenium argentatum* A. Gray), kenaf (*Hibiscus cannabinus* L.) and roselle (*H. sabdariffa* L.), guar [*Cyamopsis tetragonoloba* (L.) Taubert], grindelia (*Grindelia camporum* Greene), jojoba [*Simmondsia chinensis* (Link) C. Schneider], meadowfoam (*Limnanthes alba* Hartweg ex Benth.), crambe (*Crambe abyssinica* Hochst. ex R.E. Fries), and industrial rapeseed (*Brassica napus* L., *B. rapa* L.), buffalo gourd (*Cucurbita foetidissima* HBK), cuphea (*Cuphea* spp.), vernonia [*Vernonia galamensis* (Cass.) Less.], and Stokes aster [*Stokesia laevis* (Hill) E. Greene]. Many of the historic and current research activities on these species was initiated in 1957 by the USDA, Agricultural Research Service (ARS). More than 8000 plant species were chemically screened over a 20-yr period by the USDA-ARS National Center for Agricultural Utilization Research (NCAUR), formerly the Northern Regional Research Center (NRRC) at Peoria, IL. This research and its potential for developing new industrial crops have been well summarized (Princen, 1977, 1979, 1982, 1983; Princen & Rothfus, 1984). More than 75 new fatty acids and 40 other plant chemicals were discovered in this plant-screening effort.

In the 1970s, research activities of NCUAR and others were directed toward screening and evaluating plant species for chemicals that complement the use or substitute for petroleum-derived substances (Buchanan & Otey, 1979; Buchanan & Duke, 1981; Hoffmann, 1983, 1985; McLaughlin, 1985; McLaughlin & Hoffmann, 1982; McLaughlin et al., 1983; Roth et al., 1982). Such industrial-type feed stocks are frequently referred to as botanochemicals or energy crops. Currently, little domestication effort is being directed on energy crops, but worldwide political and economic conditions may necessitate renewed research into this area. Buchanan and Duke (1981) estimated the annual dependence of the USA on imported botanochemicals to be valued at well over $1 billion. At present, this must be a significant underestimate since annual importation cost of natural rubber alone is about $1 billion. It is further estimated that <3% of the total number of plant species have been evaluated, even in a cursory manner. It is difficult to predict how many other desirable constituents important to humanity could be found if adequate germplasm collection and evaluation were initiated and fully pursued.

Extensive reviews on the potential and progress being made on developing new industrial crops have been published by Foster et al. (1983); Hinman (1984, 1986); Kleiman (1990); Knapp (1990b); and Thompson (1985, 1990a,b). White (1977) discussed the development of many potentially new industrial crops and stressed the importance of plant introductions. Shands and White (1990) recently discussed the role of the National Plant Germplasm System (NPGS) in new crop development and the germplasm status of selected new industrial crop species. The objective of this chapter is to elaborate on the status of development, and to document the usage of plant introductions in creating new industrial crop cultivars.

To facilitate this review and compilation, the Germplasm Resources Information Network (GRIN) database of NPGS was thoroughly accessed to determine the current status of species accessions available for and involved in new industrial crop cultivar development. Many germplasm curators and plant breeders in the federal, state, and private sectors have been most helpful in providing and verifying information. Our thanks is given to them, since without their help, the project would have been extremely difficult to complete.

Each of the potentially new industrial crops, including: guayule for natural rubber and resin; kenaf and roselle for fiber, newsprint, and other paper; guar for galactomannan gum; grindelia for diterpene resins; jojoba for long straight-chain liquid wax (wax ester); meadowfoam for long-chain fatty acids; crambe and industrial rapeseed for high erucic fatty acid; buffalo and coyote gourd (*Cucurbita digitata* Gray) for edible oil and protein, starch, and cucurbitacins; cuphea for lauric acid and other medium-chain fatty acids; lesquerella [*Lesquerella fendleri* (Gray) Wats.] for hydroxy fatty acids; and vernonia and Stokes aster for epoxy fatty acids are discussed separately in following sections. A brief history on the development of specific new industrial crops is given and documented with exhaustive coverage of published references relating to germplasm resources, evaluation, enhancement, and utilization in the breeding, selection, and release of improved germplasm lines and cultivars.

GUAYULE (ASTERACEAE)

Guayule produces natural rubber that is comparable in quality to that of the rubber tree (*Hevea brasiliensis*). The small, woody perennial shrub, native to the Chihuahuan desert region of north-central Mexico and southwest Texas, is now the subject of a major commercialization effort. Importation of natural rubber into the USA currently costs about $1 billion, a significant factor in the existing unfavorable trade balance of the country.

Commercial utilization of guayule from natural plant stands dates back to the late 1880s. Domestication and development of the first guayule cultivar, 593, was initiated in 1910 (McCallum, 1941). In 1942, the Emergency Rubber Project, an intense research and development effort, was initiated to domesticate and develop guayule as an alternative rubber crop during World War II. Unfortunately, the program was abruptly terminated in 1946, but the USDA-ARS breeding program was continued until 1959 at a minimal level. Hammond and Polhamus (1965) published a comprehensive summary of the research activities and accomplishments made during the 1942 to 1959 period. Of special interest is their documentation of the germplasm collection and evaluation, and the plant genetics and breeding efforts. No cultivars were formally released during this period. Hammond and Polhamus list, describe, and provide sources of germplasm used in developing 31 guayule selections, 24 of which provide the major germplasm pool for the current USDA-sponsored cultivar developmental efforts initiated in the late 1970s.

Germplasm and cultivar development is a major component of the current commercialization effort. Breeding and genetic research in the USA is concentrated in four closely cooperating locations: Univ. of Arizona, Tucson; USDA-ARS, Phoenix, AZ; Univ. of California-Riverside; and the Texas A&M Univ. Agric. Field Station at Fort Stockton. The primary breeding objective is to develop new cultivars with a high concentration of rubber and adequate biomass to produce economically viable annual rubber yields on a given area of land. The NAS report of 1977, and the articles by Thompson and Ray (1988) and Estilai and Ray (1991) have thoroughly reviewed the past and current status, development, and future trends in the area of guayule germplasm collection, evaluation, enhancement, genetics, and breeding.

The cooperative USDA-ARS—Univ. Arizona breeding and genetic program has made good progress in developing new cultivars since its inception in 1986. Thompson et al. (1988) initiated a selection program from a diverse guayule breeding population, which contained a wide array of untested selections made previously from the USDA germplasm now held by the NPGS. Dierig et al. (1989a,b) thoroughly evaluated an array of selections from this population and determined the relationships of morphological variables to rubber production and variation among and between the various selected apomictic lines. Most of the existing germplasm in the NPGS has been found to come from a narrow base (Thompson & Ray, 1988). Twenty-one of the 26 USDA lines originated from the Mexican state of Durango. Fifteen of these descended from a bulk seed collection of only five plants at one location. Surprisingly, a rather large amount of genetic variability has been shown to exist within the facultative apomictically reproducing polyploid populations (Thompson et al., 1988; Dierig et al., 1989a,b). Ray et al. (1990) validated the model for the role of apomixis in generating genetic diversity, which may be amenable to selection.

New Arizona selections are being evaluated and reselected. Four of the six new lines in the replicated trial (Guayule Uniform Regional Variety Trial III), and four of the five observational lines planted in 1990 in Arizona, California, New Mexico, and Texas are from new selections of the cooperative Arizona-breeding and selection program. These promising new selections have the potential of producing over twice the rubber, resin, and biomass yields of the older standard lines. These lines were also selected for vigorous regeneration and regrowth after harvest by clipping, and appear to be capable of producing sustained annual rubber yields of at least 1000 kg ha^{-1} (Dierig et al., 1990). Such yields are considered to be economically viable, and should provide the basis for domestic production of rubber in the USA.

Since 1982, two Guayule Uniform Regional Variety Trials have been conducted on a cooperative basis by the various states and USDA-ARS (Ray, 1986; Ray et al., 1989a). On the basis of these evaluations, seven USDA guayule lines; 11591 (PI 478640), 11604 (PI 478642), 11605 (PI 478643), 11619 PI 478645), 12229 (PI 478652), N565 (PI 478655), and N576 (PI 478659) were jointly released by USDA-ARS, and the Arizona, California, New Mexico, and Texas Agric. Exp. Stns. (Niehaus, 1983). The California Experiment Station has officially released five germplasm lines: Cal-1 (PI 478666), Cal-2 (PI 478667), Cal-3 (PI 478664), Cal-4 (PI 478665), and Cal-5 (PI 189789) (Estilai, 1985; Tysdale et al., 1983). California has also released two cultivars, Cal-6 (NSL 202445) and Cal-7 (NSL 202446) (Estilai, 1986), which are currently being evaluated for yield and adaptation at the various locations. All PI accessions are apomictic triploids or tetraploids with the exception of Cal-3 and PI 478663 (referred to as '36-Chromosome'), which are sexual diploids.

The NPGS holdings of guayule and related species of *Parthenium* are detailed in Table 2-1. To date, only 29 accessions have received PI numbers. Two of these are guayule species hybrids. A total of 158 additional accessions are entered in the GRIN system. The majority (111) are guayule, plus three other guayule species hybrids. In addition, seven of the 17 recognized *Parthenium* spp. from two of the four generic sections are in the collection (Table 2-1). It is estimated that a total of 17 *Parthenium* accessions have been used in developing 12 released germplasm lines and two cultivars (Table 2-1).

Additional germplasm resides in the two working germplasm collections in Arizona and California. Seeds of the 1976 R.C. Rollins collection made in Mexico were rescued, and are now being grown out for evaluation in Arizona. This collection contains 43 accessions out of 122 originally collected, of which 28 are classified as pure guayule, 13 guayule introgressed with *P. incanum* (mariola), and one accession each of *P. incanum* and *P. confertum*. The major portion of the accessions outside of NPGS is located at the Univ. of California-Riverside. A significant collection of *Parthenium* spp., species hybrids, and new guayule diploids are at Riverside. In addition, progenies of accessions chiefly collected in southwestern Texas are held in a germplasm nursery at Fort Stockton, TX. The only other collection containing essentially unrelated, diverse guayule germplasm is located at the Univer-

Table 2-1. Utilization of guayule accessions in The National Plant Germplasm System (NPGS) for development of released germplasm lines and cultivars.

Species	Constituents of interest	No. of accessions in NPGS PI	No. of accessions in NPGS Other	No. of accessions used	No. of releases Germplasm lines	No. of releases Cultivars
Guayule:	Natural rubber, resins					
P. argentatum		27	111	13	8	2
Related species						
P. bipinnatifidum		0	2	0	0	0
P. confertum		0	1	0	0	0
P. fruticosum		0	7	1	0	0
P. hysterophorus		0	1	0	0	0
P. incanum		0	12	0	0	0
P. schotti		0	3	0	0	0
P. tomentosum		0	18	3	0	0
Species hybrids:		2	3	0	4	0
Total		29	158	17	12	2

sidad Autonoma Agraria in Saltillo, Coahuila, Mexico. This germplasm bank contains about 3000 accessions collected from 310 locations in six Mexican states (Kuruvadi, 1988).

KENAF AND ROSELLE (MALVACEAE)

Kenaf is on the verge of full-scale commercialization as a new industrial crop for paper pulp production. Kenaf was first introduced into the USA in the 1940s to serve as a substitute for jute (*Corchorus* spp.) to produce cordage. Research work on the utilization of kenaf for production of pulp, paper, and other fiber products began in 1960. It has been adequately demonstrated that chemi-thermomechanical pulp produced from whole stalk kenaf can be effectively used to make high-quality newsprint. Kugler (1988a,b, 1990) presents excellent reviews of the 40-yr public and private collaborative research and development efforts that have brought kenaf to the brink of full commercialization.

Kenaf and roselle are closely related species from tropical Africa. They have been grown traditionally for their bast fiber, which is used in the manufacture of jute-substitute products such as twine and carpet backing in China, USSR, and numerous other countries in Africa, Latin America, Asia, and the Middle East. Roselle is not as widely adapted as kenaf, and is slower growing and more sensitive to cool temperatures in the subtropical climate of southern Florida (F.D. Wilson, 1990, personal communication).

Kenaf and roselle have not been grown on a commercial scale in the USA, but they have been the subject of sporadic research efforts since World War II. In the late 1950s, USDA-ARS screened more than 500, mainly annual, plant species for potential usage as fiber sources for pulp and paper production. Kenaf was selected as being the most promising in 1960. From 1960 to 1978, USDA-ARS scientists at NCAUR, Peoria, IL, in close cooperation with other scientists from USDA, universities, and industry, evaluated kenaf as a new material for pulp and paper manufacture and tested several pulping techniques (Kugler, 1988a). After having demonstrated the technical feasibility of using kenaf as a renewable fiber resource and in response to the energy crisis, USDA-ARS redirected research efforts from fiber crops to the hydrocarbon program in 1978.

From 1979 to 1985, essentially no public sector research was conducted. However, private sector entities such as the American Newspaper Publishers Association and International Paper continued work on utilization of kenaf for paper production. In 1981, Kenaf International was formed, and in 1986, a cooperative agreement between Kenaf International and USDA was signed to initiate the Kenaf Demonstration Project (Kugler, 1988a). This renewed interest in kenaf placed emphasis on obtaining adaptable, high-yielding cultivars. New breeding and agronomic research projects have been initiated since 1988 in Mississippi, Oklahoma, and Texas. However, current scale up in production will have to depend upon existing kenaf cultivars developed in the earlier program of the 1950s and 1960s.

Details of the research efforts on both kenaf and roselle are well documented in numerous publications. Crane (1947, 1949) and Wilson and Menzel (1964) reviewed the early literature on the origin, distribution, genetic relationship, morphology, and utilization of 16 species of *Hibiscus* Sect. *Furcaria*. The extensive research efforts on genetic, cytogenetic, and taxonomic relationships within the genus were well covered by Menzel (1986), Menzel and Hancock (1984), Menzel and Wilson (1969), Menzel et al. (1983) and Wilson (1978). Concurrent research on all aspects of kenaf culture and harvesting conducted from 1957 was effectively summarized by White et al. (1970). This publication also serves as a good summary of the utilization and pulping characteristics of kenaf and its application for paper production. More recent research on disease resistance, and crop adaptation and production was reported by Campbell (1984), Campbell and O'Brien (1981), Campbell and White (1982), and Robinson (1988).

A reasonably adequate germplasm collection of kenaf and roselle now resides in NPGS (Table 2-2). The 195 PI accessions plus the other 111 kenaf lines came from 27 different countries. The 96 roselle accessions came from 16 countries. In addition, 106 accessions of about 30 related species of *Hibiscus* are being held by Dr. F.D. Wilson at the USDA-ARS Western Cotton Research Center, Phoenix, AZ (F.D. Wilson, 1990, personal communication). The germplasm of kenaf and related species has been in a rather precarious position since no active breeding and maintenance program had been carried out for about 10 yr. The present surge of interest has somewhat alleviated this situation, but frost-free locations are needed to maintain kenaf-related species, which are mostly perennials.

Only a limited number of kenaf cultivars have been developed and officially released. According to Wilson (F.D. Wilson, 1990, personal communication), USDA and the Cooperative Fiber Commission began a kenaf

Table 2-2. Utilization of kenaf, roselle, guar, and grindelia accessions in The National Plant Germplasm System (NPGS) for development of released germplasm lines and cultivars.

Species	Constituents of interest	No. of accessions in NPGS PI	No. of accessions in NPGS Other	No. of accessions used	No. of releases Germplasm lines	No. of releases Cultivars
Kenaf: *Hibiscus cannabinus*	Fiber, newsprint, paper	195	111	4	4	5
Roselle: *Hibiscus sabdariffa*	Fiber, newsprint, paper	54	42	3	5	0
Guar: *Cyamopsis tetragonoloba*	Galactomannan gums	1171	134	10	10	7
Grindelia: *Grindelia camporum*	Diterpene resins	0	0	0	0	0

research program in Cuba in 1943. This program led to the development of 'Cubano,' 'Cuba 108,' and 'Cuba 2032.' Cubano was the sole survivor of an anthracnose epiphytotic, and Cuba 108 was a later release of similar material. Both arose from the cv. El Salvador, which apparently was developed originally in Indonesia and introduced into Cuba in 1942, presumably from El Salvador. Cuba 2032 had a more complex history, but its anthracnose resistance also came from El Salvador. The USDA-ARS breeding program, with a major emphasis on improving kenaf as a bast-fiber crop, was initiated in southern Florida in 1951. The program depended almost completely on introduced accessions, and the most valuable germplasm source was the genetically heterogenous cv. El Salvador, also called 'Salvadorian' kenaf. An accessions (PI 249693) from Spain designated as 'Salvador' currently resides in the NPGS, but it is uncertain if this is the same germplasm.

Plant-to-row selection in El Salvador, followed by rigorous testing for yield, fiber properties, and anthracnose resistance led to the release of 'Everglades 41' (PI 532873) and 'Everglades 71' (PI 532874) in 1963 (Wilson et al., 1965). Susceptibility of kenaf to the root-knot nematode was found to be a severe constraint to its production. Some tolerance to nematode attack was found in the Salvadorian germplasm and in lines derived from this material, but a useful level of resistance was not found. Some resistance was found in interspecific hybrids of kenaf with three related *Hibiscus* spp. (Wilson & Menzel, 1964). This success led to an ambitious attempt to collect all possible species within *Hibiscus* Sect. *Furcaria*, the group to which kenaf and roselle species belong. Ultimately, the USDA-ARS world-wide *Hibiscus* collection at Belle Glade, FL and the Florida State Univ. collection at Tallahassee contained more than 1400 accessions of 37 species.

The most valuable germplasm of this extensive collection were accessions of wild kenaf from eastern Africa (Kenya and Tanzania), and a large number of cultivated and wild roselle accessions from Ghana. Screening of this material was interrupted when the USDA-ARS bast-fiber research was closed out in 1965 at Belle Glade, FL. In 1969, a new project was initiated at Savannah, GA to concentrate specifically on developing kenaf as a paper-pulp crop. Out of this program, four germplasm lines of kenaf with moderate resistance were released (unpublished mimeo, USDA-ARS and Georgia AES, 1983. Release of four strains of kenaf and five strains of fiber-type roselle.). A wild kenaf accessions from Kenya, PI 292207, was used as the source of nematode resistance in all four released kenaf lines. Line 113 (PI 468704) was a single plant selection from G7 (PI 270105 from Guatemala) × PI 292207. Line 15 (PI 468075) was derived from a single plant selection from the same cross, which was crossed to Everglades 71. The other two released selections Line 117 (PI 468076) and Line 78 (PI 468077) were selected from the same materials after one generation of backcrossing to Everglades 71. Four of the five roselle selections were derived from crosses involving two accessions PI 295598 (Niger) and PI 256038 (Pakistan). The fifth selection (PI 468412) also involved PI 295598 and an accession from Thailand designated 'THS-2' (PI 295596). A limited number of both kenaf and roselle accessions have been used to produce the small number of germplasm lines and cultivars released to date (Table 2-2).

GUAR (FABACEAE)

Guar, sometimes called cluster bean, is a summer annual legume grown primarily in the USA for the galactomannan gum from its seeds, and as a soil-improving, green manure crop. In the South Asian countries of India, Pakistan, Bangladesh, Sri Lanka, and Burma, it is grown as an annual monsoon crop and garden vegetable. It has numerous uses such as cattle forage, fuel, human food (as a legume or pulse), medicinal, and soil improvement. Galactomannan gum, which constitutes about 85% of the seed endosperm, is used as thickeners in ice cream and other food products, and a wide variety of industrial processes such as a sizing agent in paper manufacturing, an ingredient in lotions and creams in the cosmetic and pharmaceutical industries, and for purification of potash, ore flotation, and waterproofing of explosives in the mining industry. Currently, the major use is in the oil-well drilling industry as an additive to water-based drilling muds (Whistler & Hymowitz, 1979).

Guar probably originated from Africa and was domesticated in a dry region of western Asia. Guar is not found in the wild state, and probably descended from the African species *C. senegalensis* (Hymowitz, 1972). Guar was first introduced into the USA by USDA in 1903, chiefly as a soil-building crop. It has proved to be drought tolerant and well adapted to the semiarid plains of Texas and Oklahoma where it is usually grown under natural rainfall conditions. It has also been grown in southern Texas and Arizona under irrigation. Economic considerations have essentially eliminated production in Arizona at this time. Production of guar as a potential industrial crop in Australia has also been reported (Jackson & Doughton, 1982). Whistler and Hymowitz (1979) present a good review of all aspects of guar crop production. Several publications summarize recent agronomic, water use, and plant pathological research on guar (Alexander et al., 1988; Mihail & Alcorn, 1986; Stafford & McMichael, 1990; Vinizky & Ray, 1988).

The major guar-breeding effort in the USA has been centered in Texas, but only minimal research is being conducted currently. Breeding and genetics research in Arizona was phased out in the mid-1980s. Seiler and Stafford (1985) conducted research on components of yield-utilizing factor analysis, and Milligan (1984) investigated the effects of plant density on guar seed yield and its components. Paroda and Saini (1978) reviewed research on guar breeding and genetics. Ray and Stafford (1985a) briefly reviewed the more recent genetic research, and proposed a system of genetic nomenclature for guar.

Essentially all guar cultivars were developed directly or indirectly from accessions obtained in India (Table 2-2). The first cultivar of guar bred and selected in the USA in 1943 was Mesa. Mesa was developed at the Arizona Agric. Exp. Stn. at Mesa from a mixture of plant selections from several selected accessions (Whistler & Hymowitz, 1979). In 1946, 'Texsel' was released, and was developed as a selection from PI 116034, which was the first USDA guar accessions received and collected in Gowar, India in 1936. 'Groehler' was developed from a single plant selection in 1946 from Texsel at Mesa, AZ. 'Lasbella,' 'Punjab,' and 'Fine Branching' are other early cultivars for which the exact origin is unknown, but undoubtedly were selected from early accessions received from India.

The joint USDA-ARS-Texas and Oklahoma Agricultural Experiment Stations breeding effort was initiated in the late 1950s. Three cultivars from this program were derived from selections made at Iowa Park, TX. The first of these three released guar cultivars was Brooks in 1964 (Stafford et al., 1976a). Brooks originated as a single plant selection from a commercial field of Groehler in 1959, and is assumed to have been an advanced generation progeny of a natural cross between Groehler and a Texas breeding line of undetermined origin, S44-1. 'Hall,' released in 1966, is a single plant selection out of PI 179930, which was collected at Posalia, India in 1948. The third cultivar, Mills, was also released in 1966. It originated as a single plant selection from the extremely variable PI 263875, which was introduced from New Delhi, India in 1960 (Stafford et al., 1976a).

Two additional cultivars from the ARS-Texas-Oklahoma program, Kinman and Esser, were derived as single plant selections made at Chillicothe, TX from a controlled cross of Brooks × Mills at College Station, TX in 1964. Both cultivars were released in 1974 (Stafford et al., 1976b). The Brooks × Mills cross, designated as T64001, was used extensively in the later development of both released germplasm lines and cultivars.

DEVELOPING NEW INDUSTRIAL CROP CULTIVARS

Cultivar Lewis, was jointly developed and released by USDA-ARS, Arizona and Texas Agric. Exp. Stns. Lewis, released in 1984, was an F_8 selection from a controlled cross of T64001-12-1-B-3-2-B-2 × PI 338780-B made at Chillicothe, TX in 1971. PI 338780-B was a bacterial blight-resistant bulk selection from PI 338780, originally introduced from India (Stafford & Ray, 1985).

Cultivar Santa Cruz was developed and jointly released by USDA-ARS and the Arizona Agric. Exp. Stn. in 1984 (Ray & Stafford, 1985b). Santa Cruz is a result of testing and developing breeding line TX 78-3695, which was released in 1982 (Stafford et al., 1983). TX78-3695 was an F_7 selection from T64001-16-5-1-1-2-1 × PI 338780-B, which is essentially the same parentage as that of Lewis.

Five germplasm lines, with resistance to major guar diseases, were released by USDA-ARS and the Texas Agric. Exp. Stn. in 1979 (Stafford & Lewis, 1981). TX 73-2731 is a selection from T64001-14-8-3-1 × Lasbella made in 1968. TX 71-3292 is a selection from the heterogeneous Oklahoma Guar Accession, G-821, the source of which is undetermined. TX 76-3114 is a selection from T64001-12-B-3-2-B-2 × PI 338780-B made in 1971. TX76-3285 is a selection from T64002-6-1-2-3-2-2 × PI 338780-B. T64002 is the designation for the cross of Hall × PI 263875-2 made at College Station, TX in 1964. PI 263875-2 is a selection out of PI 263875, which was used in developing the cv. Mills. TX 76-2746 is a selection from PI 340651-1 × PI 338780-B made in Chillicothe, TX in 1971. PI 340651-1 is a bacterial blight-resistant selection from the Indian accession, PI 340651.

Five additional germplasm lines were developed and officially released by USDA-ARS, Arizona and Texas Agric. Exp. Stns. in 1982 (Stafford et al., 1983). All were selected from controlled crosses made at Chillicothe, TX in 1971. TX 77-3347 is a selection from T64001-7-10-1-1-B-3-1 × PI 338780-B. TX 78-3695 is from T64001-16-5-1-1-2-1 × PI 338780-B. TX 78-3337 is from T64002-6-1-2-3-2-2 × T65001-B-4-2-1-2-B. The male parent, T65001, is from a controlled backcross, Brooks[2] × Mills, made at College Station, TX in 1965. TX78-3726 is an F_6 selection from T64001-12-1-B-3-2-B-2 × PI 338780-B, and TX79-2741 is an F_8 selection from T64001-12-1-B-3-2-B-2 × PI 338780-B, and TX79-2741 is an F_8 selection from the same cross as TX78-3726.

In total, only five PI accessions (PI 116034, PI 179930, PI 263875, PI 338780, and PI 340651) were used to produce the seven officially released cultivars and 10 germplasm lines (Table 2-2). It is estimated that probably not more than five other accessions may have been used to produce the four older cultivars of undetermined origin, Mesa, Lasbella, Punjab, and Fine Branching. This probably represents usage of <1% of the total number of 1171 PI accessions in the NPGS. The other 134 accessions held by NPGS (Table 2-2) are selections, breeding and germplasm lines, and cultivars from U.S. breeding programs, which were not assigned PI numbers. Forty-five of the 134 accessions are from single plant selections made from within 18 PI accessions.

GRINDELIA, GUMWEED (ASTERACEAE)

Grindelia is truly a new crop, which has received only limited research and development as a new industrial source of resins (Thompson, 1990b). Essentially all of the research has been conducted by the Univ. of Arizona Bioresources Research Facility. Attention was focused upon plants that produced resins after they had conducted extensive research, which surveyed and evaluated a wide array of desert plants for their biocrude production potential (Hoffmann, 1983, 1985; McLaughlin & Hoffmann, 1982; McLaughlin et al., 1983). *Grindelia camporum*, an arid-adapted, herbaceous perennial native to the Central Valley area of California was determined to be the most promising of the numerous species investigated (Hoffmann et al., 1984; Hoffmann & McLaughlin, 1986).

Grindelia camporum produces significant quantities of extractable diterpene resin acids from multicellular glands on the surfaces of stems, leaves, and involucres. The diterpene resins, chiefly composed of grindelic acid and several of its derivatives, are similar chemically to the resin acids that make up rosin, a principal product of the naval stores industry. *Naval stores* is a general term for a large class of chemicals that include rosins, turpentine, fatty acids, and their derivatives. *Rosin*, a complex mixture of diperpene resin acids that is extracted from aged pine stumps and whose supply is nearly exhausted, has wide and diverse industrial applications.

Recovery of gum rosin by tapping living pine trees is labor intensive, and production has declined to almost nothing in the USA. However, the USA market used more than 500 million kg of rosin in the recent past (Hoffmann & McLaughlin, 1986). They concluded that grindelia resins most likely could substitute for rosin in numerous industrial applications, and its cultivation to meet domestic demands for rosin would have a significant impact on the agricultural economy.

A collection of germplasm accessions from California was made by the Univ. of Arizona Office of Arid Land Studies. None of these accessions, which number about 15, are currently held by the NPGS (Table 2-2). In addition, a bulk, open-pollinated, tetraploid population is also being maintained. Preliminary breeding, genetic, agronomic, and chemical research efforts were initiated in 1981. Results of this research are summarized in Hoffmann and McLaughlin (1986), McLaughlin (1985, 1986a,b,c), McLaughlin and Linker (1987), Shuck and McLaughlin (1988), and Timmermann et al. (1983). The current germplasm of *G. camporum* was shown to produce about 10% crude resin, which equates to an annual yield of around 1135 kg ha^{-1}. Economic projections indicate that crude resin yields would need to be increased to a level of 15 to 20% to be competitive (Hoffmann, 1985; Hoffmann & McLaughlin, 1986). Genetic and selection experiments indicate that such improvement in resin concentration and yield is feasible (McLaughlin, 1986a,b,c; Shuck & McLaughlin, 1987). Additionally, good tolerance to diseases, drought and salinity, the upright, herbaceous growth habit, the annual life cycle of many accessions, and the ability to regenerate growth from the root crown to produce two crops in a single growing season are favorable characteristics for domestication. No improved germplasm or cultivars of grindelia have been released.

Unfortunately, research on domestication of grindelia is now essentially nonexistent. Only private industrial sources supported the initial research, which was inexplicably terminated at a time when good progress was being made. It is regrettable that an adequate funding source for research and development is not currently available to carry forward this promising new crop.

JOJOBA (BUXACEAE)

Jojoba is becoming one of the first new arid-land industrial oilseed crops to reach commercialization. Jojoba is an evergreen woody shrub native to the Sonoran Desert in southern Arizona and California, and in northern Sonora and Baja California in Mexico. Jojoba seeds contain from 40 to 60% of a unique seed oil that is more accurately characterized as a long straight-chain liquid wax of nonglyceride esters (wax-esters). Hydrogenation converts jojoba oil into a useful white crystalline wax. The chemical structure is unique in the plant kingdom and similar to that of the wax-ester portion of sperm whale oil. At one time, jojoba oil was touted as a replacement for sperm whale oil, the importation of which has been banned in the USA since 1971. Although the chemical structure of this unique seed oil lends its utility to the development of a large array of industrial products such as high pressure and other specialty lubricants, antifoaming agents, detergents, disinfectants, emulsifiers, plasticizers, protective coatings, resins, and surfactants, the limited supply and relatively high price of the oil largely restricts current usage to the cosmetic industry.

Commercial plantings of jojoba have been made only since 1978. Planted acreage peaked at about 16 000 ha in 1984, chiefly in Arizona and California. Unfortunately, yields of many of the early plantings did not meet expectations since the planting stock was based upon unselected seed gathered from open-pollinated natural plant stands. Sizeable acreages have been abandoned, with current productive acreage now estimated at about 6000 ha (James H. Brown, President, Jojoba Growers & Processors, Inc., 1990, personal communication). Brown estimates a potential market of about 150 000 t, but Arizona, which produces about one-half of the world production, only produced about 750 t of seed in 1989, worth slightly more than $3 million.

Good reviews (Gentry, 1958; Hogan, 1979; Hogan & Bemis, 1983; Hogan et al., 1981; Kleiman, 1990; Naqvi & Ting, 1990; Nat. Res. Counc., 1985; Thompson, 1990b) summarize all aspects of jojoba natural history, culture, production, utilization, and current research and development activities and needs.

Relatively little breeding and selection research has been conducted, and lack of development of high-yielding, clonally propagated cultivars has been a severe constraint to successful commercialization of jojoba. Minimally funded, understaffed breeding and selection research programs have operated only at the Univ. of Arizona, Tucson and the Univ. of California-Riverside. The

Table 2-3. Utilization of jojoba and meadowfoam accessions in The National Plant Germplasm System (NPGS) for development of released germplasm lines and cultivars.

Species	Constituents of interest	No. of accessions in NPGS PI	No. of accessions in NPGS Other	No. of accessions used	No. of releases Germplasm lines	No. of releases Cultivars
Jojoba:	Long chain liquid wax esters					
Simmondsia chinensis		38	3	5	3	2
Meadowfoam:	Long chain fatty acids					
Limnanthes alba		22	1	2	0	3†
Related species						
L. bakeri		2	0	0	0	0
L. douglasii		13	0	0	0	0
L. floccosa		10	0	1	0	0
L. gracilis		4	0	0	0	0
L. macounii		1	0	0	0	0
L. montana		2	0	0	0	0
L. straita		2	0	0	0	0
Total		56	1	3	0	3†

† Includes one to be released in 1991.

program at Arizona was essentially terminated in 1990 due to loss of personnel and inadequacy of funding. Some clonal selection and propagation of planting stock has been assumed by private industry. USDA-ARS has a small research effort on seed oil utilization at NCAUR, Peoria.

A total of 38 jojoba PI accessions are listed on the GRIN system, but most of these are thought to be nonviable (Table 2-3). Germplasm collections in the form of seeds and nursery-grown plants of seed and clonally propagated accessions and selections are currently maintained at the Agricultural Experiment Stations of the Univ. of Arizona and Univ. of California-Riverside.

Only two cultivars have been named, Vista and Mirov. Vista, the first, originated as a selected population from a small planting in Vista, CA. Only the cv. Mirov is widely recognized in the industry, but is not widely planted (Palzkill et al., 1989). To date, only three selected and widely tested clonally propagated, pistillate jojoba germplasm lines (AT-1310, AT-1487, and AT-3365) have been officially released (Palzkill et al., 1989). These clones should be useful in future breeding programs, and will also serve as standards with which new cultivars may be compared.

MEADOWFOAM (LIMNANTHACEAE)

Species of *Limnanthes* were identified in the late 1950s by the USDA-ARS plant screening program at NCAUR, Peoria as containing a seed oil with unique long-chain fatty acids (Bagby et al., 1961; Miller et al., 1964a; Smith et al., 1960). Kleiman (1990), Smith (1979), and Purdy and Craig (1987) recently reviewed the potential of meadowfoam for industrial usage. At least 95% of its fatty acids are long chain (C20 and C22), and 85% of the fatty acids exhibit unique positions of unsaturation. The oil can be converted to liquid wax-esters similar to that produced naturally by jojoba. Meadowfoam oil may also be useful in the manufacture of specialty lubricants, detergents, and plasticizers.

The common name, meadowfoam, is descriptive since the dense flower bloom gives the fields an appearance of being covered with a white foam. The nine recognized species of *Limnanthes* are herbaceous winter annuals found on the west coast of North America from California to British Columbia (Mason, 1952). Germplasm was collected in the early 1960s, and *Limnanthes alba* was recognized by Gentry and Miller (1965) as the prime candidate for domestication due to its wide adaptation, lower water requirements, and good seed yields. In total, 58 accessions from eight species are currently held in the NPGS (Table 2-3).

The research and developmental activities on the domestication of meadowfoam have been adequately summarized (Higgins et al., 1971; Jain, 1989; Jolliff, 1981, 1988; Knapp, 1990b). Major domestication efforts have been concentrated in California and Oregon. Jain and co-workers in California have conducted extensive research on systematics, evolutionary ecology, genetics, breeding and mating systems, population structure, and yield components of *Limnanthes alba* and other related species. Jain (1989) presents an excellent summary of this research. No releases of cultivars or germplasm lines have been made from California. Much of the research on agronomy and cultivar development has been done in Oregon. Jolliff (1988) detailed the chronological development of this program.

Higgins et al. (1971) reported on the extensive germplasm and agronomic evaluation of 30 PI accessions of seven different species of meadowfoam. Domestication effort in Oregon focused on selection within *L. alba* var. *alba* for tall, upright plant types with good seed retention for mechanical harvesting. A single plant selection with good seed retention was made by W. Calhoun and J.M. Crane in 1970 from PI 283704 collected in 1962 near Perkins, CA, by Dr. H.S. Gentry. This gave rise to the release of the first meadowfoam cultivar, Foamore in 1975. The next cultivar to be released in 1984 was Mermaid, which exhibited improved seed retention. Mermaid originated as a single plant selection made in 1972 from PI 283703 also collected by Dr. Gentry near Antelope, CA (Jolliff, 1988). PI 283704 is the primary source of an improved selection currently being prepared for release under the Plant Variety Protection Program (G.D. Jolliff, 1990, personal communication).

Protandry within the highly allogamous species, *L. alba* is considered to be a constraint to high seed yields. Attempts have been made to use interspecific hybridization as a method for germplasm enhancement (Jolliff et al., 1984). Jolliff (1988) reports that oil yields of 50% above that of Mermaid have been measured in research plots in 1987 to 1988 with populations from putative interspecific hybrids of *L. floccosa* × *L. alba* initiated in 1977. These increases were attributed to increased seed size, increased seed oil content, and reduced lodging. However, hybridity of this material has not been cytogenetically confirmed.

In addition to the need for established markets for the seed oil, significant increases in seed yields are needed over the next several years for the successful commercialization of meadowfoam. Adequate funding for the necessary research has not been available. To date the breeding and selection effort has been severely constrained and restricted to a narrow germplasm base. Clearly an increased program for meadowfoam germplasm collection, evaluation, and enhancement is needed. Jain (1989) and Knapp (1990b), clearly outline measures that are needed to develop an efficient breeding and genetic program for the full commercialization of this potentially useful, new industrial oilseed crop. Currently, USDA-ARS is conducting utilization research to improve the commercialization potential of meadowfoam at NCAUR, Peoria.

CRAMBE (BRASSICACEAE)

Crambe along with industrial rapeseed are two potential new industrial crops for the production of high erucic acid (HEA) seed oil as well as a usable seed meal. According to industry estimates, more than 18 000 t of HEA oil, mostly from imported sources, are utilized annually in the USA. High erucic acid oil or its derivatives can be used in a wide array of industrial processes and products (Kramer et al., 1983; Roetheli & Blase, 1989; Van Dyne & Blase, 1989; Van Dyne et al., 1990). At present, much of the oil is processed into erucamide, which is used as an antiblock, slip-promoting additive in the manufacture of polyolefin films such as garbage bags and bread wrappers. Van Dyne et al. (1990) present an excellent review of the potential uses as well as the production, processing, marketing, and economics. They also present a thorough bibliography on all aspects of research and development of both crambe and industrial rapeseed. They further describe the activities of the HEA Oil Project, which was initiated in 1986 to focus on the commercialization of crambe and industrial rapeseed. This project involves close cooperation of Federal, state, university, and industry scientists and administrative personnel. The project is formally administered by the USDA-CSRS Office of Agricultural Materials.

White and Higgins (1966) present a review on all aspects of the earlier research and development of crambe as a new industrial oilseed crop. More recent research was reviewed by Lessman (1990), Lessman and Anderson (1981), Lessman and Meier (1972), and Shands and White (1990). *Crambe abyssinica* was first introduced into the USA in the 1940s by the Connecticut Agric. Exp. Stn. Research on crambe started earlier in Europe with agronomic testing beginning in the USSR in 1932. Promising preliminary utilization studies at NCAUR, Peoria in 1957 stimulated the initiation of field research by USDA-ARS and cooperating state agricultural experiment stations.

The major breeding and genetic research was conducted by USDA-ARS at Beltsville, MD and by the Purdue Univ. Agric. Exp. Stn. (Campbell et al., 1986a,b; Leppik & White, 1975; Meier & Lessman, 1973a,b; White, 1975; White & Solt, 1978). Most of the initial evaluation in the USA was conducted on PI 247310 received in 1958 from Sweden. A second, much used accession (PI 279346) was collected in Ethiopia in 1962. Soon after, 10 accessions were obtained from the USSR. These earliest received accessions were the primary source of the selection program initiated by Meier and Lessman at Purdue Univ. in 1965, and are also a major germplasm source for Dr. Lessman's current program at New Mexico State Univ. (K.J. Lessman, 1990, personal communication). Three cultivars were released by the Purdue Univ. Agric. Exp. Stn. Indy was a selection for early maturity and heavy seed size from PI 279346. Prophet (PI 514650) was developed by mass selection for large seed size from PI 247310. The cv. Meyer (PI 514649) was selected from progeny of a cross involving both PI 247310 and PI 279346.

The germplasm enhancement and cultivar development program at USDA-ARS at Beltsville culminated in the release of two cultivars (Campbell et al., 1986a) and three germplasm lines (Campbell et al., 1986b). Cultivars BelAnn (PI 533667) and BelEnzian (PI 533668) were derived from introgressing germplasm from four wild populations (PI 384523, PI 384529, PI 384530 all from Ethiopia, and PI 370747 from Turkey) into the cv. Indy. The line C-37 (PI 533666) was derived from the same breeding population from which cultivars BelAnn and BelEnzian were selected. The other two lines C-22 (PI 533664) and C-29 (PI 533665) were derived from a comparable crossing scheme as above, but involved four different wild accessions (PI 384522, PI 384524, PI 384527 all from Ethiopia, and PI 392327 from Turkey), which were also subsequently crossed to Indy.

In total, five cultivars and three germplasm lines have been released, but only 10 germplasm lines were used (Table 2-4). A total of 65 PI accessions plus 100 other accessions of *C. abyssinica* are currently held by the NPGS. Sixty-three additional PI accessions of the related species *C. hispanica* are also in the system plus 55 other accessions of at least 12 additional species within the genus.

Shands and White (1990) concluded that limited genetic diversity in available crambe germplasm is a major constraint to development of new cultivars. Only a few accessions are known to have come directly from the wild, and accessibility for collection of wild germplasm in Ethiopia, the center of origin, is very limited. Successful commercialization of crambe will require a sustained breeding program to increase yield and disease resistance, especially to *Alternaria*. Crambe seed meal has promise as a good protein-rich feed supplement (Carlson & Tookey, 1983). Genetic diversity is needed to allow for screening and selection for low or zero thioglucosides in the seed meal to enhance economic value, as has been accomplished in both sources of industrial rapeseed, *Brassica napus* and *B. rapa*. Brzezinski and Mendelewski (1984) recently developed a rapid method for determining total

Table 2-4. Utilization of crambe, industrial rapeseed and other erucic acid containing *Brassica* spp., and buffalo and coyote gourd accessions in The National Plant Germplasm System (NPGS) for development of released germplasm lines and cultivars.

Species	Constituents of interest	No. of accessions in NPGS PI	Other	No. of accessions used	No. of releases Germplasm lines	Cultivars
Crambe:	High erucic acid oil					
Crambe abyssinica		65	100	10	3	5
Related species						
C. aspera		1	0	0	0	0
C. cordifolia		1	0	0	0	0
C. filiformis		24	0	0	0	0
C. grandiflora		1	0	0	0	0
C. hispanica		63	0	0	0	0
C. juncea		2	0	0	0	0
C. koktebelica		1	0	0	0	0
C. kralikii		11	0	0	0	0
C. maritima		1	0	0	0	0
C. orientalis		1	0	0	0	0
C. strigosa		1	0	0	0	0
C. tataria		4	0	0	0	0
C. spp.		4	3	0	0	0
Total		180	103	10	3	5
Brassica:	High erucic acid oil					
Brassica napus (winter rapeseed)		555	60	10	0	2
B. rapa (spring rapeseed)		502	730	0	0	0
B. carinata (abyssinian mustard)		49	0	0	0	0
B. elongata		1	0	0	0	0
B. juncea (Indian mustard)		337	654	0	0	0
B. narinosa		1	0	0	0	0
B. nigra (black mustard)		68	8	0	0	0
B. tournifortii		12	4	0	0	0
B. spp.		10	15	0	0	0
Total		1535	1471	10	0	2
Cucurbita:	Industrial and vegetable oil, starch, cucurbitacins					
Curcubita foetidissima (buffalo gourd)		27	4	8	0	1
C. digitata (coyote gourd)		1	0	3	1	0
Total		28	4	11	1	1

glucosinolate content in rapeseed meals. Dr. K.J. Lessman (1990, personal communication) has used a slight modification of this method for screening crambe germplasm.

INDUSTRIAL RAPESEED (BRASSICACEAE)

Industrial or HEA rapeseed is not an unknown crop, and has been grown in Europe for hundreds of years. Basically, two *Brassica* species are grown to produce industrial rapeseed oils; *B. napus* L. (winter rapeseed), which produces the major quantity, and *B. rapa* L. (formerly *B. campestris*) (spring rapeseed) (McNaughton, 1976). Considerable research was conducted in Canada to develop rapeseed as a world-class commodity (Downey, 1971). Recently, research in Canada developed a rapeseed with an edible type of seed oil called *canola*, which has essentially no erucic acid and a seed meal with very low glucosinolatees (Downey, 1988). Röbbelen and Thies (1980) present further information on the biosynthesis of seed oil and breeding of rapeseed.

Most species of *Brassica* produce seed oils with relatively high quantities of erucic acid. Auld and co-workers in Idaho have evaluated more than 2100 accessions of *Brassica* spp. from 23 worldwide germplasm collections (Auld et al., 1988, 1989; Mahler & Auld, 1989). Data extracted from Mahler and Auld (1989) indicate that none of the species evaluated had low (<2.0%) erucic acid except *B. napus*. Only 0.8% of 130 *B. napus* accessions tested from NPGS had low erucic acid. The 130 accessions represent about 21% of the total number of 615 accessions held by NPGS (Table 2-4). In contrast, 2.9% of 34 accessions in the Univ. of California-Davis collection, and 23.4% of 188 accessions from worldwide collections had <2.0% erucic acid. This clearly reflects the intensity of breeding effort for canola-type rapeseed outside the USA prior to the current developmental upswing in this country. None of the 130 *B. napus* accessions tested from NPGS had high (>50%) erucic acid. In contrast, 23.5% of the 34 accessions from the Univ. of California-Davis, and 24.5% of 188 accessions from worldwide collections had seed oil containing more than 50% erucic acid.

A total of 9.6% of the 230 tested NPGS accessions of *B. rapa* (listed as *B. campestris*) had high erucic acid (Mahler & Auld, 1989). The 230 accessions tested represent about 19% of the total 1232 *B. rapa* accessions held by NPGS. Two of seven accessions from the Univ. of California-Davis collection and 70% of the 74 accessions from worldwide collections were high in erucic acid. No accessions in either *B. napus* or *B. rapa* were found to contain more than 60% erucic acid in their seed oils. In contrast, about 47% of the 294 NPGS accessions of *B. oleracea* var. *botrytis* (broccoli and cauliflower) had more than 50%, and 5% of these were measured as having more than 60% erucic acid. Of the 351 NPGS cabbage (*B. oleracea* var. *capitata*) accessions tested, only 8.3% had HEA. None of the *B. oleracea* types are grown for oilseed production.

None of the 27 accessions from UC-Davis and 107 accessions from worldwide collections of the Abyssinian mustard (*B. carinata*), nor four (NPGS) accessions of Indian mustard (*B. juncea*), or five (UC-Davis) accessions of black mustard (*B. nigra*) had seed oils with erucic acid above 50%. Two of 37 accessions of Chinese cabbage types listed as *B. rapa* from worldwide collections, and one of the eight UC-Davis accessions of the wild species *B. tournifortii* contained higher than 50% erucic acid (Mahler & Auld, 1989).

With the wealth of germplasm available within the genus *Brassica* (Table 2-4), it should be possible to produce new cultivars of industrial rapeseed with even higher levels of erucic acid. Imaginative uses of genetic engineering techniques in combination with conventional breeding and selection should prove to be productive in the future.

Until recently, most of the rapeseed breeding and genetics was conducted in Europe and Canada. The recent interest in developing a domestic source of HEA industrial rapeseed oil has stimulated breeding and cultivar development in both the private and public sectors. Calgene and Agrigenetics have developed sizable research and development programs to obtain high-yielding cultivars for both industrial and food oil usage. The first U.S. low glucosinolate, HEA rapeseed cultivar, Indore, a *B. rapa* type, was released by the Oregon Agric. Exp. Stn. (Calhoun et al., 1983). Currently, Auld and co-workers at the Univ. of Idaho have the only active public sector breeding program. The Idaho Agric. Exp. Stn. has released two *B. napus* cultivars, Cascade (PI 509072) a canola type and Bridger (PI 509073) a HEA type (Auld & Mahler, 1987; Auld et al., 1987).

BUFFALO GOURD AND COYOTE GOURD (CUCURBITACEAE)

The buffalo gourd and coyote gourd are feral, xerophytic cucurbits native to semiarid and arid areas of western North America that produce seeds rich in edible oil and protein. The perennial plants develop large fleshy storage roots that contain more than 50% starch. Unlike the buffalo gourd, the coyote gourd is a polytypic species composed of four subspecies originally classified as *C. digitata* Gray, *C. palmata* Wats., *C. cylindrata* Bailey, and *C. cordata* Wats. (A.C. Gathman, 1990, personal communication).

The possibility of domesticating and using semiarid and arid adapted perennial cucurbits, such as the buffalo gourd or the coyote gourd, as new sources of vegetable seed oils and proteins was first proposed by Dr. L.C. Curtis (1946). During the late 1940s and early 1950s, some research was initiated, but the activity waned until the early 1970s. At this time, the late Dr. William P. Bemis and co-workers at the Univ. of Arizona recognized the attractive potential of a single plant species producing edible seed oils, seed proteins, root starches, and other byproducts. The potential of the buffalo gourd and related species was enunciated in a series of review papers by Bemis et al. (1978, 1979), Hogan and Bemis (1983), DeVeaux and Schultz (1985), and Hinman (1984, 1986).

A multidisciplinary team of scientists and students at the Univ. of Arizona conducted an excellent, sustained, broad-based research effort for more than 15 yr. This research was well focused and has been documented in a series of papers that include: germplasm collection and evaluation (Scheerens et al., 1978, 1989, 1991); composition and functionality of potential food and industrial feedstock ingredients (DeVeaux & Schultz, 1985; Scheerens

& Berry, 1986; Scheerens et al., 1978, 1987a; Vasconcellos et al., 1981); plant growth, fruiting, and agronomic research (Nelson et al., 1983, 1988; Scheerens et al., 1987b, 1990); disease resistance (Rosemeyer et al., 1986); breeding, genetics, taxonomic relationships, and domestication (Bemis et al., 1978, 1979; Gathman & Bemis, 1990; Scheerens et al., 1978, 1989, 1991).

Essentially all research effort on the development of the buffalo gourd and coyote gourd as a new crop has ceased. The high expectations of a unique cultural system proposed by Bemis et al. (1978), which would allow for both harvest of seeds for oil and protein and roots for starch, was not realized. Problems associated with the perennial growth habit as related to susceptibility to soil-borne fungi and build up of viral diseases proved to be a major constraint. Another major factor was low seed yields that fell well below the projected yields of 2000 kg ha^{-1} (Nelson et al., 1988). Nelson et al. (1988) also demonstrated that buffalo gourds grown under intensive culture had relatively low water use efficiency and peak consumptive use rates similar to that of conventional crops. They were reasonably successful in obtaining high root and starch production (up to 34 550 kg ha^{-1} root yield with starch content of 63.5% on a dry weight basis) when grown as an annual crop with high density plantings (Nelson et al., 1983).

Thompson (1990b) addressed the question of why such a developmental program should essentially fail after such a good, sustained effort was expended on species with such potentially desirable characteristics. He concluded that neither the seed oil or proteins were unique enough in character to stimulate interest in their utilization by industry. The unique fine-grained character and the acceptable yields of the root starch were positive, but the economic feasibility of growing buffalo gourds solely for starch production was not fully demonstrated. The only unique chemical constituent of the buffalo gourd is the presence of quantities of cucurbitacins found in all parts of the plant. Cucurbitacins impart bitter flavor to plant parts and are potent attractants to certain beetles and other insects. Gathman and Bemis (1990) speculate that they may be of value as sources of medicinal and pharmaceutical products. However, more research is needed to determine the economic potential and useful applications. It is reasonable to assume that future political and economic changes may provide a favorable environment for the full development and commercial utilization of these multifaceted aridland adapted plant species.

During the course of this research program, significant efforts were expended on germplasm collection and evaluation in addition to breeding and cultivar development. Scheerens et al. (1978) details evaluation of 33 accessions of buffalo gourd collected in Arizona in 1975, and 52 additional accessions collected in 1976 from the southern Rocky Mountains and the Great Plains region of the USA. Currently, 25 PI accessions and four Arizona breeding lines are held by the NPGS (Table 2-4). Three of the later accessions are selections and one is a hybrid of two of the three selections. Synthetic No. 1, the only buffalo gourd cultivar developed, was not officially released, but is being maintained by the Univ. of Arizona. Only one accession of coyote gourd (*C. digitata*), PI 240879, is currently held by the NPGS. However,

1985 seed of a *C. digitata* composite, which contains germplasm of the four subspecies (*C. digitata, C. palmata, C. cordata,* and *C. cylindrata*), is still available at the Univ. of Arizona (J.M. Nelson, 1990, personal communication).

CUPHEA (LYTHRACEAE)

The U.S. chemical industry is heavily dependent upon imported coconut and palm kernel oils as the primary source of lauric acid (C12:0) and other medium-chain fatty acids for manufacturing soaps, detergents, lubricants, and other related products. The USDA-ARS plant screening program at NCAUR, Peoria, in the 1960s discovered that seed oils from species of the genus *Cuphea* contained high levels of lauric, capric (C10:0) caprylic (C8:0), and other medium-chain fatty acids (Miller et al., 1964b). After conducting preliminary evaluation of *Cuphea* germplasm (Lythraceae), excessive seed shattering and dormancy, indeterminate flowering, and sticky glandular hairs were serious constraints to domestication. Currently, the only remaining constraint is seed shattering (S.J. Knapp, 1990, personal communication).

Essentially no agronomic research was initiated until industry began to generate strong interest and support in the late 1970s to develop cuphea as an industrial oilseed crop. The first research effort was started in Europe (Röbbelen & Hirsinger, 1982). U.S. industry worked closely with USDA-ARS and financially supported germplasm collections in Mexico and Brazil in 1981 and 1982, respectively. Seed oils of 73 species sampled from 11 of the 12 sections of the genus were analyzed, revealing unparalleled diversity for fatty acid composition (Graham et al., 1981; Graham & Kleiman, 1985; Kleiman, 1990; Wolf et al., 1983). In 1983, USDA-ARS pooled resources with Oregon State Agric. Exp. Stn. and member companies of the Soap and Detergent Association to develop cuphea as a new domestic industrial oilseed crop (Arndt, 1985; Graham, 1989; Knapp, 1990b; Thompson, 1984, 1985; Thompson & Dierig, 1988a). Germplasm evaluation for agronomic characteristics, adaptation and yields of seed, oil, and fatty acids was initiated (Hirsinger, 1985; Hirsinger & Knowles, 1984; Jaworski et al., 1988; Knapp, 1990b; Thompson & Kleiman, 1988; Thompson et al., 1990). Preliminary evaluation of some cuphea species and interspecific hybrids have also indicated considerable potential for usage as new ornamental pot and bedding plants (Thompson, 1984, 1986, 1989; Thompson et al., 1987; Ray & Thompson, 1988).

Graham (1988) published an extensive revision of the generic section, Heterodon, in which the most promising species for domestication reside. Graham is currently working on taxonomic revision of other sections of the genus. Additional germplasm collections have contributed to the program. Several species within section Heterodon were collected by S.J. Knapp (1990, unpublished data) in 1986. Two major collections of germplasm were made in Brazil in 1989 by Roath and co-workers (W.W. Roath, 1989, 1990, un-

Table 2-5. Utilization of cuphea accessions in The National Plant Germplasm System (NPGS) for development of released germplasm lines, cultivars, and interspecific hybrids.

Species	No. of accessions in NPGS PI	No. of accessions in NPGS Other	No. of accessions used	No. of releases Germplasm lines	No. of releases Cultivars
Lauric acid-rich species:					
Cuphea laminuligera	3	6	3†	0	0
C. lutea	4	0	2	0	0
C. tolucana	29	42	1	0	0
C. wrightii	21	20	1	0	0
Capric acid-rich species:					
C. angustifolia	3	1	1†	0	0
C. caeciliae	0	1	1	0	0
C. crassiflora	1	0	1	0	0
C. ignea	7	1	1†	0	0
C. lanceolata	27	5	6	1	0
C. leptopoda	6	6	4†	0	0
C. llavea	7	3	5†	0	0
C. lophostoma	1	2	1	0	0
C. procumbens	18	7	6†	0	0
C. viscosissima	46	39‡	2	5	0
Other species (n = 76):	78	523§	0	0	0
Interspecific hybrids (n = 21):	0	21	(32)	3†	0
Total	249	677	35	9	0

† One accession each of six parental species involved in developing three released interspecific hybrids (1006 = C. leptopoda × C. laminuligera, 1016 = C. procumbens × C. llavea, and 1070 = C. ignea × C. angustifolia).
‡ Includes 33 new accessions collected in 1989.
§ Includes 468 accessions of 40 (29 previously uncollected) species collected in Brazil in 1989.

published data). A total of 486 accessions of 40 (29 previously uncollected) species were collected during these two expeditions, which were made cooperatively with Brazilian scientists. Roath and Widrlechner (1989, unpublished data) made two domestic collections of C. viscosissima, the only species native to the USA. Forty accessions were collected in 1987 and 33 more in 1989. Knapp et al. (1991b) has documented the oil and fatty acid diversity of the C. viscosissima germplasm collection.

Considerable effort on germplasm enhancement is now in progress (Graham, 1989; Knapp, 1990a,b; Thompson, 1990a; Thompson & Dierig, 1988a). Species receiving most attention are listed in Table 2-5. Research has been centered at Phoenix and Tucson, AZ; Corvallis, OR, and Ames, IA. Germplasm maintenance and storage is at the North Central Plant Introduction Station at Ames, IA. Research in Arizona has been essentially phased out and transferred to Iowa and Oregon. One approach emphasized in Arizona was an attempt to recombine and release new sources of genetic variability through interspecific hybridization and cytogenetic investigations (Gathman & Ray, 1987; Ray et al., 1988, 1989b). Graham (1988, 1989) has made significant contributions to characterization of species chromosome numbers and species relationships. Gathman is continuing cytogenetic and molecular biological research relative to speciation at Southeast Missouri State Univ., Cape Girardeau, MO. The fertile interspecific hybrid of *C. lanceolata* × *C. viscosissima* and its reciprocal (Ronis et al., 1990; Thompson & Dierig, 1988a) are now being used by Knapp and co-workers in Oregon and Roath in Iowa to accelerate domestication of *C. viscosissima* through genetic introgression.

Relatively little genetic information is available on the diverse group of species within the genus. Thompson (1989) reported on a single recessive gene designated *si* for shortened internodes, which conditions a compact growth habit within populations of *C. leptopoda*. Heritable isozyme variation has been characterized and used to determine systems of mating and outcrossing rates within *C. lanceolata, C. laminuligera, C. lutea*, and *C. viscosissima* in Oregon (Knapp & Tagliani, 1989a; Knapp et al., 1991a; Krueger & Knapp, 1990, 1991). Ronis et al. (1990) used isozyme variability to verify hybridity within three interspecific cuphea hybrids. Webb and Knapp (1990) have made significant progress in development of efficacious methods for DNA extraction from *Cuphea*, which had been previously characterized as recalcitrant. Restriction fragment length polymorphism (RFLP) and allozyme linkage maps of *C. lanceolata* are being constructed (S.J. Knapp, 1990, personal communication).

To date, no significant reduction in the rate of seed shattering has resulted through selection and breeding, and no meaningful genetic variability has been identified. The characteristic seed-shattering mechanism is one of the primary taxonomic descriptors that clearly differentiates *Cuphea* from other taxa in the Lythyraceae. Significant progress has been made to remove the constraint of seed dormancy in several of the species under investigation (Knapp, 1990a,b; Knapp & Tagliani, 1989b; Roath & Widrlechner, 1988). Selection is being employed to overcome dormancy and other constraints to domestication. A completely nondormant genetic stock of *C. lanceolata* is being registered and released (S.J. Knapp, 1990, personal communication).

Major attention is being given to variations in fatty acid biosynthesis and its possible modification by mutation breeding and molecular biological techniques. Webb and Knapp (1991) reported on genetic variability and heritability of oil seed among half-sib families of the allogamous species, *C. lanceolata*. Research is now centered on the domestication of *C. viscosissima*, which is a potentially high yielding, capric acid-rich (C10:0), autogamous species. Characteristically, this species has a severe dormancy problem and viscous trichomes on plant and flower parts. Sticky hairs on plants are not now considered to be a serious constraint to production, and may well provide an effective defense against aphids and other potentially harmful insects (S.J. Knapp, 1990, personal communication). Significant progress has been made in the modification of fatty acid biosynthesis in *C. viscosissima* by mutation breeding techniques. The fatty acid phenotypes of five mutant genetic stocks have been found to transgress the range found in wild populations. *Cuphea viscosissima* typically has a seed oil containing about 70% C10:0 and <3% C12:0. One of the true breeding mutant lines, VSCPY1, produces more than 14% C12:0 while still producing the same level of C10:0.

Two other lines VSCPR1 and VSCPR2 produce about 6% C12:0 and a reduced level of about 40% C10:0. Two of these mutants have been fully characterized (Knapp & Tagliani, 1991), and all five are currently being released and registered (S.J. Knapp, 1990, personal communication). These studies point out the possibilities of altering and developing new, useful cuphea germplasm tailored to supplying feedstock for various industrial applications and uses.

In total, about 926 accessions of 90 *Cuphea* spp. are held in the NPGS (Table 2-5). Of this total, 249 accessions from 39 species have received PI numbers. In addition, 21 interspecific hybrids are in the system. Three of these hybrids have been released jointly in 1990 by USDA-ARS and the Univ. of Arizona Agric. Exp. Stn. (unpublished "Release of Germplasm of Three *Cuphea* Interspecific Hybrids with Ornamental Potential"). Of the 35 accessions utilized, 32 accessions of 14 species were used in the development of the 21 interspecific hybrids. The Oregon Agric. Exp. Stn. is in the process of releasing a nondormant *C. lanceolata* in addition to the five fatty acid mutant germplasm lines of *C. viscosissima*. To date, no improved cultivars have been released, but an extensive breeding effort is in progress.

LESQUERELLA (BRASSICACEAE)

The seed oil of *Lesquerella* spp. is a good source of hydroxy fatty acids (lesquerolic, densipolic, and auricolic), and may serve as a replacement for imported castor oil. Ricinoleic and sebacic acids from castor oil are classified as critical materials by the U.S. Department of Defense. Lesquerella oil contains only minor quantities of ricinoleic acid, and sebacic acid cannot be produced from lesquerolic acid. However, lesquerella seed oil is believed to have broader utility than castor oil, and may serve as an essential chemical feedstock for production of a wide array of lubricants, plastics, protective coatings, surfactants, cosmetics, and pharmaceuticals. For example, dodecanedioic acid, currently only made from petroleum, can be produced readily from lesquerolic acid. A thorough study sponsored by the USDA Office of Agricultural Materials is in progress to assess fully the potential for commercialization of lesquerella as a new industrial crop and material source.

The USDA-ARS plant chemical screening program in the early 1960s at NCAUR, Peoria identified the seed oils of an array of *Lesquerella* spp. as good sources of three new hydroxy fatty acids (Kleiman et al., 1972; Mikolajczak et al., 1962; Miller et al., 1962; Smith et al., 1961, 1962). Kleiman (1990) and Smith (1979) present a good discussion on chemical aspects and utilization of the unique fatty acids of lesquerella. Using modern chromatographic techniques, Kleiman (1990, unpublished data) recently reassessed the seed oil composition of the current *Lesquerella* germplasm collection, including nine previously unreported species. He concluded that the genus contained significant amounts of chemical variation. Seed oil contents varied from 11 to 39%. Lesquerolic acid varied from zero to 78.7%. *Lesquerella fendleri*, which is the primary species targeted for domestication, had variation in lesquerolic acid from 55 to 60% in four accessions tested.

Rollins and Shaw (1973) recognized 69 species of *Lesquerella* native to North America. The greatest concentration of species is in southwestern USA, Northern Mexico, and the Rocky Mountain and intermontane basin region of the western USA. About 12 species also occur in South America, but they are not represented in the germplasm collection. Nothing is known about these species in regard to their seed oil and fatty acid content.

A concerted effort was made to assemble a comprehensive collection of germplasm (Barclay et al., 1962; Gentry & Barclay, 1962). The NPGS currently holds a total of 96 accessions of 22 different species (Table 2-6). Of the total, 10 PI and 21 other accessions not listed in GRIN are held in the USDA-ARS working germplasm collection at Phoenix, AZ. Active research on the domestication of species of *Lesqurella* as a new source of hydroxy fatty acids was initiated in 1984 at the USDA-ARS U.S. Water Conservation Laboratory, Phoenix, AZ. Prior to that time, some research on germplasm evaluation, selection, and cultural research was conducted by Dr. D.D. Rubis at the Univ. of Arizona from 1966 to 1977, but no published information is available on this effort. A working germplasm collection of 90 accessions of 23 *Lesquerella* spp. was assembled and evaluated (Thompson, 1985, 1988a). From this initial and subsequent evaluations, *L. fendleri* was clearly superior in agronomic commercialization potential to all the other species tested (Thompson & Dierig, 1988b; Thompson et al., 1989). A small selection and breeding program was initiated in 1985, which has resulted in significant increases in seed yield. Yields of 1400 kg ha^{-1} from an essentially unselected population have been obtained regularly in replicated yield trials (Thompson & Dierig, 1988b; Thompson et al., 1989). Half-sib families from single plant selections have been evaluated. A second cycle of a simple recurrent selection program is currently undergoing tests. Seed yields of 2000 kg ha^{-1} appear to be readily attainable. Abundant genetic variability is apparent within the species. Two putative male-sterile plants have been identified. The genetic basis for male sterility, yellow seed coat, and lemon-yellow flower color is currently under investigation. Isozyme variation both within *L. fendleri* and the other species in the germplasm collection is being assessed. Isozyme variation within *L. fendleri* is also being used to characterize the mating system within the species. To date, no breeding lines or cultivars have been released (Table 2-6).

The possibility of interspecific hybridization as a means for germplasm enhancement is being explored. Rollins and Solbrig (1973) document instances of interspecific hybridization among densipolic acid-rich *Lesquerella* spp. Steps are being taken to increase seed of 25 accessions of 13 *Lesquerella* spp. for further germplasm evaluation and utilization. A proposal is being developed to initiate a new germplasm collection of previously uncollected *Lesquerella* spp. and to recollect selected species currently held in the NPGS. As many as 16 *Lesquerella* spp., most of which have not been evaluated for seed oil or fatty acid content, are considered to be rare, and their future existence is either threatened or endangered.

Table 2-6. Utilization of lesquerella accessions in The National Plant Germplasm System (NPGS) for development of released germplasm lines and cultivars.

Species	No. of accessions in NPGS PI	No. of accessions in NPGS Other	No. of accessions used	No. of releases Germplasm lines	No. of releases Cultivars
Lesquerolic acid-rich species					
Lesquerella angustifolia	2	1†	0	0	0
L. argyraea	3	1	0	0	0
L. engelmannii	3†	1†	0	0	0
L. fendleri	21†	6†	0	0	0
L. globosa	0	1	0	0	0
L. gordonii	15†	13†	0	0	0
L. gracilis	3	0	0	0	0
L. grandiflora	3†	0	0	0	0
L. lasiocarpa	2†	0	0	0	0
L. ludoviciana	1	0	0	0	0
L. mirandiana	0	1	0	0	0
L. ovalifolia	0	1	0	0	0
L. palmeri	3	0	0	0	0
L. pinetorum	1	0	0	0	0
L. purpurea	1	0	0	0	0
L. recurvata	0	1	0	0	0
Densipolic acid-rich species					
L. densipila	5	0	0	0	0
L. lescurii	1	0	0	0	0
L. lyrata	1	0	0	0	0
L. perforata	2	0	0	0	0
L. stonensis	2†	0	0	0	0
Auricolic acid-rich species					
L. auriculata	1	0	0	0	0
Total	70†	26†	0	0	0

† Number of accessions held in the USDA-ARS working germplasm collection at Phoenix, AZ includes 10 PI and 21 other accessions not listed by GRIN.

In addition to the current USDA-ARS *Lesquerella* breeding and genetics effort in Arizona, research is also being conducted to develop a practical crop production system using conventional farm equipment similar to that used for winter wheat production in central Arizona. Research on processing and utilization is also in progress at NCAUR, Peoria (Carlson et al., 1990; Kleiman, 1990). Considerable interest in the utilization of *Lesquerella* seed oil is being indicated by several industrial companies. About 8 ha were planted in October 1990 at the Univ. of Arizona Maricopa Agricultural Center to provide seed for initial pilot oil extractions for industrial evaluation. Other plantings totalling more than 10 ha were also made in 1990 by private industry in Arizona, California, Oklahoma, and Texas.

VERNONIA (ASTERACEAE)

The seed oil of *Vernonia galamensis* (Cass.) Less. is a rich source of a naturally epoxidized fatty acid, vernolic acid. Epoxidized fatty acids are used in industry as plasticizers and stabilizers in the manufacture of plastics, and in the formulation of protective coatings and other products. Existing needs have been met with chemical modification of petrochemicals or through the epoxidation of fats and oils, chiefly soybean and linseed oils.

Gunstone (1954) originally discovered that seeds of *V. anthelmintica* from India and Pakistan contained substantial amounts of oil (23-31%) containing a naturally occurring epoxidized fatty acid (68-75%), which was subsequently named vernolic acid. A program was initiated in the mid-1950s by USDA-ARS, to introduce and evaluate germplasm, and to develop cultivars and crop production practices suitable to American agriculture. Information on use of specific accessions in the germplasm enhancement effort is not available, but more than 200 selections were made at Purdue University and evaluated from 1965 to 1967 (Berry et al., 1970). They concluded from a detailed study of 40 selections that significant genotypic variation existed for most characters evaluated. Utilization research on the oil and its components was also initiated concurrently. Uneven maturity of flowers and severe seed loss through shattering proved to be severe constraints to the development of usable cultivars in this species. Large-scale plantings in Nebraska and North Carolina were successfully harvested with farm combines, but losses from seed shattering were high. Seed storage studies by White and Bass (1971) showed that an adequate postharvest afterripening period effectively dissipated dormancy. Seeds placed in cold storage soon after harvest lost dormancy slowly. Post frost harvest resulted in reduced yields and lower germination. Another study (White & Earle, 1971) demonstrated that good quality vernonia seeds can be stored for relatively long periods without appreciable reduction in oil content or quality. Both utilization and agronomic research were concurrently phased out since economic crop production in the USA was judged to be unlikely. Details of this phase of the commercialization efforts of vernonia are well documented by Perdue et al. (1986). In total, 26 accessions of *V. anthelmintica* are currently being held in the NPGS (Table 2-7).

Germplasm explorations were undertaken in 1966 to 1967 in eastern and southern Africa to acquire seeds of related *Vernonia* spp. within the generic section Stenglia (Smith, 1971). Many species were collected, but none had good seed retention, and the seed oil yields were not impressive. Serendipitously, Dr. Robert E. Perdue, Jr., was collecting germplasm in Ethiopia in 1964 and discovered an annual nonstengloid species of *Vernonia* in a semi-arid area near Harar, which had excellent seed retention. The plant, initially identified as *V. pauciflora* (Willd.) Less., is now known as *V. galamensis* spp. *galamensis* var. *ethiopica* M. Gilbert. Details of the limited evaluation, agronomic and utilization research on this new germplasm are documented by Perdue (1988), Perdue et al. (1986), and Aziz et al. (1984). Seeds contained 41.9% oil with 72.6% vernolic acid, which was about 30% higher than

Table 2-7. Utilization of vernonia and Stokes aster accessions in The National Plant Germplasm System (NPGS) for development of released germplasm lines and cultivars.

Species	Constituents of interest	No. of accessions in NPGS PI	Other	No. of accessions used	No. of releases Germplasm lines	Cultivars
Vernonia:	Epoxy fatty acid					
Vernonia galamensis†						
spp. *galamensis*						
var. *galamensis*		1	3	0	0	0
var. *petitiana*		0	7	0	0	0
var. *ethiopica*		1	0	0	0	0
var. *australis*		2	1	0	0	0
spp. *nairobensis*		1	6	0	0	0
spp. *lushotoensis*		0	2	0	0	0
spp. *mutomensis*		0	3	0	0	0
spp. *afromontana*		3	2	0	0	0
spp. *gibbosa*		2	3	0	0	0
Total (*galamensis*)		10†	27†	0	0	0
V. anthelmintica		18	8	0	0	0
Other *Vernonia* spp. (*n* = 14)		33	15	0	0	0
Total		61	50	0	0	0
Stokes aster:	Epoxy fatty acid					
Stokesia laevis		35‡	0	29	4‡	0

† Number classified as *Vernonia galamensis* listed in the GRIN systems are 10 PI and three other accessions. A total of 24 other accessions are held in the USDA-ARS working germplasm collection at Phoenix, AZ.
‡ Four germplasm lines released and assigned PI numbers.

the best improved germplasm of *V. anthelmintica*. Unfortunately, the plants had a short-day photoperiodic requirement for flower and subsequent seed production, and was not adapted for production in the continental USA. However, agronomic research was initiated in Zimbabwe in 1983 on the unimproved germplasm, and significant seed yields have been obtained (Cunningham, 1987; Perdue, 1988; Perdue et al., 1986).

Interest has also been revived in vernonia utilization research (Afolabi et al., 1989; Ayorinde et al., 1988, 1989; Carlson & Chang, 1985; Carlson et al., 1981; Perdue, 1988; Perdue et al., 1986). A pilot plant extraction of oil from seed produced in Zimbabwe has recently been completed (K.D. Carlson, 1990, personal communication), which provided both oil and meal for further research and evaluation by industry. The Coatings Research Institute, Eastern Michigan Univ., Ypsilanti, MI, has recently initiated research on vernonia oil to develop "reactive diluents" for use in "high-solids" coatings (R.E. Perdue, 1990, personal communication). They believe the low viscosity of the oil will permit it to be used as a solvent or additive to alkyd-resin paints with the expectation that emissions of volatile organic compounds (VOC) will be greatly reduced. Volatile organic compounds react with N oxides in the presence of sunlight to create ground-level ozone, a deleterious component of smog. Other potential uses of vernonia oil in industrial products are baked coatings on metal panels (Carlson et al., 1981), and the synthesis of dibasic acids and interpenetrating polymer networks (Afolabi et al., 1989; Ayorinde et al., 1988, 1989).

This success stimulated interest in obtaining new germplasm within the highly diverse *V. galamensis* spp. complex that includes six subspecies, one of which has four varieties (Gilbert, 1986; Jeffrey, 1988; Perdue, 1988). Special attention was given to obtaining new germplasm that would be day neutral and flower under long day growing conditions with high mature seed retention. In addition to the 10 PI and three other accessions listed in the GRIN system, 24 new, additional accessions are held in the USDA-ARS working germplasm collection and are undergoing evaluation at Phoenix, AZ. Most of these new accessions have only received preliminary evaluation, and most have not yet been assigned PI numbers (Table 2-7). Seed supply of most accessions is currently limited. Some of the new accessions of several subspecies and varieties of *V. galamensis* have been found to be quantitative short day plants (Phatak et al., 1989). Field observations in Arizona as well as Georgia, Oregon, Iowa, Colorado, Texas, and Virginia indicate that some accessions of *V. galamensis* ssp. *galamensis* var. *petitiana* flower under long day growing conditions. Single plant selection and seed increases are being made within this material, which should provide the basis for a new, major domestication effort.

In addition to the two species that have received major attention, *V. anthelmintica* and *V. galamensis*, the NPGS has holdings of 48 accessions of 14 other species, which may have value in the newly activated germplasm enhancement efforts. To date no germplasm or cultivar releases have been made of any of the vernonias.

STOKES ASTER (ASTERACEAE)

Stokes aster, like vernonia, is also a potential source of vernolic acid. *Stokesia* is a monotypic genus in the tribe *Vernonia*, and is native to the southeastern USA (Gunn & White, 1974). Both seeds and plants of Stokes aster, an attractive cross-pollinated, perennial ornamental, are commercially available. The agronomic potential of Stokes aster was summarized by Campbell (1981) who reported that seed oil content of 20 *Stokesia laevis* accessions ranged from 27.0 to 44.0% with a mean of 38.5 ± 0.97%. Vernolic acid content ranged from 63.1 to 78.8% with a mean of 71.3 ± 1.03%. One accession, PI 383891, had both the highest oil and vernolic acid content.

Campbell (1981) further discussed studies on the mode of pollination, the evaluation of genetic variability within the germplasm collection, and provided a description of the breeding program being conducted at Beltsville, MD. The breeding approach was based upon recurrent selection primarily for seed retention and yield, and plant stand longevity. A total of 29 of the 32 then available PI accessions were used in the development of six populations, three early and three late flowering. Field-selected plants were evaluated for oil, vernolic acid, and protein content. Superior plants within each population were intercrossed in the greenhouse. From this material, Campbell officially released four germplasm populations in 1989, which subsequently received PI numbers in 1990 (Table 2-7.). BSLE 1 (PI 537295) involved a total of 16 PI accessions in its development. The other early flowering population BSLE 2 (PI 537296) only involved three PI accessions, which were also used for development of BSLE 1. The two late-flowering populations released as BSLL 1 (PI 537297) and BSLL 2 (PI 537298) both involved the same 17 accessions of which four were in common with BSLE 1 and only one in common with BSLE 2. One accession, PI 347645 was used in the creation of all four populations. Accessions PI 383876, 383893, and 391385 were involved in the development of three of the populations, BSLE 1, BSLL 1, and BSLL 2. This represents the highest percentage usage (90%) of accessions in the development of new released germplasm or cultivars of any of the new crops herein described.

Since the release of these four new accessions, little if any research has been conducted to develop Stokes aster as a new crop and source of epoxy fatty acids. Most of the recent interest in this area has been focused on *Vernonia*. However, some interest is being generated in a reevaluation of Stokes aster along with that of *V. galamensis* at Virginia State Univ., Petersburg, VA as part of the new 1890 Institution Capacity Building Research Grant Program. Management studies using these improved lines are needed to assess yield and productive longevity under field conditions. While the wild stands of *Stokesia* are rather limited and some threatened, germplasm is readily available especially from widespread populations in Mississippi.

SUMMARY AND FUTURE DEVELOPMENTS

Considerable variation exists among the various new industrial crops in the current level of research and developmental activity. Differences also exist in regard to the number of accessions available for domestication and new crop development. In total, about 6481 accessions of the 14 crop species are in the NPGS (3701 PI accessions plus 2780 other accessions). For guar, more than 1300 accessions are held by NPGS, whereas for buffalo and coyote gourd only 32 are in the system. As for grindelia, only 15 accessions are available, and none are currently in the NPGS.

The number of accessions held by NPGS may not necessarily be a good indication of the germplasm diversity of the candidate species. In general, too limited research has been done on most of these species to assess genetic diversity with any degree of accuracy. It is probably safe to conclude that genetic diversity for most of the 14 crop species in the germplasm collection is far from adequate with the exception of rapeseed, guar, guayule, and possibly kenaf and roselle.

The number of accessions held by NPGS is also not necessarily a good indicator of the number of accessions used to develop new improved germplasm and cultivars. Overall, only 137 (2.1%) of the total 6481 accessions of the 14 new crops have been used in developing new germplasm lines and cultivars. In total, only 51 ($\bar{x} = 3.6$) new germplasm lines and 27 ($\bar{x} = 1.9$)

cultivars have been released for the 14 crops. However, the range for germplasm lines is from 0 to 14 and from 0 to 7 for released cultivars for the 14 crops. No cultivars have been released for 6, and no germplasm lines have been released for 5 of the 14 crops. For grindelia, lesquerella, and vernonia, which have received minimal research attention to date, no germplasm line or cultivars have yet been released. Even though 10 germplasm lines and seven cultivars of guar have been released, only about 10 accessions out of a total of 1300 were used in their development.

It is apparent that the variability in numbers and adequacy of the available germplasm pool for development of improved germplasm and cultivars of these 14 potential new industrial crops is a reflection of the priority and financial resources allocated for research and development. It is true that underinvestment is the rule, and allocation of resources for research and development on even conventional food, feed, and fiber crops is currently inadequate. Numerous studies have documented annual high rates of return on investment in agricultural research from 20 to 50% (Evenson et al., 1979). Historically, only a very small proportion of agricultural research effort has been allocated for development of new or alternative crops. Since 1957, the USA has invested <1% of public sector agricultural research funds for this purpose (Sampson, 1987; Thompson, 1988b). This is difficult to rationalize since domestic production of only two of these new crops, natural rubber by guayule, and lauric acid and other medium-chain fatty acids by cuphea would offset the current annual cost of importation of about $1.5 billion worth of commodities. This is clearly a "catch-22" situation. Essentially all new industrial crops are expected to be economic successes before they are fully commercialized. They are expected to compete with little or no subsidy with imported or petroleum-derived products on the one hand, and conventional crops on the other. It is general knowledge that the production of most conventional agronomic crops are subsidized in one way or another, and supported by strong commodity organizations. With most new crops, major agricultural research and development funding is not forthcoming until the new crops have achieved a substantial production base and developed an established constituency. New mechanisms, funding, and organizational structure, such as those authorized by the FY 1990 Farm Bill, are clearly needed.

A new development, which should have impact on the development of new crops, is the authorization and formation of a new Crop Advisory Committee (CAC) for New Crops. The initial, organizational meeting of this CAC was held at the Agronomy Meetings at San Antonio, TX in October 1990. The opportunity now exists for effective recognition and evaluation of the wide array of germplasm needs for the wide array of new crops. Sound recommendations of the CAC to the NPGS should greatly improve the probability of positive action and success in full commercialization of a signficant number of these new industrial crops.

REFERENCES

Afolabi, O.A., M.E. Aluko, W.A. Anderson, and F.O. Ayorinde. 1989. Synthesis of a toughened elastomer from *Vernonia galamensis* seed oil. J. Am. Oil Chem. Soc. 66:983-985.

Alexander, W.L., D.A. Bucks, and R.A. Backhaus. 1988. Irrigation water management for guar seed production. Agron. J. 80:447-453.

Arndt, S. 1985. *Cuphea*, diverse fatty acid composition may yield oleochemical feedstock. J. Am. Oil Chem. Soc. 62:6-12.

Auld, D.L., and K.A. Mahler. 1987. Bridger and Cascade winter rapeseed varieties. Current Information Ser. 801. Univ. of Idaho, Moscow.

Auld, D.L., K.A. Mahler, B.L. Bettis, and J.C. Crock. 1987. Registration of 'Bridger' rapeseed. Crop Sci. 27:1310.

Auld, D.L., K.A. Mahler, and D.J. LeTourneau. 1989. Evaluation of four *Brassica* germplasm collections for fatty acid composition. J. Am. Oil Chem. Soc. 66:1475-1479.

Auld, D.L., K.A. Mahler, and A.A. Voorhis. 1988. Evaluation of the USDA collection of *Brassica* for fatty acid composition and glucosinolate content. Idaho Agric. Exp. Stn. Misc. Ser. 141.

Ayorinde, F.O., G. Osman, R.L. Shepard, and F.T. Powers. 1988. Synthesis of azelaic acid and suberic acid from *Vernonia galamensis* oil. J. Am. Oil Chem. Soc. 65:1774-1777.

Ayorinde, F.O., F.T. Powers, L.D. Streete, R.L. Shepard, and D.N. Tabir. 1989. Synthesis of dodecanedioic acid from *Vernonia galamensis* oil. J. Am. Oil Chem. Soc. 66:690-692.

Aziz, P., S.A. Kahn, and A.W. Sabir. 1984. Experimental cultivation of *Vernonia pauciflora*—a rich source of vernolic acid. Pak. J. Sci. Ind. Res. 27:215-219.

Bagby, M.O., C.R. Smith, Jr., T.K. Miwa, R.L. Lohmar, and I.A. Wolff. 1961. A unique fatty acid from *Limnanthes douglasii* seed oil: the C_{22} diene. J. Org. Chem. 26:1261-1265.

Barclay, A.S., H.S. Gentry, and Q. Jones. 1962. The search for new industrial crops II: *Lesquerella* (Cruciferae) as a source of new oilseeds. Econ. Bot. 16:95-100.

Bemis, W.P., J.W. Berry, and C.W. Weber. 1979. The buffalo gourd: a potential arid land crop. p. 65-87. *In* G.A. Ritchie (ed.) New agricultural crops. Westview Press, Boulder, CO.

Bemis, W.P., J.W. Berry, C.W. Weber, and T.W. Whitaker. 1978. The buffalo gourd: A new potential horticultural crop. HortScience 13:235-240.

Berry, C.D., K.J. Lessman, G.A. White, and F.R. Earle. 1970. Genetic diversity inherent in *Vernonia anthelmintica* (L.) Willd. Crop Sci. 10:178-180.

Brzezinski, W., and P. Mendelewski. 1984. Determination of total glucosinolate content in rapeseed meal with thymol reagent. Z. Pflanzenzucht. 93:177-183.

Buchanan, R.A., and J.A. Duke. 1981. Botanochemical crops. p. 157-179. *In* T.A. McClure and E.S. Lipinsky (ed.) CRC handbook of biosolar resources. Vol. II. Resource material. CRC Press, Boca Raton, FL.

Buchanan, R.A., and F.H. Otey. 1979. Multi-use oil- and hydrocarbon-producing crops in adaptive systems for food, material, and energy production. Biosources Dig. 1:176-202.

Calhoun, W., G.D. Jolliff, and J.M. Crane. 1983. Registration of Indore rapeseed. Crop Sci. 23:184-185.

Campbell, T.A. 1981. Agronomic potential of Stokes aster. p. 287-295. *In* E.H. Pryde et al. (ed.) New sources of fats and oils. Am. Oil Chem. Soc. Monogr. 9. Am. Oil Chem. Soc., Champaign, IL.

Campbell, T.A. 1984. Inheritance of seedling resistance to gray mold in kenaf. Crop Sci. 24:733-734.

Campbell, T.A. et al. 1986a. Registration of 'Belann' and 'BelEnzian' crambe. Crop Sci. 26:1082-1083.

Campbell, T.A. et al. 1986b. Registration of C-22, C-29, and C-37 crambe germplasm. Crop Sci. 26:1088-1089.

Campbell, T.A., and M.J. O'Brien. 1981. Differential response of kenaf to gray mold. Crop Sci. 21:88-90.

Campbell, T.A., and G.A. White. 1982. Population density and planting date effects on kenaf performance. Agron. J. 74:74-77.

Carlson, K.D., and S.P. Chang. 1985. Chemical epoxidation of a natural unsaturated epoxy seed oil from *Vernonia galamensis* and a look at epoxy oil markets. J. Am. Oil Chem. Soc. 62:934-939.

Carlson, K.D., A. Chaudhry, and M.O. Bagby. 1990. Analysis of oil and meal from *Lesquerella fendleri* seed. J. Am. Oil Chem. Soc. 67:438-442.

Carlson, K.D., W.J. Schneider, S.P. Chang, and L.H. Princen. 1981. *Vernonia galamensis* seed oil: A new source for epoxy coatings. p. 297-318. *In* E.H. Pryde et al. (ed.) New sources of fats and oils. Am. Oil Chem. Soc. Monogr. 9. Am. Oil Chem. Soc., Champaign, IL.

Carlson, K.D., and H.L. Tookey. 1983. Crambe meal as a protein source for feeds. J. Am. Oil Chem. Soc. 60:1979-1985.

Crane, J.C. 1947. Kenaf-fiber plant rival of jute. Econ. Bot. 1:334-350.

Crane, J.C. 1949. Roselle—a potentially important plant fiber. Econ. Bot. 3:89-103.

Cunningham, I. 1987. Zimbabwe and U.S. develop vernonia as a potentially valuable new industrial crop. Diversity 10:18-19.

Curtis, L.C. 1946. The possibilities of using species of perennial cucurbits as a source of vegetable fats and protein. Chemurgic Dig. 5:221-224.

DeVeaux, J.S., and E.B. Schultz, Jr. 1985. Development of buffalo gourd (*Cucurbita foetidissima*) as a semiaridland starch and oil crop. Econ. Bot. 39:454-472.

Dierig, D.A., D.T. Ray, and A.E. Thompson. 1989a. Variation of agronomic characters among and between guayule lines. Euphytica 44:265-271.

Dierig, D.A., A.E. Thompson, and D.T. Ray. 1989b. Relationship of morphological variables to rubber production in guayule. Euphytica 44:259-264.

Dierig, D.A., A.E. Thompson, and D.T. Ray. 1990. Estimated yield performance of new Arizona guayule selections. El Guayulero 12(1&2):12-20.

Downey, R.K. 1971. Agricultural and genetic potentials of cruciferous oilseed crops. J. Am. Oil Chem. Soc. 48:718-722.

Downey, R.K. 1988. From rapeseed to canola and beyond. p. 17-31. *In* L.L. Hardman and L. Waters (ed.) Strategies of alternative crop development: Case histories. Center for Alternative Plant and Animal Products. Univ. of Minnesota, St. Paul.

Estilai, A. 1985. Registration of Cal-5 guayule germplasm. Crop Sci. 25:369-370.

Estilai, A. 1986. Registration of Cal-6 and Cal-7 guayule germplasm. Crop Sci. 26:1261-1262.

Estilai, A., and D.T. Ray. 1991. Genetics, cytogenetics, and breeding of guayule. p. 47-92. *In* J.W. Whitworth and E.E. Whitehead (ed.) Guayule natural rubber. USDA-CSRS and Guayule Adm. Manage. Comm., Washington, DC.

Evenson, R.F., P.E. Waggoner, and V.W. Ruttan. 1979. Economic benefits from research. Science 205:1101-1107.

Foster, K.E., M.M. Karpiscak, J.G. Taylor, and N.G. Wright. 1983. Guayule, jojoba, buffalo gourd and Russian thistle: Plant characteristics, products and commercialization potential. Desert Plants 5:112-117, 126.

Gathman, A.C., and W.P. Bemis. 1990. Domestication of buffalo gourd, *Cucurbita foetidissima*. p. 335-348. *In* D.M. Bates et al. (ed.) Biology and utilization of the Cucurbitaceae. Cornell Univ. Press, Ithaca, NY.

Gathman, A.C., and D.T. Ray. 1987. Meiotic analysis of fourteen *Cuphea* species and two interspecific hybrids. J. Hered. 78:315-318.

Gentry, H.S. 1958. The natural history of jojoba (*Simmondsia chinensis*) and its cultural aspects. Econ. Bot. 12:261-295.

Gentry, H.S., and A.S. Barclay. 1962. The search for new industrial crops III: Prospectus of *Lesquerella fendleri*. Econ. Bot. 16:206-211.

Gentry, H.S., and R.W. Miller. 1965. The search for new industrial crops IV: Prospectus of *Limnanthes*. Econ. Bot. 19:25-32.

Gilbert, M.G. 1986. Notes on east African *Vernonieae* (Compositae). A revision of the *Vernonia galamensis* complex. Kew Bull. 41:19-24.

Graham, S.A. 1988. Revision of *Cuphea* section Heterodon (Lythraeceae). Syst. Bot. Monogr. 20:1-168.

Graham, S.A. 1989. *Cuphea*: A new plant source of medium-chain fatty acids. Crit. Rev. Food Sci. Nutr. 28:139-173.

Graham, S.A., F. Hirsinger, and G. Röbbelen. 1981. Fatty acids of *Cuphea* (Lythraceae) seed lipids and their systematic significance. Am. J. Bot. 68:908-917.

Graham, S.A., and R. Kleiman. 1985. Fatty acid composition in *Cuphea* seed oils from Brazil and Nicaragua. J. Am. Oil Chem. Soc. 62:81-82.

Gunn, C.R., and G.A. White. 1974. *Stokesia laevis*: Taxonomy and economic value. Econ. Bot. 28:130-135.

Gunnstone, F.D. 1954. Fatty acids. Part II. The nature of the oxygenated acid present in *Vernonia anthelmintica* (Willd.) seed oil. J. Chem. Soc. (London) May: 1611-1616.

DEVELOPING NEW INDUSTRIAL CROP CULTIVARS

Hammond, B.L., and L.G. Polhamus. 1965. Research on guayule (*Parthenium argentatum*): 1942-1959. USDA Agric. Tech. Bull. 1327. U.S. Gov. Print. Office, Washington, DC.

Higgins, J.J., W. Calhoun, B.C. Willingham, D.H. Dinkel, W.L. Raisler, and G.A. White. 1971. Agronomic evaluation of prospective new crop species. II. The American *Limnanthes*. Econ. Bot. 25:44-54.

Hinman, C.W. 1984. New crops for arid lands. Science 225:1445-1448.

Hinman, C.W. 1986. Potential new crops. Sci. Am. 255:33-37.

Hirsinger, F. 1985. Agronomic potential and seed composition of cuphea, an annual crop for lauric and capric seed oils. J. Am. Oil Chem. Soc. 62:76-80.

Hirsinger, F., and P.F. Knowles. 1984. Morphological and agronomic descriptions of selected *Cuphea* germplasm. Econ. Bot. 38:439-451.

Hoffmann, J.J. 1983. Arid lands plants as feedstocks for fuel and chemicals. Crit. Rev. Plant Sci. 1:95-116.

Hoffmann, J.J. 1985. Resinous plants as an economic alternative to bioenergy plantations. Energy 10:1139-1143.

Hoffmann, J.J., B.E. Kingsolver, S.P. McLaughlin, and B.N. Timmermann. 1984. Production of resins by arid-adapted Asteraceae. p. 251-271. *In* B.N. Timmermann et al. (ed.) Phytochemical adaptations to stress. Plenum, New York.

Hoffmann, J.J., and S.P. McLaughlin. 1986. *Grindelia camporum*: Potential cash crop for the arid Southwest. Econ. Bot. 40:162-169.

Hogan, L. 1979. Jojoba: A new crop for arid regions. p. 177-205. *In* G.A. Ritchie (ed.) New agricultural crops. Westview Press, Boulder, CO.

Hogan, L., and W.P. Bemis. 1983. Buffalo gourd and jojoba: Potential new crop for arid lands. Adv. Agron. 36:317-349.

Hogan, L., D.A. Palzkill, and R.E. Dennis. 1981. Production of jojoba in Arizona. Arizona Agric. Exp. Stn. Coop. Ext. Serv. Publ. 81132.

Hymowitz, T. 1972. The transdomestication concept as applied to guar. Econ. Bot. 26:49-60.

Jackson, K.J., and J.A. Doughton. 1982. Guar: A potential industrial crop for the dry tropics of Australia. J. Austr. Inst. Agric. Sci. 48:17-32.

Jain, S.K. 1989. Domestication of *Limnanthes* (meadowfoam) as a new oil crop. p. 121-134. *In* Plant domestication by induced mutation. Int. Atomic Energy Agency, Vienna.

Jaworski, C.A., M.H. Bass, S.C. Phatak, and A.E. Thompson. 1988. Differences in leaf intumescences between *Cuphea* species. HortScience 23:908-909.

Jeffrey, C. 1988. The Vernonieae in East Tropical Africa. Notes on Compositae: V. Kew Bull. 43:195-277.

Jolliff, G.D. 1981. Development and production of meadowfoam (*Limnanthes alba*). p. 269-285. *In* E.H. Pryde et al. (ed.) New sources of fats and oils. Am. Oil Chem. Soc. Monogr. 9. Am. Oil Chem. Soc., Champaign, IL.

Jolliff, G.D. 1988. Meadowfoam domestication in Oregon: A chronological history. p. 53-56. *In* L.L. Hardman and L. Waters (ed.) Strategies for alternative crop development: Case histories. Center for Alternative Crops and Products. Univ. of Minnesota, St. Paul.

Jolliff, G.D., W. Calhoun, and J.M. Crane. 1984. Development of a self-pollinated meadowfoam from interspecific hybridization. Crop Sci. 24:369-370.

Kleiman, R. 1990. Chemistry of new industrial oilseed crops. p. 196-203. *In* J. Janick and J.E. Simon (ed.) Advances in new crops. Timber Press, Portland, OR.

Kleiman, R., G.F. Spencer, F.R. Earle, H.J. Nieschlag, and A.S. Barclay. 1972. Tetra-acid triglycerides containing a new hydroxy eicosadienoyl moiety in *Lesquerella auriculata* seed oil. Lipids 7:660-665.

Knapp, S.J. 1990a. Recurrent mass selection for reduced seed dormancy in *Cuphea laminuligera* and *Cuphea lanceolata*. Plant Breed. 104:46-52.

Knapp, S.J. 1990b. New temperate industrial oilseed crops. p. 203-310. *In* J. Janick and J.E. Simon (ed.) Advances in new crops. Timber Press, Portland, OR.

Knapp, S.J., and L.A. Tagliani. 1989a. Genetics of allozyme variation in *Cuphea lanceolata* Ait. Genome 32:57-63.

Knapp, S.J., and L.A. Tagliani. 1989b. Genetic variation for seed dormancy in *Cuphea laminuligera* and *Cuphea lanceolata*. Euphytica 47:65-70.

Knapp, S.J., and L.A. Tagliani. 1991. Two medium-chain fatty acid mutants of *Cuphea viscosissima* Plant Breed. 106:338-341.

Knapp, S.J., L.A. Tagliani, and B.H. Liu. 1991a. Outcrossing rates of experimental populations of *Cuphea lanceolata*. Plant Breed. 106:334-337.

Knapp, S.J., L.A. Tagliani, and W.W. Roath. 1991b. Fatty acid and oil diversity of *Cuphea viscosissima:* A source of medium-chain fatty acids. J. Am. Oil Chem. Soc. 68:515-517.

Knowles, P.F., et al. 1984. Development of new crops: Needs, procedures, strategies, and options. Rep. 102. Counc. Agric. Sci. Technol. Ames, IA.

Knox, E.G., and A.A. Theisen (ed.) 1981. Feasibility of introducing new crops: Production-Marketing-Consumption (PMC) systems. A report prepared for the Natl. Sci. Found. by Soil and Land Use Technol., Columbia, MD. Rodale Press, Emmaus, PA.

Kramer, J.K.G., F.D. Sauer, and W.J. Pigden (ed.) 1983. High and low erucic rapeseed oils: Production, usage, chemistry and toxicological evaluation. Academic Press, New York.

Krueger, S.K., and S.J. Knapp. 1990. Genetics of allozyme variation in *Cuphea laminuligera* and *Cuphea lutea.* J. Hered. 81:351-358.

Krueger, S.K., and S.J. Knapp. 1991. Mating systems of *Cuphea laminuligera* and *Cuphea lutea.* Theor. Appl. Genet. 82:221-226.

Kugler, D.E. 1988a. Kenaf newsprint: Realizing commercialization of a new crops after four decades of research and development. USDA-CSRS, Spec. Projects and Program Systems, Washington, DC.

Kugler, D.E. 1988b. Development and commercialization of kenaf: Newsprint leads the way. p. 67-72. *In* L.L. Hardman and L. Waters (ed.) Strategies of alternative crop development: Case histories. Center for Alternative Plant and Animal Products. Univ. of Minnesota, St. Paul.

Kugler, D. 1990. Kenaf: Nonwoody fiber crop. Commercialization of kenaf for newsprint. p. 289-292. *In* J. Janick and J.E. Simon (ed.) Advances in new crops. Timber Press, Portland, OR.

Kuruvadi, S. 1988. Identification and evaluation of consistently high rubber yielding genotypes in native guayule populations. El Guayalero 10(3&4): 10-14.

Leppik, E.E., and G.A. White. 1975. Preliminary assessment of *Crambe* germplasm resources. Euphytica 24:681-689.

Lessman, K.J. 1990. Crambe: A new industrial crop in limbo. p. 217-222. *In* J. Janick and J.E. Simon (ed.) Advances in new crops. Timber Press, Portland, OR.

Lessman, K.J., and W.P. Anderson. 1981. Crambe. p. 223-246. *In* E.H. Pryde et al. (ed.) New sources of fats and oils. Am. Oil Chem. Soc. Monogr. 9. Am. Oil Chem. Soc., Champaign, IL.

Lessman, K.J., and V.D. Meier. 1972. Agronomic evaluation of crambe as a source of oil. Crop Sci. 12:224-227.

Mahler, K.A., and D.L. Auld. 1989. Fatty acid composition of 2,100 accessions of *Brassica.* Idaho Agric. Exp. Stn. Misc. Ser. 125.

Mason, C.T., Jr. 1952. A systematic study of the genus *Limnanthes* R. Br. p. 455-507. *In* Univ. of California Publ. Bot. 25. Univ. of California Press, Berkeley.

McCallum, W.B. 1941. The cultivation of guayule. I. and II. India Rubber World 105:33-36, 153-156.

McLaughlin, S.P. 1985. Economic prospects for new crops in the southwestern United States. Econ. Bot. 39:473-481.

McLaughlin, S.B. 1986a. Heritabilities of traits determining resin yield in gumweed (*Grindelia camporum*). J. Hered. 77:368-370.

McLaughlin, S.B. 1986b. Mass selection for increased resin yield in *Grindelia camporum* (Compositae). Econ. Bot. 40:155-161.

McLaughlin, S.P. 1986c. Differentiation among populations of tetraploid *Grindelia camporum.* Am. J. Bot. 73:1748-1754.

McLaughlin, S.P., and J.J. Hoffmann. 1982. Survey of biocrude-producing plants from the Southwest. Econ. Bot. 36:323-339.

McLaughlin, S.P., B.E. Kingsolver, and J.J. Hoffmann. 1983. Biocrude production in arid lands. Econ. Bot. 37:150-158.

McLaughlin, S.P., and J.D. Linker. 1987. Agronomic studies of gumweed (*Grindelia camporum*); seed germination, planting densities, planting dates, and biomass and resin production. Field Crops Res. 15:357-368.

McNaughton, I.H. 1976. Swedes and rapes. *Brassica napus* (Cruciferae). p. 53-56. *In* N.W. Simmonds (ed.) Evolution of crop plants. Longman, New York.

Meier, V.D., and K.J. Lessman. 1973a. Breeding behavior for crosses of *Crambe abyssinica* and a plant introduction designated *C. hispanica.* Crop Sci. 13:49-51.

Meier, V.D., and K.J. Lessman. 1973b. Heritabilities of some agronomic characters for the interspecific cross of *Crambe abyssinica* and *C. hispanica.* Crop Sci. 13:237-240.

DEVELOPING NEW INDUSTRIAL CROP CULTIVARS

Menzel, M.Y. 1986. Genetic relationships among the relatives of *Hibiscus cannabinus* and *H. sabdariffa*: Sources of new germplasm for kenaf and roselle. p. 445-456. *In* K.A. Siddiqui and A.M. Faruqui (ed.) New genetical approaches to crop improvement. PIDC Print. Press (Pvt) Ltd., Karachi, Pakistan.

Menzel, M.Y., P.A. Fryxell, and F.D. Wilson. 1983. Relationships among New World species of *Hibiscus* sect. *Furcaria* (Malvaceae). Brittonia 35:204-221.

Menzel, M.Y., and J.F. Hancock. 1984. Cytotaxonomy of the octoploid and decaploid species of *Hibiscus* sect. *Furcaria* (Malvaceae). The Nucleus 27:48-63.

Menzel, M.Y., and F.D. Wilson. 1969. Genetic relationships in *Hibiscus* sect. *Furcaria*. Brittonia 21:91-125.

Mihail, J.D., and S.M. Alcorn. 1986. *Macrophomina phaseolina* from guar in Arizona. Can. J. Bot. 64:11-12.

Mikolajczak, K.L., F.R. Earle, and I.A. Wolff. 1962. Search for new industrial oils. VI. Seed oils of the genus of *Lesquerella*. J. Am. Oil Chem. Soc. 39:78-80.

Miller, R.W., M.E. Daxenbichler, F.R. Earle, and H.S. Gentry. 1964a. Search for new industrial oils. VIII. The genus *Limnanthes*. J. Am. Oil Chem. Soc. 41:167-169.

Miller, R.W., F.R. Earle, I.A. Wolff, and Q. Jones. 1964b. Search for new industrial oils. IX. *Cuphea*, a versatile source of fatty acids. J. Am. Oil Chem. Soc. 41:279-280.

Miller, R.W., C.H. Van Etten, and I.A. Wolff. 1962. Amino acid composition of *Lesquerella* seed meals. J. Am. Oil Chem. Soc. 39:115-117.

Milligan, S.B. 1984. Effect of plant density in guar seed yield and its components. M.S. thesis. Univ. of Arizona, Tucson.

Naqvi, H.H., and I.P. Ting. 1990. Jojoba: A unique liquid wax producer from the American desert. p. 247-251. *In* J. Janick and J.E. Simon (ed.) Advances in new crops. Timber Press, Portland, OR.

National Academy of Science. 1975. Underexploited tropical plants with promising economic value. Natl. Acad. of Sci., Washington, DC.

National Academy of Science. 1977. Guayule: An alternative source of natural rubber. Natl. Acad. of Sci., Washington, DC.

National Research Council. 1985. Jojoba: New crop of arid lands, new raw material for industry. Natl. Acad. Press, Washington, DC.

Nelson, J.M., J.C. Scheerens, J.W. Berry, and W.P. Bemis. 1983. The effects of plant population and planting date on root and starch production of buffalo gourd grown as an annual. J. Am. Soc. Hortic. Sci. 108:198-201.

Nelson, J.M., J.C. Scheerens, T.L. McGriff, and A.C. Gathman. 1988. Irrigation and plant spacing effects on seed production of buffalo and coyote gourds. Agron. J. 80:60-65.

Niehaus, M.H. 1983. The role of the Guayule Administrative Management Committee in guayule commercialization research. El Guayulero 5(2&3):15-19.

Palzkill, D.A., M.H. Younes, and L. Hogan. 1989. AT-1310, AT-1487, and AT-3365: Clonal jojoba germplasm selected for horticultural use. HortScience 24:526-527.

Paroda, R.S., and M.L. Saini. 1978. Guar breeding. Forage Res. 4A:9-39.

Perdue, R.E., Jr. 1988. Systematic botany in the development of *Vernonia galamensis* as a new industrial oilseed crop for the semi-arid tropics. Acta Univ. Uppsala Symb. Bot. Ups. XXVIII (3):125-135.

Perdue, R.E., Jr., K.D. Carlson, and M.G. Gilbert. 1986. *Vernonia galamensis*, potential new crop source of epoxy acid. Econ. Bot. 40:54-68.

Phatak, S.C., A.E. Thompson, C.A. Jaworski, and D.A. Dierig. 1989. Response of *Vernonia galamensis* to photoperiod. Abstr. 8. *In* Abstracts of First Annual Conf. Assoc. for the Advancement of Industrial Crops, Peoria, IL. 2-6 Oct. Assoc. for the Advancement of Ind. Crops, Peoria, IL.

Princen, L.H. 1977. Need for renewable coatings raw materials and what could be available today. J. Coat. Technol. 49:88-93.

Princen, L.H. 1979. New crop developments for industrial oils. J. Am. Oil Chem. Soc. 56:845-848.

Princen, L.H. 1982. Alternate industrial feedstocks from agriculture. Econ. Bot. 36:302-312.

Princen, L.H. 1983. New oilseed crops on the horizon. Econ. Bot. 37:478-492.

Princen, L.H., and J.A. Rothfus. 1984. Development of new crops for industrial raw materials. J. Am. Oil Chem. Soc. 61:281-289.

Purdy, R.H., and C.D. Craig. 1987. Meadowfoam: New source of long-chain fatty acids. J. Am. Oil Chem. Soc. 64:1493-1494, 1496-1497.

Ray, D.T. (chm.). 1986. Preliminary report of the first guayule uniform regional variety trials (1982-1985). El Guayulero 7(3&4):10-27.

Ray, D.T., D.A. Dierig, and A.E. Thompson. 1990. Facultative apomixis in guayule as a source of genetic diversity. p. 245-247. In J. Janick and J.E. Simon (ed.) Advances in new crops. Timber Press, Portland, OR.

Ray, D.T., D.A. Dierig, A.E. Thompson, F.S. Nakayama, G.E. Hamerstrand, M.A. Foster, J. Moore, A. Estilai, J.G. Waines, C.L. Gonzalez, and J.R. Mulkey. 1989a. The second guayule uniform regional yield trials. El Guayulero 11(3&4):45-54.

Ray, D.T., A.C. Gathman, and A.E. Thompson. 1989b. Cytogenetic analysis of interspecific hybrids in *Cuphea*. J. Hered. 80:329-332.

Ray, D.T., and R.E. Stafford. 1985a. Genetic nomenclature in guar. Crop Sci. 25:177-179.

Ray, D.T., and R.E. Stafford. 1985b. Registration of Santa Cruz guar. Crop Sci. 25:1124-1125.

Ray, D.T., and A.E. Thompson. 1988. *Cuphea*—A new ornamental plant. Ariz. Land People 38(4):12.

Ray, D.T., A.E. Thompson, and A.C. Gathman. 1988. Interspecific hybridization in *Cuphea*. HortScience 23:751-753.

Roath, W.W., and M.P. Widrlechner. 1988. Inducing germination of dormant *Cuphea* seeds and the effects of various induction methods on seedling survival. Seed Sci. Technol. 16:699-703.

Röbbelen, G., and F. Hirsinger. 1982. *Cuphea*, the first annual oil crop for the production of medium-chain triglycerides (MCT). p. 161-170. In Improvement of oilseed and industrial crops by induced mutations. Panel Proc. Ser. Int. Atomic Energy Agency, Vienna.

Röbbelen, G., and W. Thies. 1980. Biosynthesis of seed oil and breeding for improved seed oil quality of rapeseed. p. 253-283. In *Brassica* crops and wild allies. Japan Sci. Soc. Press, Tokyo.

Robinson, F.E. 1988. Kenaf: A new fiber crop for paper production. Calif. Agric. 42(5):31-32.

Roetheli, J., and M. Blase. 1989. Vegetable oils high in erucic acid—crambe and industrial rapeseed. Growing Industrial Materials (unnumbered series), USDA-CSRS, Office of Agric. Ind. Materials, Washington, DC.

Rollins, R.C., and E.A. Shaw. 1973. The genus *Lesquerella* (Cruciferae) in North America. Harvard Univ. Press, Cambridge, MA.

Rollins, R.C., and O.T. Solbrig. 1973. Interspecific hybridization in *Lesquerella*. Contrib. Gray Herb. 203:3-48.

Ronis, D.H., A.E. Thompson, D.A. Dierig, and E.R. Johnson. 1990. Isozyme verification of interspecific hybrids of *Cuphea*. HortScience 25:1431-1434.

Roth, W.B., I.M. Cull, R.A. Buchanan, and M.O. Bagby. 1982. Whole plants are renewable energy resources: Checklist of 508 species analyzed for hydrocarbon, oil, polyphenol, and protein. Trans. Ill. State Acad. Sci. 75:217-231.

Rosemeyer, M.E., J.K. Brown, and M.R. Nelson. 1986. Five viruses isolated from field-grown buffalo gourd (*Cucurbita foetidissima*), a potential crop for semiarid lands. Plant Dis. 70:405-409.

Sampson, R.L. (chm.) 1987. New farm and forest products. Response to the challenges and opportunities facing American agriculture. A Report from the New Farm and Forest Product Task Force to the Sec. of Agric. USDA, Washington, DC.

Scheerens, J.C., W.P. Bemis, M.L. Dreher, and J.W. Berry. 1978. Phenotypic variation in fruit and seed characteristics of buffalo gourd. J. Am. Oil Chem. Soc. 55:523-525.

Scheerens, J.C., and J.W. Berry. 1986. Buffalo gourd: Composition and functionality of potential food ingredients. Cereal Foods World 31:183-192.

Scheerens, J.C., M.J. Kopplin, I.R. Abbas, J.M. Nelson, A.C. Gathman, and J.W. Berry. 1987a. Feasibility of enzymatic hydrolysis and alcoholic fermentation of starch contained in buffalo gourd (*Cucurbita foetidissima*) roots. Biotechnol. Bioeng. 29:436-444.

Scheerens, J.C., T.L. McGriff, A.E. Ralowicz, M.H. Wilkins, and J.M. Nelson. 1989. Variation in seed yield components of buffalo gourd (*Cucurbita foetidissima* HBK.) grown as an annual. Euphytica 40:55-62.

Scheerens, J.C., A.E. Ralowicz, T.L. McGriff, K.E. Bee, J.M. Nelson, and A.C. Gathman. 1991. Phenotypic variation of agronomic traits among coyote gourd accessions and their progeny. Econ. Bot. 45:365-378.

Scheerens, J.C., Y.M.R. Yousef, A.E. Ralowicz, A.C. Gathman, and H.M. Scheerens. 1987b. Floral development, flowering patterns and growth rate of monoecious and gynoecious buffalo gourd. J. Am. Soc. Hortic. Sci. 112:574-578.

Schuck, S.M., and S.P. McLaughlin. 1988. Flowering phenology and outcrossing in tetraploid *Grindelia camporum* Greene. Desert Plants 9:7-16.

Seiler, G.J., and R.E. Stafford. 1985. Factor analysis of components of yield in guar. Crop Sci. 25:905-908.

Shands, H.L., and G.A. White. 1990. New crops in the U.S. National Plant Germplasm System. p. 70-75. *In* J. Janick and J.E. Simon (ed.) Advances in new crops. Timber Press, Portland, OR.

Smith, C.E., Jr. 1971. Observations on Stengeloid species of *Vernonia*. USDA-ARS Agric. Handb. 396, U.S. Gov. Print. Office, Washington, DC.

Smith, C.R., Jr. 1979. Unusual seed oils and their fatty acids. p. 29-47. *In* E.H. Pryde (ed.) Fatty acids. Am. Oil Chem. Soc., Champaign, IL.

Smith, C.R., Jr., M.O. Bagby, T.K. Miwa, R.L. Lohmar, and I.A. Wolff. 1960. Unique fatty acids from *Limnanthes douglasii* seed oil: the C_{20}- and C_{22}-monoenes. J. Org. Chem. 25:1770-1774.

Smith, C.R., Jr., T.L. Wilson, R.B. Bates, and C.R. Schofield. 1962. Densipolic acid: A unique hydroxydienold acid from *Lesquerella densipila* seed oil. J. Org. Chem. 27:3112-3117.

Smith, C.R., Jr., T.L. Wilson, T.K. Miwa, H. Zobel, R.L. Lohmar, and I.A. Wolff. 1961. Lesquerolic acid. A new hydroxy acid from *Lesquerella* seed oil. J. Org. Chem. 26:2093-2095.

Stafford, R.E., M.L. Kinman, L.E. Brooks, and C.R. Lewis. 1976a. Registration of Brooks, Hall, and Mills guar. Crop Sci. 16:309.

Stafford, R.E., J.S. Kirby, M.L. Kinman, and C.R. Lewis. 1976b. Registration of Kinman and Esser guar. Crop Sci. 16:310.

Stafford, R.E., and C.R. Lewis. 1981. Registration of five guar germplasm lines. Crop Sci. 21:147-148.

Stafford, R.E., and B.L. McMichael. 1990. Primary root and lateral root development in guar seedlings. Environ. Exp. Bot. 30:27-34.

Stafford, R.E., and D.T. Ray. 1985. Registration of Lewis guar. Crop Sci. 25:365.

Stafford, R.E., D.T. Ray, D.L. Johnson, and R.K. Thompson. 1983. Five guar germplasm lines. Crop Sci. 23:808.

Theisen, A.A., E.G. Knox, and F.L. Mann. 1978. Feasibility of introducing food crops better adapted to environmental stress. Vol. I. Vol. II (Individual crop report, with H.B. Sprague as junior author). Report prepared for the National Science Foundation. U.S. Gov. Print. Office, Washington, DC.

Thompson, A.E. 1984. *Cuphea*—A potential new crop. HortScience 19:352-354.

Thompson, A.E. 1985. New native crops for the arid Southwest. Econ. Bot. 39:436-453.

Thompson, A.E. 1986. Germplasm evaluation of *Cuphea*, a potentially new ornamental crop. HortScience 21:884 (Abstr.).

Thompson, A.E. 1988a. Lesquerella—A potential new crop for arid lands. p. 1311-1320. *In* E.E. Whitehead et al. (ed.) Arid lands: Today and tomorrow. Westview Press, Boulder, CO.

Thompson, A.E. 1988b. Alternative crop opportunities and constraints on development efforts. p. 1-9. *In* L.L. Hardman and L. Waters (ed.) Strategies of alternative crop development: Case histories. Ctr. for Alternative Plant and Animal Products, Univ. of Minnesota, St. Paul.

Thompson, A.E. 1989. Nature and inheritance of compact plant habit in *Cuphea leptopoda* Hemsley. HortScience 24:368-370.

Thompson, A.E. 1990a. Breeding new industrial crops. p. 100-103. *In* J. Janick and J.E. Simon (ed.) Advances in new crops. Timber Press, Portland, OR.

Thompson, A.E. 1990b. Arid-land industrial crops. p. 232-241. *In* J. Janick and J.E. Simon (ed.) Advances in new crops. Timber Press, Portland, OR.

Thompson, A.E., and D.A. Dierig. 1988a. *Cuphea* for medium-chain fatty acids. El Guayulero 10(1&2):5-7.

Thompson, A.E., and D.A. Dierig. 1988b. *Lesquerella*—A new arid land industrial oil seed crop. El Guayulero 10(1&2):16-18.

Thompson, A.E., D.A. Dierig, and E.R. Johnson. 1989. Yield potential of *Lesquerella fendleri* (Gray) Wats., a new desert plant resource for hydroxy fatty acids. J. Arid Environ. 16:331-336.

Thompson, A.E., D.A. Dierig, S.J. Knapp, and R. Kleiman. 1990. Variation in fatty acid content and seed weight in some lauric acid rich *Cuphea* species. J. Am. Oil Chem. Soc. 67:611-617.

Thompson, A.E., and R. Kleiman. 1988. Effect of seed maturity on seed oil, fatty acid and crude protein content of eight *Cuphea* species. J. Am. Oil Chem. Soc. 65:139–146.

Thompson, A.E., and D.T. Ray. 1988. Breeding guayule. Plant Breed. Rev. 6:93–165.

Thompson, A.E., D.T. Ray, M. Livingston, and D.A. Dierig. 1988. Variability of rubber production and plant growth characteristics among single plant selections from a diverse guayule breeding population. J. Am. Soc. Hortic. Sci. 113:608–611.

Thompson, A.E., D.T. Ray, and M.S. Roh. 1987. Evaluation of *Cuphea procumbens* × *C. llavea* hybrids as new floral and bedding plants. HortScience 22:1142–1143. (Abstr.).

Timmermann, B.N., D.J. Luzbetak, J.J. Hoffmann, S.D. Joland, K.H. Schram, R.B. Bates, and R.E. Klenck. 1983. Grindelane diterpenoids from *Grindelia camporum* and *Chrysothamnus paniculatus*. Phytochemistry 22:523–525.

Tysdal, H.M., A. Estilai, I.A. Siddiqui, and P.F. Knowles. 1983. Registration of four guayule germplasms. Crop Sci. 23:189.

Van Dyne, D.L., and M.G. Blase. 1989. Commercializing high erucic acid oil crops. Trans. Mo. Acad. Sci. 23:13–22.

Van Dyne, D.L., M.G. Blase, and K.D. Carlson. 1990. Industrial feedstocks and products from high erucic acid oil: crambe and industrial rapeseed. Unnumbered bull. Univ. of Missouri, Columbia.

Vasconcellos, J.A., W.P. Bemis, J.W. Berry, and C.W. Weber. 1981. The buffalo gourd *Cucurbita foetidissima* HBK, as a source of edible oil. p. 55–68. *In* E.H. Pryde et al. (ed.) New sources of fats and oils. Monogr. 9. Am. Oil Chem. Soc., Champaign, IL.

Vinizky, I., and D.T. Ray. 1988. Germination of guar seed under salt and temperature stress. J. Am. Soc. Hortic. Sci. 113:437–440.

Webb, D.M., and S.J. Knapp. 1990. DNA extraction from a previously recalcitrant plant genus. Plant Mol. Biol. Rep. 8:180–185.

Webb, D.M., and S.J. Knapp. 1991. Estimates of genetic parameters for oil yield of a *Cuphea lanceolata* population. Crop Sci. 31:621–624.

Wheaton, E.R. (chair). 1984. Growing industrial materials: Renewable resources from agriculture and forestry. Report of the Critical Materials Task Force on the role of American agriculture and forestry in maintaining supplies of critical materials. USDA, Washington, DC.

Wheaton, E.R. 1990. Industrial crops commercialization. p. 41–46. *In* J. Janick and J.E. Simon (ed.) Advances in new crops. Timber Press, Portland, OR.

Whistler, R.L., and T. Hymowitz. 1979. Guar: Agronomy, production, industrial use, and nutrition. Purdue Univ. Press, West Lafayette, IN.

White, G.A. 1975. Distinguishing characteristics of *Crambe abyssinica* and *C. hispanica*. Crop Sci. 15:91–93.

White, G.A. 1977. Plant introductions—A source of new crops. p. 17–24. *In* D.S. Seigler (ed.) Crop resources. Academic Press, New York.

White, G.A., and L.N. Bass. 1971. *Vernonia anthelmintica*: A potential seed oil source of epoxy acid. III. Effects of line, harvest date, and seed storage on germination. Agron. J. 63:439–441.

White, G.A., et al. 1970. Cultural harvesting methods of kenaf—An annual crop source of pulp in the Southeast. USDA Prod. Res. Rep. 113. USDA-ARS, Washington, DC.

White, G.A., and F.R. Earle. 1971. *Vernonia anthelmintica*: A potential seed oil source of epoxy acid. IV. Effects of line, harvest date, and seed storage on quantity and quality of oil. Agron. J. 63:441–443.

White, G.A., and J.J. Higgins. 1966. Culture of crambe, a new industrial oilseed crops. USDA-ARS Prod. Res. Rep. 95. USDA-ARS, Washington, DC.

White, G.A., and M. Solt. 1978. Chromosome numbers in *Crambe, Crambella*, and *Hemicrambe*. Crop Sci. 18:160–161.

Wilson, F.D. 1978. Wild kenaf. *Hibiscus cannabinus* L. (Malvaceae), and related species in Kenya and Tanzania. Econ. Bot. 18:80–91.

Wilson, F.D., and M.Y. Menzel. 1964. Kenaf (*Hibiscus cannabinus*), roselle (*Hibiscus sabdariffa*). Econ. Bot. 18:80–91.

Wilson, F.D., T.E. Summers, J.F. Joyner, D.W. Fisher, and C.C. Seale. 1965. 'Everglades 41' and 'Everglades 71'—two new varieties of kenaf (*Hibiscus cannabinus* L.) for fiber and seed. Florida Agric. Exp. Stn. Cir. S-168.

Wolf, R.B., S.A. Graham, and R. Kleiman. 1983. Fatty acid composition of *Cuphea* seed oils. J. Am. Oil Chem. Soc. 60:27–28.

3 Use of Introduced Germplasm in Cool-Season Food Legume Cultivar Development

F. J. Muehlbauer
USDA-ARS
Washington State University
Pullman, Washington

Cool-season food legumes, including pea (*Pisum sativum* L.), lentil (*Lens culinaris* Medik.), chickpea (*Cicer arietinum* L.), faba bean (*Vicia faba* L.), and grasspea (*Lathyrus sativus* L.), had their origin in the Mediterranean basin and the near-east arc. Carbonized remains in that region indicate that pea, lentil, and chickpea were cultivated with cereals as early as the seventh millennium B.C. (Ladizinsky & Adler, 1976; Smartt, 1990; Williams et al., 1974; Zohary, 1972, 1973). The eastern Mediterranean region to Asia Minor into central Asia are considered important areas where these crops were likely domesticated; however, the eastern Mediterranean seems most important for the evolution and domestication of the cool-season food legumes (Khvostova, 1975; Makasheva, 1973; Smartt & Hymowitz, 1985).

From their centers of origin, cultivation of the cool-season food legumes spread to other areas. The pea spread to the cool-temperate areas of central and northern Europe and particularly to the USSR where they became a major pulse crop. The pea also found its way to northern India and China where it is now grown extensively as a green vegetable or dry edible pulses. Apparently, pea was one of the first crops introduced into the New World soon after Columbus' voyage (Hedrick, 1928). Since domestication, the pea has been used mainly as dry pulses; however, the development of a succulent garden pea, canning pea, freezing pea, edible podded pea, and most recently, the "snap pea" have demonstrated their genotypic versatility and popularity as food crops. The greatly expanded use of pea in recent years as a protein supplement for livestock feeding in the European Economic Community underscores their value as a feed crop. Pea production in the USA has stabilized at about 500 000 acres including all types of peas. The pea seed industry is also important in the northwestern states and provides high-quality pea seed to U.S. processors and overseas users as well.

Cultivation of lentil also spread to other areas soon after domestication. Lentil has acquired the reputation as a crop that can produce some yield

---

Copyright © 1992 Crop Science Society of America, 677 S. Segoe Rd., Madison, WI 53711, USA. *Use of Plant Introductions in Cultivar Development, Part 2,* CSSA Special Publication no. 20.

under adverse conditions of poor fertility and limited moisture; while alternate crops often fail completely under the same conditions. Lentil is a major food crop and a dietary staple in India, Pakistan, Bangladesh, Afghanistan, Iran, the Middle East, Turkey, Ethiopia, and northern Africa. The crop was introduced into South America by the Spaniards and into North America by immigrants from north and central Europe. The crop is now produced over large areas in the western hemisphere, usually in rotation with cereals. Production of lentil in the USA has fluctuated in response to market demands at about 150 000 acres annually, 85 to 90% of which is exported.

Domestication of the chickpea apparently was in the same region of southwest Asia as lentil and pea. From its presumed center of origin in the Near East and Asia Minor, chickpea quickly spread to the Indian subcontinent where it now is the major cool-season food legume grown on over 20 million acres annually and is a dietary mainstay. Chickpea remains an important crop in the Mediterranean basin and the Middle East. Two distinct types of chickpea have evolved since domestication. The "desi" type is by far the most important in the subcontinent of India and Ethiopia, and is characterized by small seeds that are angular and variously pigmented. The preference for desi types in these areas may relate to the pigments in the testa that appear to impart certain fungistatic properties. These fungistatic properties appear to prevent seed rotting when planted in pathogen-infected soils, and ensure seedling emergence and plant establishment in regions where the crop is important to local populations. In contrast, the "kabuli" type, popular in most other parts of the world where chickpea is grown, is characterized by large seeds that have a rounded appearance and lack pigmentation. In most areas where kabuli types are grown, it is necessary to use fungicidal seed treatments to obtain satisfactory seedling emergence.

Chickpea was brought to North and South America by the Spaniards and Portuguese. In the USA, production is confined to coastal areas of southern California and the Palouse region of eastern Washington and northern Idaho. In these areas, the kabuli type predominates; however, a small but increasing acreage of desi types is developing. In contrast to the use of chickpea worldwide as a dietary staple, U.S. consumption is mainly as an additional attraction in salad bars.

Faba bean was domesticated in western Asia or central Asia (Bond et al., 1985), but its exact origin and its wild progenitor are still unknown. Domestication probably occurred during the Neolithic period. By the third millennium B.C., the crop was already widely distributed throughout the Mediterranean region and into northern Europe. The crop spread along the Nile valley and into Ethiopia soon after domestication. The introduction of faba bean into China was more recent and it was not until the silk trade around 1200 A.D. that the large-seeded "major" type was introduced to China. The crop was introduced to the western hemisphere soon after Columbus and became an important food crop in South America. *Favism*, a disease characterized by haemolytic anemia, is not uncommon in the Mediterranean region where the faba bean is consumed in large quantities. Toxic compounds in faba bean seeds are believed responsible for favism (Kay, 1979).

Faba bean has not become an important crop in the USA. The small amount produced is mainly used as feed and forage for livestock. Faba bean is often used as a winter forage. Grazing is usually discontinued in early spring and the plants can then produce a seed crop in early summer. During the era of the draft horse (*Equus* spp.), the crop was an important source of feed and hence it became known in the USA as "horse beans."

Grasspea is of unknown origin, but is considered native to southern Europe and western Asia (Duke, 1981, p. 107-110). The crop is widely grown in dry regions of India, the Middle East, and South America. The crop is especially drought tolerant and can be grown under adverse conditions of poor soil, low fertility, and limited soil moisture. The crop is not grown to any extent in the USA, but an interest in the crop has developed in the prairies of central and western Canada. Grasspea is adapted to dry areas and it may possibly be successfully grown in the arid western USA. The major use for the crop would be as a protein supplement for animal feeding. Use of grasspea for human food is limited because of its high content of B-N-oxalyl-L-2,B diaminopropionic acid (ODAP) that acts as an antagonist in amino acid metabolism (Smartt, 1990), causing a condition commonly referred to as *Lathyrism*. Promising results have been obtained through breeding for low concentrations of ODAP acids in Canada (A.E. Slinkard, 1990, personal communication). Selections with low ODAP concentration may lead to the development of grasspea as a food crop for dry areas.

Germplasm collections and their utilization have enabled public and private breeders to solve critical disease problems with the cool-season food legumes. Genetic variation for disease resistance, stress tolerance, morphological and quality traits found in land races and wild forms has contributed to cultivar development in these crops. These and other aspects relative to improving cool-season food legumes are discussed in this chapter.

STATUS OF GERMPLASM COLLECTIONS

Location of Major Germplasm Collections

Major collections of the cool-season food legumes are maintained in the USA by the National Plant Germplasm System, at the International Centers in Syria and India, and at facilities of national programs in several countries (Table 3-1).

Germplasm collections of pea are available from several sources. The Weibullsholm genetic stocks collection maintained by the Nordic Gene Bank at Alnarp, Sweden has been designated by the International Board of Plant Genetic Resources (IBPGR) as the World *Pisum* germplasm collection (Bettencourt et al., 1989). This World collection is the work of the late Professor Herbert Lamprecht and more recently, Dr. Stig Blixt. The collection is particularly well characterized genetically and samples of accessions are available on request. Another well-defined genetic stocks collection resulted from the work of the late Dr. Gerry A. Marx at Geneva, NY. The Marx collection

Table 3-1. Major collection of cool-season food legumes. (From van der Maesen et al., 1988, revised.)

Institute and Location	Pisum	Lens	Cicer	Vicia sect. faba	Lathyrus
Ege Agric. Res. Introd. Centre, Menemen, Turkey	2 000				
Ethiopian Genebank, Addis Abab, Ethiopia	1 860	413	717	1 298	
Marx Genetic Stocks Collection, Geneva, NY	>500				
Germplasm Lab., Bari, Italy	5 000			2 000	
ICARDA, Aleppo, Syria		6 000	4 500	5 000	100
ICRISAT, Patancheru, India			14 000		
INIA, Mexico City, Mexico			1 600		
John Innes Inst., Norwich, England	2 000				
NBPGR, New Delhi, India	1 400				
Netherlands Genebank, Wageningen, Netherlands	800			700	
Nordic Genebank, Alnarp, Sweden	5 000				
Natl. Seed Storage Lab., Fort Collins, CO	2 213	702	2 698	18	
Pakistan Agric. Res. Counc., Islamabad, Pakistan	10	144	626	13	
Reg. Plant Introduction Stn., Geneva, NY	2 800				
Reg. Plant Introduction Stn., Pullman, WA		1 973	3 431	295	330
Vavilov Inst., Plant Industry, Leningrad, USSR	5 550	2 470	1 685	2 525	
ZG Kulturpfl., Gatersleben, Germany	2 000	160	40	1 300	
Inst., of Crop Germplasm Resources, Beijing, Peoples Republic of China	1 677	336	23	1 999	

includes many cultivars, PI accessions, mutants, and enhanced stocks. Much of the G.A. Marx germplasm has been made available to both basic and applied researchers. A catalog describing the G.A. Marx genetic stock collection is being prepared by Dr. James McFerson of the Northeast Regional Plant Introduction Station, Geneva, NY. Other genetically well-defined *Pisum* collections are maintained at Waitrowo, Poland by Dr. W.K. Swiecicki and at Hobart, Tasmania, Australia by Dr. Ian Murfet.

Important *Pisum* germplasm collections are also maintained at Edinburgh, Scotland, UK; the John Innes Institute at Norwich, England; the Vavilov Institute at Leningrad, USSR: Gatersleben, Germany; and Bari, Italy. The U.S. *Pisum* collection is currently maintained by the Northeast Regional Plant Introduction Station, Geneva, NY. The collection numbers more than 2800 accessions and includes cultivars, land races, and wild and primitive forms.

By far the largest germplasm collection of lentil is maintained by the International Center for Agricultural Research in the Dry Areas (ICARDA),

Aleppo, Syria and numbers 4700 accessions (Table 3-1). The ICARDA collection includes many accessions from the national collections of India, Turkey, Ethiopia, and the USA. The U.S. collection contains more than 2250 accessions from 40 countries. The U.S. and ICARDA collections now include wild *Lens* spp. that were recently collected in the centers of origin.

The International Crops Research Institute for the Semi-Arid Tropics (ICRISAT), Hyderabad, India and ICARDA have extensive collections of chickpea (Table 3-1). The initial material used to establish these collections was made available by the former USDA Regional Pulse Improvement Project centered in Iran and India in the late 1960s. That project assembled 4177 accessions of cultivated types that were then made available to the ICARDA and ICRISAT collections. Most of these accessions were also added to the *Cicer* collection maintained in the USDA-ARS Regional Plant Introduction Station at Pullman, WA. The USDA-ARS collection currently numbers more than 3800 accessions of cultivated and wild forms from more than 20 countries. Many of the wild forms in the collection were obtained from the ICRISAT collection. The wild forms in the ICRISAT collections were largely the result of collection efforts of Dr. L.J.G. van der Maesen. Also included among the wild *Cicer* spp. in the USDA collection are the collections made by F.J. Muehlbauer, W.J. Kaiser, and C.R. Sperling in Turkey in 1985 and 1989.

An extensive collection of faba bean is maintained at ICARDA (Table 3-1). Other centers also have sizeable collections of faba bean, most important of which are the collections maintained at Bari, Italy; Leningrad, USSR; and Beijing, People's Republic of China. The origin of faba bean is still unknown and no extant wild species are cross compatible with the cultivated type. Ladizinsky et al. (1988) speculated that the origin of faba bean might be northern Pakistan.

The USDA-ARS *Lathyrus* collection maintained at Pullman, WA contains 330 accessions of 13 species (Table 3-1). Little information is available concerning other *Lathyrus* collections, but sizeable collections are maintained at ICRISAT and ICARDA. These collections represent important sources of germplasm for development of this drought-tolerant crop.

Availability of Wild Species in Germplasm Collections and Their Cross-compatibility to Cultivated Types

The germplasm collections of the cool-season food legumes include many accessions of wild species of *Pisum, Lens*, and *Cicer*. The number of wild species was augmented by collections made by G. Ladizinsky, F.J. Muehlbauer, W.J. Kaiser, and C.R. Sperling during the 1970s and 1980s. Accessions of wild species are duplicated in the ICARDA, ICRISAT, and USDA-ARS collections and are available for breeding purposes. Evaluations of wild species accessions for disease resistance resulted in identified resistance to chickpea Ascochyta blight in perennial accessions of wild *Cicer* spp., and to root knot nematode in accessions of annual wild species of *Cicer*. However, systematic evaluation of the wild species collections of the food legumes for other important traits are yet to be undertaken.

Cross-compatibility Groups in the Cool-season Food Legumes

Cross-compatibility studies between wild and cultivated species have been reported for *Pisum, Lens, Cicer,* and *Vicia* (Ben Ze'ev & Zohary, 1973; Ladizinsky & Adler, 1976; Ladizinsky et al., 1985; Ladizinsky et al., 1988; Pickersgill et al., 1985; Polhill & van der Maesen, 1985; Smartt, 1990). Cross-compatibility groups for pea, lentil, chickpea, faba bean, and grasspea are as follows:

Pea

The genus *Pisum* comprises the species *P. sativum* and *P. fulvum* Sibth & Sm. both with $2n = 14$ chromosomes (Polhill & van der Maesen, 1985). *Pisum sativum* comprises subspecies *sativum*, the cultivated species and ssp. *elatius* (M. Bieb.) Alef. Aschers & Graebn. Cultivated *P. sativum* ssp. *sativum* has been divided into var. *sativum*, that contains the horticultural types, and var. *arvense* that contains fodder peas and winter pea types. Subspecies *elatius* comprises var. *elatius* (M. Bieb.) Alef., var. *pumilio* Meikle (*P. humile* Boiss. & Noe) and var. *brevipedunculatum* Davis & Meikle (Smartt, 1990). All subspecies of *P. sativum* are at least partially cross-compatible and, with the exception of certain chromosomal translocations, show full chromosome homology. A distinctive form endemic in Ethiopia has in the past been classified as *P. abyssinicum* A. Br., however, it is more properly considered as a subspecies of *P. sativum* (Smartt, 1990).

The second biological species of *Pisum, P. fulvum* Sibth & Sm., comprises relatively small plants with yellow-brownish flowers and small pods. Crosses between *P. fulvum* and members of *P. sativum* subspecies can be made with little difficulty, but *P. fulvum* must be the pollen parent.

Lentil

The genus *Lens* comprises two biological species (Ladizinsky et al., 1984, 1988). Similar to the *pisum* spp., all *Lens* spp. have $2n = 14$ chromosomes. The preeminant biological species, *L. culinaris*, comprises three subspecies including ssp. *culinaris*, the cultivated type; ssp. *orientalis* (Boiss.) Handel-Mazzeti, the presumed progenitor of the cultivated type; and ssp. *odemensis* Ladizinsky, a newly discovered subspecies that differs from ssp. *orientalis* and ssp. *culinaris* by three chromosomal translocations, but is still partially fertile when intercrossed with ssp. *culinaris*.

The other biological species of *Lens, L. nigricans* (Bieb.) Godron, comprises two subspecies including ssp. *nigricans* and ssp. *ervoides* (Brign.) Grande. These two subspecies produce partially fertile hybrids when intercrossed presumably because they differ by two to four chromosomal rearrangements (Ladizinsky et al., 1988). Crosses of ssp. *ervoides* with *L. culinaris* ssp. *culinaris* have been made with the assistance of embryo rescue and embryo culture (Ladizinsky et al., 1985). Crosses of the cultivated types with ssp. *nigricans* have been reported; but, because ssp. *nigricans* is cross-compatible with ssp. *ervoides*, the latter subspecies can be used as a bridge to obtain gene flow to cultivated types.

Chickpea

The genus *Cicer* was originally included in the Vicieae tribe, but was removed from that tribe and placed in a monogeneric tribe Cicereae Alef. (Kupicha, 1977). The genus *Cicer* comprises nine annual and 31 perennial species. All annual species have $2n = 16$ chromosomes.

The nine annual species of *Cicer* have been divided into four cross-compatibility groups on the basis of fertility of the interspecific hybrids (Ladizinsky et al., 1988). The first cross-compatibility group includes *C. arietinum*, the cultivated chickpea and two closely related wild species, *C. reticulatum* Lad. and *C. echinospermum* Dav. Crosses among these species produce fertile or partially fertile hybrids. *Cicer reticulatum* is the presumed progenitor based on morphological similarities between the two species and the nearly complete fertility of F_1 hybrids. Cytological examinations indicate that *C. echinospermum* differs from *C. reticulatum* and *C. arietinum* by a reciprocal translocation (Ladizinsky, 1975; Ladizinsky & Adler, 1976).

The other annual *Cicer* spp., including *C. bijugum* K.H. Rech., *C. pinnatifidum* Jaub. & Spach, *C. judaicum* Boiss., *C. yamashitae* Kitam., *C. chorassanicum* (Bge.) M. PoP., and *C. cuneatum* Hochst. are all cross-incompatible with the cultivated species, and therefore constitute a tertiary gene pool of chickpea.

Faba bean

Vicia is a large genus comprising more than 130 species (Smartt, 1990). *Vicia faba*, the cultivated species with $2n = 12$ chromosomes, is included in section Faba along with *V. narbonensis* L., *V. hyaeniscyamus* Mouterde, *V. galilaea* Plitm. and Zohary, *V. johannis* Tamamschian, and *V. bithynica* (L.) L. (Ladizinsky et al., 1988; Smartt, 1990). However, *V. faba* is reproductively isolated from other *Vicia* spp. and successful crosses involving *V. faba* and other *Vicia* spp. have not been possible.

Grasspea

The chromosome complement of *Lathyrus* spp. is most commonly $2n = 14$, although some polyploidy has been reported (Smartt, 1990). Few attempts have been made to obtain interspecific hybrids among the *Lathyrus* spp.; however, successful hybridizations have been reported, including crosses of *L. sativus* with *L. cicera* L., and *L. odoratus* L. with *L. hirsutus* L. (Smartt, 1990).

SOURCES OF RESISTANCE TO STRESSES THAT REDUCE PRODUCTIVITY OF COOL-SEASON FOOD LEGUMES

The diseases and pests that reduce productivity of the cool-season food legumes worldwide were recently reviewed (Bos et al., 1988; van Emden et al., 1988; Kraft et al., 1988; Nene et al., 1988). A large number of these diseases and insect pests cause serious problems with production of food legumes in the USA (Tables 3-2, 3-3, 3-4).

Disease Resistance

Pea

The pea crop has the longest history of production in the USA and by far the largest number of production problems. Foremost among these problems are the diseases that affect the crop. Pea root rots caused by *Pythium, Aphanomyces,* and *Fusarium* spp., have been a chronic problem and have been studied for more than 30 yr (Kraft et al., 1988). Germplasm, resistant or tolerant to these root pathogens, has been identified (Table 3-5) and used to develop resistant or tolerant cultivars. Unfortunately, when improved or enhanced germplasm is used by private breeders, the use of such publicly developed germplasm is usually not acknowledged. It is difficult, therefore, to determine the impact of introduced material on sustaining pea productivity.

Table 3-2. Important diseases and pests of pea in the USA.

Disease/Pest	Scientific notation
Diseases:	Causative organism(s)
Root rot	*Aphanomyces euteiches* f. sp. *pisi* Drechs., *Fusarium solani* f. sp. *pisi* (F.R. Jones) Synd. & Hans., *Pythium ultimum* Trow
Fusarium wilt	*Fusarium oxysporum* Schl. f. sp. *pisi* Snyd. & Hans. races 1, 2, 5 & 6
Powdery mildew	*Erysiphe pisi* Syd.
Downy mildew	*Peronospora pisi* Syd.
Sclerotinia white mold	*Sclerotinia sclerotiorum* (Lib.) de Bary
Bacterial blight	*Pseudomonas pisi* Sackett
Pea enation mosaic virus	
Bean leaf roll virus	
Pea streak virus	
Pea seed-borne mosaic virus	
Insects:	Genus and species
Pea aphid	*Acrythosiphon pisum* (Harris)
Pea seed weevil	*Bruchus pisorum* L.
Pea leaf weevil	*Sitona lineatus* L.
Loopers	*Autographa californica* (Speyer) *Anagrapha falcifera* (Kirby)
Nematodes:	
Root knot nematode	*Meliodogyne* spp.

Table 3-3. Important diseases and pests of lentil in the USA.

Disease/Insect	Scientific notation
Diseases:	Organism
Pea enation mosaic virus	
Bean (pea) leaf roll virus	
Pea streak virus	
Insects:	Genus and species
Lygus bugs	*Lygus hesperus* Knight, *L. elisus* Van duzee
Pea aphids	*Acyrthosiphon pisum* (Harris)

Breeding lines of pea, released by public plant breeders, have played an important role in developing improved cultivars. A good example is the recent development of Minn. 108 (Davis et al., 1976), a breeding line that has been used extensively in public and private breeding programs. Minn. 108 was preceded by the development of Minn. 494A-11 (King et al., 1981), a germplasm line with moderate-to-high resistance to Aphanomyces root rot incited by *Aphanomyces eutieches* f. sp. *pisi* Drechs. Minn. 494A-11 was apparently developed by intercrossing eight PI lines identified by King et al. (1960) as resistant to Fusarium and Pythium root rot (Table 3-5), followed by field testing and intercrossing surviving plants. In addition, 378A, also prominent in the pedigree of Minn. 108, was a progeny line developed from intercrossing and testing those original eight resistant PI lines (Fig. 3-1).

Most of the other germplasm lines released as sources of wilt resistance, root rot tolerance, or other diseases (Gritton, 1990; Gritton & Hagedorn, 1971; Kraft, 1981, 1984, 1989; Kraft & Giles, 1978a,b; Kraft & Tuck, 1986) have PI material in their parentage either directly or indirectly. Many of these lines have resistance to Fusarium root rot incited by *F. solani* (Mart.) Appel & Wr. f. sp. *pisi* (F.R. Jones) Snyd. & Hans. and Pythium root rot incited by *Pythium ultimum* Trow. For example, the germplasm lines released by Kraft (1989) were developed from previously released germplasm that used PI material. The parentage of 86-638 was 691008 (a Race 5 wilt resistant selection from PI 244113 made by Dr. W.A. Haglund at Mt. Vernon, WA) crossed with PH-91-3, a germplasm line released by Kraft et al. (1972) which

Table 3-4. Important diseases and pests of chickpea in the USA.

Disease/Insect	Scientific notation
Diseases:	Organism
Ascochyta blight	*Ascochyta rabiei* (Pass.) Lab.
Seed rot	*Pythium ultimum* Trow
Fusarium wilt	*Fusarium oxysporum* Schl. f. sp. *ciceri* Snyd. & Hans.
Pea enation mosaic virus	
Pea streak virus	
Bean (pea) leaf roll virus	
Insects:	Genus and species
Pea aphid	*Acrythosiphon pisum* (Harris)

Table 3-5. Germplasm lines of pea resistance or tolerance to root rots and wilts.

Disease	Sources of resistance or tolerance	Reference(s)
Common root rot incited by *Aphanomyces eutieches*	PI 116159, PI 167250, PI 169604, PI 176721, PI 180693, PI 180702, PI 180868, PI 784129	Lockwood, 1960
	PI 175227 (sel)	Marx et al., 1972
	Minn. 108	Davis et al., 1976
	Minn. 494A-11	King et al., 1981
	792022	Kraft, 1981
	75-786, 85-1638, 84-1930	Kraft & Tuck, 1986
	WIS 8901-RR, WIS 8902-RR, WIS 8903-RR, WIS 8904-RR, WIS 8905-RR	Gritton, 1990
	86-638; 86-2197; 86-2231; 86-2236	Kraft, 1989
Fusarium root rot	PI 164417-India; PI 164837-India; PI 164917-Turkey; PI 165577-India; PI 165965-India; PI 169606-Turkey; PI 171816-Turkey; PI 173507-Turkey	King et al., 1960
	PI 140165; PI 174921; PI 174922; PI 179969; PI 196013; PI 196021; PI 196022; PI 242028; PI 257593	Kraft, 1975
	PI 140165; PI 183910; PI 194006; PI 210587; PI 223285	Kraft & Roberts, 1970
	PH 14-119; PH 91-3	Kraft et al., 1972
	VR 410-2; VR 1492-1	Kraft & Giles, 1978b
	RR-178; WR-1167	Kraft, 1984
	792022	Kraft, 1981
Fusarium wilt	PI 203066; PI 171816; PI 164971; PI 280616; PI 210568; PI 169606; PI 169006; PI 162693; PI 164837	Haglund, 1976
	PI 189171	Kraft & Tuck, 1986
	PI 280616 (res to races 5 & 6); WSU 31 (res to all races); PI 244092 (res to all races); PI 206789 (res to races 5 & 6)	Haglund & Anderson, 1987
	74SN3; 74SN4; 74SN5; (691005); (691009); PI 210568; PI 203066	Kraft & Giles, 1976

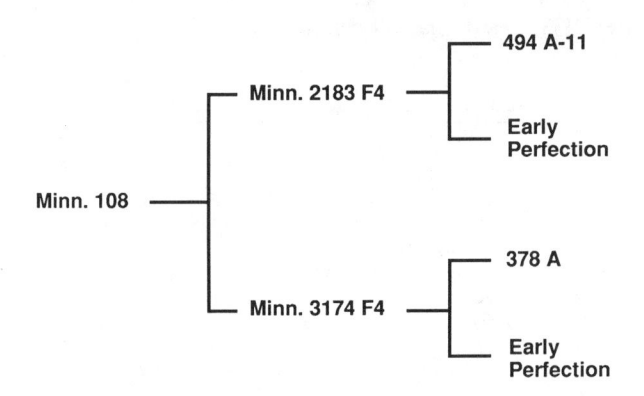

```
                                    ┌── 494 A-11
                 ┌── Minn. 2183 F4 ──┤
                 │                  └── Early Perfection
Minn. 108 ───────┤
                 │                  ┌── 378 A
                 └── Minn. 3174 F4 ──┤
                                    └── Early Perfection
```

Fig. 3-1. Pedigree of Minn. 108 Pea. (From Davis et al., 1976.)

had PI 166159 in its parentage, and PI 257593, a root rot resistant line identified by Kraft (1975). Similarly, the parentage of 84–1638 (Kraft & Tuck, 1986) included PI 189171, a line resistant to Fusarium wilt race 1 and tolerant to Fusarium root rot. Also, 84–1930 was derived from the cross of PH-91-3 × 792022. Germplasm line PH-91-3, as previously mentioned, has two PI lines in its parentage while 792022 was derived from a cross involving PH-14-119 with the original "afila" line of Goldenberg (1965). The recent releases of Gritton (1990) have used Minn. 494 and Minn. 108, both germplasm lines developed from PI material, in their parentage (Table 3–5).

A common problem in the use of introduced material for cultivar development is the difficulty in transferring genes of interest while leaving behind undesirable or deleterious traits. The lines of Gritton (1990) were further enhanced toward improved quality cultivars by the inclusion in their parentage the so-called CSC lines that were identified as "quality cultivars." The common root rot resistant/tolerant germplasm lines used in those crosses were derived from PI material from India and Turkey identified as resistant more than 30 yr earlier by King et al. (1960) (Table 3–5). Another problem that can be associated with introduced germplasm is seed-borne pathogens (fungal, bacterial, or viral). Such pathogens may persist and spread within breeding nurseries.

Fusarium wilt race 1 of pea, incited by *F. oxysporum* Schl. f. sp. *pisi* Snyd. & Hans., first appeared in 1924 and was described by Linford (1928). The disease was soon discovered in Washington, Idaho, and New York (Wade et al., 1938). Screening of 1024 available cultivars showed that resistance to the disease was five times more common than susceptibility, and the disease was quickly brought under control by resistant cultivars. However, a second race of the fungus appeared that rendered race 1 resistant cultivars susceptible (Snyder & Walker, 1935). This second race was designated as "near wilt" because of its similarities to race 1 wilt. Near wilt was controlled through a dominant resistance gene found in 'Delwiche Commando' (Hare et al., 1948). Races 1 and 2 were the only economically important wilt races in the USA until race 5 appeared in Northwest Washington in 1963 (Haglund & Kraft, 1970) and race 6 appeared in the same area in 1979 (Haglund & Kraft, 1979).

Resistance to race 5 of Fusarium wilt was found in the PI collection of pea and led to the release of three germplasm lines (Haglund, 1976). The lines were developed from crosses of resistant PI material with 'NWR Hyalite,' a cultivar from the Galatin Valley Seed Company that had resistance to races 1 and 2. Subsequently, other germplasm lines were released by Kraft and Giles (1976) and Haglund and Anderson (1987), some of which were also resistant to race 6. Resistance to each of the four economically important races is controlled by a single dominant gene in each case. In the cases of Fusarium wilt races 1 and 2, resistance was quickly found in commercial-type cultivars; however, resistance to races 5 and 6 was not and hybridization and selection were required to develop acceptable resistant cultivars.

Ascochyta blight incited by *Ascochyta* spp. is an especially severe disease of pea in midwestern USA (Lawyer, 1984). However, even though extensive screening for resistance has been conducted, no reliable sources of resistance have been discovered. Resistance and partial resistance to *Phoma medicaginis* var. *pinodella* (Jones) Boerema (= *Ascochyta pinodella*) was reported by Sakar (1980) (Table 3-6). The resistance found was primarily in Austrian winter-type pea with pigmented seeds, flowers, and stems. The most resistant germplasm with horticultural type was 74SN3 previously released by Kraft and Giles (1976) as a multiple root rot and wilt resistant germplasm line. Several cultivars are reportedly resistant to Ascochyta blight (Table 3-6); however, the level of resistance is not sufficient for adequate control of the disease under field conditions.

Powdery mildew of pea, incited by *Erysiphe pisi* Syd. (syn. *E. polygoni* DC), is widely distributed in the USA. Disease development is enhanced by dry and warm days with cool nights. The disease causes reduced yields and reduced seed quality. Good sources of resistance are now available, many of which trace to Peruvian material or the immune selection made by the former Walt Pierce (Asgrow Seed Co., Twin Fall, ID) in the old cv. Strategem (Hagedorn, 1984). Numerous germplasm lines have since been released that carry one of these sources of resistance (Gritton & Hagedorn, 1971).

Several viral diseases of pea important in the USA and sources of resistance were listed (Table 3-7) by Kraft and Kaiser (1990). These include sources of resistance to bean leaf roll (BLRV), pea enation mosaic (PEMV), pea seedborne mosaic (PSbMV), and pea streak (PSV) viruses. Sources of resistance to alfalfa mosaic (AMV), Wisconsin pea streak (WPSV), and red clover vein mosaic (RCVMV) viruses were identified by Hagedorn (1968). Bean leaf roll virus, also known as pea top yellows or pea leaf roll virus, caused significant yield losses in pea seed fields in southern Idaho in 1980 (Hampton, 1983). Several cultivars have exhibited either tolerance or resistance to the virus (Table 3-7), and many of them have dark green foliage.

Pea enation mosaic virus has long been a problem in the USA. Fortunately, good resistance was found in PI 140295 and used by breeders to develop resistant germplasm and cultivars (Fig. 3-2). Breeding line G168, found in numerous pedigrees (Baggett, 1976b, 1977, 1982a,b; Baggett & Kean, 1988; Marx et al., 1979) is a PEMV-resistant selection made from PI 140295.

Pea seedborne mosaic virus is the only important seedborne virus of pea in the USA. This disease has often been found in breeders nurseries, less

Table 3-6. Germplasm lines of peas resistance to foliar fungal diseases.

Disease	Sources of resistance	References
Ascochyta blight	Romack, Melrose, 74SN3, PI 429349, PI 429348	Saker et al., 1982
	PI 179019, PI 163131, PI 236493, PI 173052, Cobri, Recette, Sun Valley	Ali et al., 1978
	PI 343971	Darby et al., 1986
	Rondo	Bretag, 1989
Powdery mildew	OSU 42, Geneva 59-29, PI 142775, PI 142777, PI 180792, PI 203064	Sakr, 1989
	Stragegem, Mexique 4	Cousin, 1965

INTRODUCED GERMPLASM IN COOL—SEASON LEGUMES

Table 3-7. Pea germplasm accessions, breeding lines, and cultivars with resistance or tolerance to bean leaf roll (BLRV), pea enation mosaic (PEMV), pea seedborne mosaic (PSbMV) and pea streak viruses (PSV). (From Kraft and Kaiser, 1990, with additions.)[†]

BLRV	PEMV	PSbMV	PSV
Abador	Aurora	B442-15	PI 116944
Alderman	Canner 50	B442-66	PI 140297
Almota	Canner 695	OSU 547-29	PI 193845
Burpeeana	Canner 69141	OSU 559-6	PI 195405
Centurion	Commando	OSU 564-3	PI 203066
Champ	Corvallis	OSU 584-16	PI 212029
Climax	Freezer 50	OSU 589-12	PI 261677
Cobri	Freezer 52	OSU 615-15	PI 140295
Coquette	Freezer 6650	OSU 620-1	M176
Elf	H286-1-1	VR-410-2	S423
Frisky	H294-5-1-1	VR-1492-1	S434
Jubilee	H312-2-3	WIS7105	S441
Juwell	H543-3-1-11	WIS7106	
Lincoln	H890-3-2	X78006	
OSU 559-6	Honeypod	X78122	
OSU 564-3	Maestro	X78123	
OSU 584-16	Mohawk	X78124	
OSU 589-12	New Era	X78125	
Perfected 400	Novella II	X78126	
Perfection	Olympia	X78127	
Pioneer	OSU 547-29	X78128	
Pride	OSU 559-6	PI 193586	
Rika	OSU 564-3	PI 193835	
Sparkle	OSU 584-16	PI 347328	
Splendor	OSU 589-12	PI 347442	
Superalaska	OSU 615-15	PI 347452	
Surpass	OSU 620-1	PI 347465	
Sybo	Perfected freezer 60	PI 347485	
Telephone	PI 140295	PI 347487	
Wando	Pluperfect	PI 347494	
Wisconsin Pride	Shoshone	PI 356984	
Wyola	Surprise 60	PI 357003	
	Tempter	PI 357005	
	Trident	PI 357015	
	M176	PI 357023	
	S423	PI 357026	
	S434	PI 357038	
	S441	PI 378158	

[†] References used to prepare this table:
  BLRV: Drijfhout, 1968; Hagedorn, 1974, 1984; Hubbeling, 1956.
  PEMV: Baggett, 1984; Baggett & Hampton, 1983; Baggett & Kean, 1988; Hagedorn & Hampton, 1975; Schroeder & Barton, 1958; Baggett, 1976b.
  PSbMV: Baggett & Hampton, 1977; Baggett & Kean, 1988; Hagedorn, 1974; Hagedorn & Gritton, 1973; Hampton & Braverman, 1979; Kraft & Giles, 1978b; Muehlbauer, 1983; Provvidenti & Alconero, 1988a,b,c; Stevenson & Hagedorn, 1971.
  PSV: Ford & Baggett, 1965; Baggett, 1976b; Hagedorn, 1968.

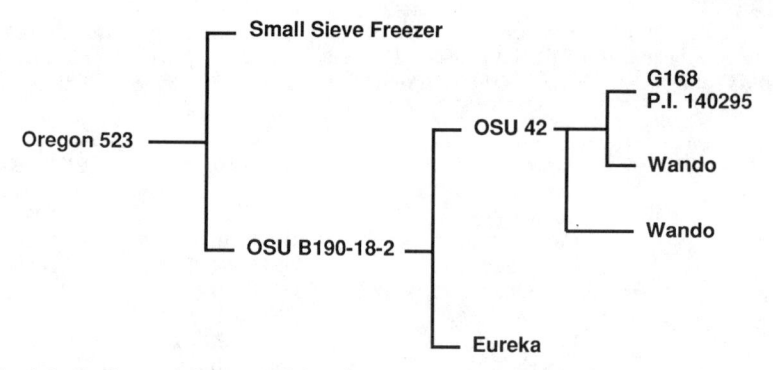

```
                    ┌── Small Sieve Freezer
                    │
                    │                              ┌── G168
                    │                    ┌── OSU 42 ──┤   P.I. 140295
Oregon 523 ─────────┤                    │         └── Wando
                    │                    │
                    │                    │         ─── Wando
                    └── OSU B190-18-2 ───┤
                                         │
                                         └── Eureka
```

Fig. 3-2. Pedigree of Oregon 523 freezing pea. (From Baggett and Kean, 1988.)

often in commercial fields. Stevenson and Hagedorn (1971) screened part of the PI collection and identified PI 193586 and green axiled plants of PI 193835, a heterogenous land race accession, as being symptomless under repeated inoculation with an isolate of PSbMV. These two PI lines were used as sources of PSbMV resistance to develop Wis 7105 and Wis 7106 (Hagedorn & Gritton, 1971b) germplasm lines in a 'New Season' and a 'Dark Skin Perfection' background, respectively. Numerous other PSbMV-resistant germplasm lines were developed using the resistance of Wis 7105 and Wis 7106 or the original PI lines (Baggett & Hampton, 1977; Baggett & Kean, 1988; Kraft & Giles, 1978b; Muehlbauer, 1983). Additional sources of resistance to several strains of PSbMV were identified and reported (Provvidenti & Alconero, 1988a,b,c).

Multigenic resistance to PSV and RCVMV has been identified in the PI collection. G168, a selection from PI 140295, has proved to be a good source of resistance to PSV (Baggett, 1976b). Sources of resistance and the inheritance of resistance to clover yellow vein virus in pea has been reported (Provvidenti, 1987b).

Lentil

Sources of resistance to PSbMV in lentil were identified by systematic screening of the collection (Haddad et al., 1978; Muehlbauer, 1977). Four PI lines with immunity to the virus were identified (Table 3-8) and are being used in breeding resistant cultivars.

Pea enation mosaic virus (PEMV) is probably the most important disease of the lentil crop in the USA. The disease was especially severe in 1983 and 1990 when weather conditions were conducive to survival of aphid vectors (personal observation). Good sources of tolerance were identified in material introduced from India (Table 3-8). The two most resistant lines, PI 472547 and PI 472609, were short, had highly pubescent leaves and relatively small seeds when compared to cultivars commonly grown in the USA. The lines have been used in hybridization programs to develop resistant cultivars. Screening of the lentil core collection for resistance to PEMV (F.J. Muehlbauer et al., 1990, unpublished data) indicated a good level of resistance

Table 3-8. Sources of disease resistance found in introduced germplasm of lentil and chickpea..

Crop and disease	PI accession(s) or cultivars	Reference
Lentil:		
Pea seedborne mosaic virus	PI 212610, PI 251786, PI 297745, PI 368648	Muehlbauer, 1977 Jermyn, 1980
Pea enation mosaic virus	PI 472547, PI 472609	Aydin et al., 1987
Rust (*Uromyces fabae*)	'Tekoa,' 'Laird' 'Araucana-INIA' 'Pant-L-406'	Muehlbauer & Slinkard, 1985 Tay et al., 1981 Pandya et al., 1980
Chickpea:		
Ascochyta blight	PI 251781, PI 292006, PI 343014, PI 383626, PI 379217, PI 451653, PI 458869, PI 471915	F.J. Muehlbauer & W.J. Kaiser (1990, unpublished data)

in accessions from Iran. Further screening of accessions from that region seems promising for identifying sources of resistance to the virus.

Ascochyta blight of lentil is an important disease in western Canada, Turkey, and parts of the Middle East. In Canada, the disease is especially prevalent when frequent rains occur between flowering and harvest. In such instances, infection of seeds can be so severe that the lentils are not marketable. An intermediate level of resistance to the disease has been identified in 'Laird' (Slinkard, 1978). Breeders are currently using Laird and ILL5588 to develop additional resistant cultivars.

Rust of lentil, incited by *Uromyces fabae* (Pers.) Shroet f. sp. *lentis*, is an important disease in India, Pakistan, Ethiopia, Morocco, Argentina, and Chile; however, it has not been reported in North America. Resistance to the disease was found in Tekoa and Laird by breeders in Chile (Tay et al., 1981). Tekoa and Laird were developed in the USA and Canada, respectively, from PI lines (Table 3-9). Resistance to lentil rust was found in PI 299127 (ILL 358) which is currently being used in the breeding program at ICARDA (Dr. Willie Erskine, 1989, personal communication).

Fusarium wilt of lentil, incited by *Fusarium oxysporum* Schl. f. sp *lentis* Snyd. & Hans. is a serious problem in the Middle East and the Indian subcontinent, but it is not a problem in the USA. The ICARDA program, however, has identified two sources of resistance to Fusarium wilt in the PI colleciton. These include PI 254554 (ILL 241) and PI 370633 (ILL 632).

Chickpea

Ascochyta blight of chickpea, incited by *Ascochyta rabiei* (Pass.) Lab., can devastate crops in the Mediterranean region, Pakistan, India, West Asia, and the USA. Resistance in germplasm from the USSR has been effectively used by ICARDA to develop resistant/tolerant breeding lines. These lines are being used in the USA to develop Ascochyta blight resistant cultivars. In addition, systematic screening of PI lines from the USSR, Turkey, Ethio-

Table 3-9. Pea, lentil, and chickpea cultivars developed from plant introductions.

Crop and cultivars	Plant introduction accession	References
Pea:		
Knight	PI 140295	Marx et al., 1979
Corvallis	PI 140295	Baggett, 1977
Oregon Sugar Pod	PI 140295	Baggett, 1976a
Oregon Sugar Pod II	PI 140295	Baggett, 1982b
Oregon 605	PI 140295	Baggett, 1982b
Oregon 523	PI 140295	Baggett & Kean, 1988
Alaska 81	PI 193835	Muehlbauer, 1987b
Umatilla	PI 244241	Muehlbauer, 1987b
Garfield	PI 244104	Muehlbauer et al., 1977
Lentil:		
Laird	PI 343028	Slinkard, 1978
Eston	PI 179307	Slinkard, 1981
Tekoa	PI 251784	Wilson & Law, 1972
Redchief	PI 181886 PI 329171	Wilson & Muehlbauer, 1983
Brewer	PI 251784	Muehlbauer, 1987a
Emerald	Bulk of PI lines	Muehlbauer, 1987a
Chickpea:		
Garnet	PI 273879	Muehlbauer & Kaiser, 1987
Tammany	PI 458872	Muehlbauer & Kaiser, 1987
Sarah	PI 315787	Muehlbauer & Kaiser, 1991

pia, Iran, Israel, and Syria was successful in identifying eight lines with good resistance to the disease (Table 3-8).

Insect Resistance in Peas

Evaluations of germplasm have been made for resistance to insects that attack pea crops. Pesho et al. (1977) were able to identify 16 lines of pea from the *Pisum* collection (more than 1600 accessions) as having a useful amount of resistance to *Bruchus pisorum* L. Similarly, Smith et al. (1980) found resistance to *Sitona lineatus* L. in the same collection. The resistance to bruchids was associated with short peduncles. Resistance to Sitona weevil apparently was associated with the rapid development of large leaf area. Attempts have been made to incorporate these traits into improved cultivars with limited success.

Other Considerations

Winter hardiness in lentil was found at Pullman, WA in several PI lines from Turkey including PI 370630, PI 370632, and PI 370633. Several sources of cold tolerance have been identified by ICARDA and include PI 299366 (ILL 465), PI 339319 (ILL 590), and PI 283604 (ILL 1918).

Resistance to a broad leaf weed herbicide was identified by Slinkard (1980) in PI 179310.

There has not been any systematic use of germplasm to improve the faba bean or the grasspea crop in the USA.

VALUABLE MORPHOLOGICAL OR QUALITY TRAITS AVAILABLE IN GERMPLASM COLLECTIONS

New plant and leaf types of pea became possible with the discovery of the afila (*Af*) gene (Goldenberg, 1965). The recessive *Af* gene converts leaflets to tendrils; whereas the recessive *st* and *tl* genes impart reduced stipule size and leaflets on the ends of the tendrils, respectively. The *Af* gene reduces leaf area by about 25 to 30%, while greatly improving the standing ability of the plants by the profusion of tendrils that intertwine to form a dense upright canopy. The improved mutual support allows for better air movement in the lower canopy that results in reduced severity of foliar diseases, particularly Sclerotinia white mold, incited by *Sclerotinia sclerotiorum* (Lib.) de Bary, and Botrytis grey mold, incited by *Botrytis cinerea* Pers. ex Fr., (Davies et al., 1985). The afila types hold particular promise for the dry pea crop because the plants mature rapidly and the open more upright canopy facilitates harvest, which often results in improved seed quality.

A new type of pea-utilizing genes for reduced pod parchment, *v* and *p*, and the gene for cylindrical pod shape, *n*, was developed during the 1980s by the Galatin Valley Seed Co., Twin Falls, ID. Their cv. Snap Pea was the first to combine these genes in a horticultural-type background. A germplasm release by Kraft and Giles (1978a) of a line selected from PI 244219 carried the genes for reduced pod parchment and cylindrical pod. This new type of pea has gained ready acceptance as a new fresh vegetable and a commodity for freezing.

Nonshattering lentil cultivars would provide a means of overall yield improvement without increased yield potential. Shattering, either pod drop or pod dehiscence, has reduced seed yield by an estimated 17% in the USA. Pod drop was the most serious of the two types of shattering (Erskine, 1985). Germplasm collections contain numerous small-seeded accessions in which the pods remain intact during threshing. This is considered a valuable trait for developing pod indehiscent large-seeded types. A gene for reduced pod parchment, *rpp*, was identified by Vandenberg (1987). Recessive *rpp* is considered to be an important gene for breeding lentil cultivars with reduced shattering.

CULTIVARS DEVELOPED FROM INTRODUCED GERMPLASM

While it is not possible to identify and list all the cultivars of cool-season food legumes that have been developed from introduced germplasm, selected releases illustrating this use of germplasm resources are listed (Table 3-9).

Pea

A dominant gene for resistance to pea enation mosaic virus was found in PI 140295. PI 140295 was also the source of G168, a breeding line used to develop germplasm lines and cultivars, both in the public and private sector. 'Alaska 81' was developed as a PSbMV-resistant cultivar. Resistance to the virus was obtained from Wis 7105, a germplasm line with PI 193835 in its parentage (Hagedorn & Gritton, 1971b).

'Umatilla', developed from a cross involving PI 244251, has a unique combination of large smooth yellow seeds and pods with reduced parchment. The reduced pod parchment trait was obtained from J.I.34, a germplasm line obtained from the John Innes Institute, Norwich, UK. The reduced pod parchment trait imparts excellent resistance to pod shattering compared to previously grown cultivars.

'Garfield' was a pure line selection from PI 244104, a predominantly small-seeded accession. Garfield has good resistance to Fusarium and Pythium root rot and is high yielding compared to other dry pea cultivars. Unfortunately, poor seed and cooking qualities have prevented Garfield from being widely grown.

Lentil

Several lentil cultivars have been released that were either the result of pure line selection or hybridization. The first lentil cultivar released in the USA was 'Tekoa' (Wilson & Law, 1972). Tekoa was the result of pure line selection within PI 251784 and represented a significant improvement in seed size and color compared to the commonly grown 'Chilean'. Unfortunately, Tekoa was susceptible to mechanical damage during harvesting and processing and it quickly lost favor with lentil processors and production was discontinued.

'Laird', a tall upright and large-seeded cultivar, was the result of pure line selection within PI 343028. The cultivar was developed by A.E. Slinkard (1978) for the prairies of western Canada. The late maturity of Laird has prevented the cultivar from being grown on large acreages in the USA.

'Brewer' was a selection from a cross between Tekoa, a selection from PI 251784, and an unknown PI line (Muehlbauer, 1987a). Brewer has exceptionally high yields when compared to the commonly grown Chilean type. As a result of its yield advantage, Brewer has become the predominant cultivar grown in the USA and now occupies more than 90% of the lentil acreage.

'Redchief' originated from a cross between PI 181886 and PI 329171 that was selected for large nonmottled seeds with bright red cotyledons (Wilson & Muehlbauer, 1983). Since most lentil cultivars in use in the USA and Canada are yellow cotyledon types, the development of Redchief represented an entirely new type of lentil for the USA. Currently, the production of Redchief is <2000 acres; however, production has increased at the rate of about 10% per year from 1986-1991.

'Emerald' originated as a selection from a bulk population of PI lines (Muehlbauer, 1987a). Emerald is characterized by large seeds with dark green seedcoats and green cotyledons. These features are desirable traits that should improve its acceptance in domestic and foreign markets.

'Eston' was selected from PI 179307 (Slinkard, 1981). The cultivar is especially high yielding and its plant habit retains erectness at maturity. The medium seed size of Eston has prevented the cultivar from being widely grown. However, Eston has been used extensively as a parent in crosses to improve the standing ability of otherwise acceptable cultivars.

Chickpea

'Garnet' chickpea was developed by pureline selection from PI 273879, a high-yielding line introduced from Ethiopia (Muehlbauer & Kaiser, 1987). Garnet is a desi type with typically small, angular, and pigmented seeds. Garnet was released to provide U.S. producers an adapted desi-type chickpea that might be produced in dry areas.

'Tammany' chickpea originated as a selection from PI 458872, a line introduced from Pakistan (Muehlbauer & Kaiser, 1987). Tammany has a unifoliate leaf structure that differs from the fern leaf structure that is typical of most chickpea cultivars. Tammany is earlier maturing than 'Surutato 77' and 'UC-5' and has larger seed size. These two traits make the cultivar well suited to the dryland farming systems of the Pacific Northwest.

'Sarah' was developed by pure line selection from PI 315787, an accession originating from India (Muehlbauer & Kaiser, 1991). In India, this accession was developed as an Ascochyta blight resistant desi-type chickpea and designated as 'C235'. This selection is being grown as an Ascochyta blight-resistant cultivar in other areas of the Indian subcontinent, Ethiopia and Australia. In Australia, it has been given the name 'Tyson'. Sarah was highly resistant to Ascochyta blight in field-screening tests conducted at Pullman, WA.

Faba Bean and Grasspea

The faba bean cultivars in use in the USA were imported from Europe where extensive breeding programs to improve the crop are underway. Similarly, the grasspea cultivars that have been used in agronomic tests originated in the Mediterranean basin.

PRIORITIES FOR GERMPLASM EVALUATION

Evaluation of existing germplasm collections for traits of importance is a high priority as set forth by the Crop Advisory Committees for these crops. The U.S. *Pisum* germplasm collection has long been plagued by infections of PSbMV. The virus, because of its seedborne nature, has seriously impeded germplasm utilization by public and private breeders because of the risks of introducing the virus into breeding nurseries. Contamination of entire breeding programs of public and private breeders has occurred in the past, and caused large investments of time and funds for cleanup, as well as losses of valuable breeding stocks. For this reason, the *Pisum* CAC has placed high priority on eliminating PSbMV from the collection. A PSbMV-eradication program was initiated in which plants used for seed production were tested by enzyme-linked immunosorbent assay (ELISA) for the presence of the virus. Plants containing the virus were discarded and plants free of virus were used to produce seed. Nearly all of the *Pisum* accessions have undergone this virus eradication process and nuclear virus-free seed has been produced. Following seed increase of the nuclear seed, evaluation for traits of interest can proceed. The following is a brief list of the priorities for evaluation of the *Pisum* collection.

1. Evaluate the collection for resistance or tolerance to the Ascochyta blight complex.
2. Evaluate the collection for resistance to common root rot caused by *Aphanomyces euteiches*.
3. Evaluate the collection for resistance to Fusarium root rot.

The Special Purpose Food Legume Crop Advisory Committee has accepted the responsibility for the lentil, chickpea, faba bean, lupine, and *Lathyrus* collections. Of these, the lentil, chickpea, and lupine collections have had the most interest.

Priority for evaluation of these collections is as follows:

1. Evaluate the lentil collection for resistance or tolerance to pea enation mosaic virus. This virus causes the most important disease problem limiting lentil production in the USA.
2. Evaluate the chickpea collection for resistance to Ascochyta blight.
3. Evaluate certain accessions of the lupine collection for adaptation to various areas throughout the USA.

SUMMARY AND PROSPECTS

Introduced germplasm has been used extensively in the development of improved cultivars of pea, lentil, and chickpea in the USA. New improved pea cultivars benefited most from introduced germplasm. Resistance or tolerance to root-rotting fungi (*Aphanomyces* and *Fusarium*), wilt, foliar pathogens, and viruses has been found in introduced germplasm and has been deployed in a large number of superior cultivars. Most lentil cultivars in use in North America were selected directly from introduced germplasm or crosses involving introduced germplasm and locally adapted cultivars. Resistance to Ascochyta blight of chickpea identified in germplasm introduced from the USSR is currently being used to develop resistant cultivars. A core collection of lentil germplasm is currently being evaluated for resistance to pea enation mosaic virus, the most serious virus affecting lentils in the USA. No active breeding programs are under way in the USA on faba bean or grasspea (*Lathyrus*). Grasspea, because of its tolernace of dry conditions, could become an important protein crop for dry situations.

Critical needs for cool-season food legume crop improvement programs include; resistance to the Ascochyta blight complex in pea, better resistance to common root rot of pea incited by *Aphanomyces* and *Fusarium*, pea enation mosaic virus resistance in lentil, sources of good resistance to Ascochyta blight of chickpea; and agronomic evaluations of faba bean and grasspea. Exploration and collection of cool-season food legume germplasm in obviously underrepresented regions is proceeding. Additional wild types and land races from such areas as the USSR and China probably contain important genes for further enhancement of food legume germplasm and the development of improved cultivars.

ACKNOWLEDGMENT

The author gratefully acknowledges the suggestions for improving the draft manuscript made by Drs. R.O. Hampton, A.E. Slinkard, N.F. Weeden, and S. Kresovich, and the contributions made by Drs. W.J. Kaiser and J.M. Kraft. Assistance of Mrs. Joy Barbee is also gratefully acknowledged.

REFERENCES

Ali, S.M., L.F. Nitschke, A.J. Dube, M.R. Krause, and B. Cameron. 1978. Selection of pea lines for resistance to pathotypes of *Ascochyta pinodes, A. pisi* and *Phoma medicaginis* var. *pinodella*. Aust. J. Agric. Res. 29:841-849.

Aydin, H., F.J. Muehlbauer, and W.J. Kaiser. 1987. Pea enation mosaic virus resistance in lentils (*Lens culinaris*). Plant Dis. 71:635-638.

Baggett, J.R. 1976a. 'Oregon Sugarpod' pea. HortScience 11:619.

Baggett, J.R. 1976b. Oregon M176, S423, S434, S441 disease resistant pea breeding lines. HortScience 11:620.

Baggett, J.R. 1977. 'Corvallis' pea. HortScience 12:170.

Baggett, J.R. 1982a. 'Oregon Sugarpod II' edible pod pea. HortScience 17:93-94.

Baggett, J.R. 1982b. 'Oregon 605' pea. HortScience 17:94-95.

Baggett, J.R. 1984. Cultivar differences in susceptibility to Ascochyta stem blight, enation mosaic, and red clover vein mosaic. Pisum Newsl. 16:4-5.

Baggett, J.R., and R.O. Hampton. 1977. Oregon B442-15 and B445-66 pea seedborne mosaic virus-resistant breeding lines. HortScience 12:506.

Baggett, J.R., and R.O. Hampton. 1983. Pea enation mosaic virus: Variation in resistance conferred by *En*. Pisum Newsl. 15:3-6.

Baggett, J.R., and D. Kean. 1988. Seven pea seedborne mosaic virus resistant pea breeding lines. HortScience 23:630-631.

Ben Ze'ev, N., and D. Zohary. 1973. Species relationships in the genus *Pisum* L. Isr. J. Bot. 22:73-91.

Bettencourt, E., J. Konopka, and A.B. Damania. 1989. Directory of germplasm collections 1.1 Food legumes. Int. Board for Plant Genet. Resourc., Rome.

Bond, D.A., D.A. Lawes, G.C. Hawtin, M.C. Saxena, and J.H. Stephens. 1985. Faba bean (*Vicia faba* L.). p. 199-265. *In* R.J. Summerfield and E.H. Roberts (ed.) Grain legume crops. Collins Professional and Tech. Books, London.

Bos, L., R.O. Hampton, and K.M. Makkouk. 1988. Viruses and virus diseases of pea, lentil, faba bean and chickpea. p. 591-616. *In* R.J. Summerfield (ed.) World crops: Cool season food legumes Kluwer Academic Publ., Dordrecht, Netherlands.

Bretag, T.W. 1989. Resistance of pea cultivars to Ascochyta blight caused by *Mycosphaerella pinoides, Phoma medicaginis* and *Ascochyta pisi*. Annu. Appl. Biol. 114 (Suppl.):156-157.

Cousin, R. 1965. Etude de la resistance l'oidium chez le pois. Ann. Amelior. Plantes 15:93-97.

Darby, P., B.G. Lewis, and P. Matthews. 1986. Diversity of virulence within *Ascochyta pisi* and resistance in the genus *Pisum*. Plant Pathol. 35:214-223.

Davies, D.R., G.J. Berry, M.C. Heath, and T.C.K. Dawkins. 1985. Pea (*Pisum sativum* L.). p. 147-198. *In* R.J. Summerfield and E.H. Roberts (ed.) Grain legume crops. Collins Professional and Tech. Books, London.

Davis, D.W., M.A. Shehata, and H.L. Bissonnette. 1976. Minnesota 108 pea breeding line. HortScience 11:434.

Drijfhout, E. 1968. Testing for pea leaf roll virus and the inheritance of resistance in peas. Euphytica 17:224-235.

Duke, J.A. 1981. Handbook of legumes of world economic importance. Plenum Press, New York.

Erskine, W. 1985. Selection for pod retention and pod indehiscence in lentils. Euphytica 34:105-112.

Ford, R.E., and J.R. Baggett. 1965. Reactions of plant introduction lines of *Pisum sativum* to alfalfa mosaic, clover yellow mosaic, and pea streak viruses, and to powdery mildew. Plant Dis. Rep. 49:787-789.

Goldenberg, J.B. 1965. "Afila", a new mutation in pea (*Pisum sativum* L.). Bol. Genet. 1:27-31.

Gritton, E.T. 1990. Registration of five root rot resistant germplasm lines of processing pea. Crop Sci. 30:1166-1167.

Gritton, E.T., and D.J. Hagedorn. 1971. Registration of Wisconsin pea cultivars. Crop Sci. 11:941.

Haddad, N.I., F.J. Muehlbauer, and R.O. Hampton. 1978. Inheritance of resistance to pea seed-borne mosaic virus in lentils. Crop Sci. 18:613-615.

Hagedorn, D.J. 1968. Disease reaction of *Pisum sativum* plant introductions to three legume viruses. Plant Dis. Rep. 52:160-162.

Hagedorn, D.J. 1974. Virus diseases of pea, *Pisum sativum*. APS Monogr. 9. Am. Phytopathol. Soc., St. Paul.

Hagedorn, D.J. (ed.). 1984. Compendium of pea diseases. Am. Phytopathol. Soc., St. Paul.

Hagedorn, D.J., and E.T. Gritton. 1971. Registration of Wisconsin 7105 and 7106 pea germplasm. Crop Sci. 11:946.

Hagedorn, D.J., and E.T. Gritton. 1973. Inheritance of resistance to the pea seed-borne mosaic virus. Phytopathology 63:1130-1133.

Hagedorn, D.J., and R.O. Hampton. 1975. Pea enation mosaic virus resistance among commercial breeding lines of *Pisum sativum*. Plant Dis. Rep. 59:895-899.

Haglund, W.A., and W.C. Anderson. 1987. WSU 28 and WSU 31 pea inbred lines with resistance to specific races of Fusarium wilt. HortScience 22:513-514.

Haglund, W.A., and J.M. Kraft. 1970. *Fusarium oxysporum* f. *pisi*, race 5. Phytopathology 60:1861-1862.

Haglund, W.A., and J.M. Kraft. 1979. *Fusarium oxysporum* f. sp. *pisi*, race 6: Occurrence and distribution. Phytopathology 69:818-820.

Hampton, R.O. 1983. Pea leaf roll in northwestern U.S. pea seed production areas. Plant Dis. 67:1306-1310.

Hampton, R.O., and S.W. Braverman. 1979. Occurrence of pea seedborne mosaic virus and new virus-immune germplasm in the plant introduction collection of *Pisum sativum*. Plant Dis. Rep. 63:95-99.

Hare, W.W., J.C. Walker, and E.J. Dewiche. 1948. Inheritance of a gene for near-wilt resistance in garden pea. J. Agric. Res. 78:239-250.

Hedrick, U.P. 1928. Vegetables of New York. Vol. I. Peas of New York. J.B. Lyon Co., Albany, NY.

Hubbeling, N. 1956. Resistance to top yellows and Fusarium wilt in peas. Euphytica 5:71-86.

Jermyn, W.A. 1980. P.I.212610 resistant to aphids and viruses. Lentil Exp. News Serv. 7:65.

Kay, D.E. 1979. Food legumes. Crop and Product Dig. 3. Trop. Prod. Inst., London.

King, T.H., D.W. Davis, M.A. Shehata, and F.L. Pfleger. 1981. Minnesota 494-A22 pea germplasm. HortScience 16:100.

King, T.H., H.G. Johnson, H.L. Bissonnette, and W.A. Haglund. 1960. Development of lines of *Pisum sativum* resistant or tolerant to Fusarium root rot and wilt. Proc. Am. Soc. Hortic. Sci. 75:510-516.

Khvostova, V.V. 1975. Genetics and breeding of peas. Nauka Publ., Novosibirsk. (Translated from Russian by B.R. Sharma, Oxonian Press, New Delhi, 1983.)

Kraft, J.M. 1975. A rapid technique for evaluating pea lines for resistance to Fusarium root rot. Plant Dis. Rep. 59:1007-1011.

Kraft, J.M. 1981. Registration of 792022 and 792024 pea germplasm (Reg. nos. GP21 and GP 22). Crop Sci. 21:352-353.

Kraft, J.M. 1984. Registration of WR1158, WR1167, and RR-1178 pea germplasm. Crop Sci. 24:389.

Kraft, J.M. 1989. Registration of 86-638, 86-2197, 86-2231, and 86-2236 pea germplasms. Crop Sci. 29:494-495.

Kraft, J.M., and R.A. Giles. 1976. Registration of 74SN3, 74SN4 and 74SN5 pea germplasm. Crop Sci. 16:126.

Kraft, J.M., and R.A. Giles. 1978a. Registration of 244219-13 pea germplasm. Crop Sci. 18:1098.

Kraft, J.M., and R.A. Giles. 1978b. Registration of VR74-410-2 and VR74-1492-1 pea germplasm. Crop Sci. 18:1099.

Kraft, J.M., and W.J. Kaiser. 1990. Screening peas for disease resistance. In Proc. Int. Workshop, Breeding cool season food legumes for stress resistance, Ravello, Italy. 9-12 Sept. Int. Ctr. for Agric. Res. in the Dry Areas (ICARDA), Aleppo, Syria.

Kraft, J.M., and D.D. Roberts. 1970. Resistance in peas to Fusarium and Pythium root rot. Phytopathology 60:1814-1817.

Kraft, J.M., and J.A. Tuck. 1986. Registration of 75-786, 84-1638 and 84-1930 pea germplasms. Crop Sci. 26:1262-1263.

Kraft, J.M., M.P. Haware, and M.M. Hussein. 1988. Root rot and wilt diseases of food legumes. p. 565-576. In R.J. Summerfield (ed.) World crops: Cool season food legumes. Kluwer Acad. Publ., Dordrecht, Netherlands.

Kraft, J.M., M.J. Silbernagel, and F.J. Muehlbauer. 1972. Registration of Ph-14-119 and Ph-91-3 pea germplasm. Crop Sci. 12:399.

Kupicha, F.K. 1977. The delimitation of the tribe *Vicieae* (Leguminosae) and the relationship of *Cicer* L. Bot. J. Linn. Soc. 74:131-132.

Ladizinsky, G. 1975. A new *Cicer* from Turkey. Notes R. Bot. Gardens. 34:201-202.

Ladizinsky, G., and A. Adler. 1976. The origin of chickpea (*Cicer arietinum* L.). Euphytica 25:211-217.

Ladizinsky, G., D. Cohen, and F.J. Muehlbauer. 1985. Hybridization in the genus *Lens* by means of embryo culture. Theor. Appl. Genet. 70:97-101.

Ladizinsky, G., B. Pickersgill, and K. Yamamato. 1988. Exploitation of wild relatives of the food legumes. p. 967-978. In R.J. Summerfield (ed.) World crops: Cool season food legumes. Kluwer Acad. Publ., Dordrecht, Netherlands.

Ladizinsky, G., D. Braun, D. Goshen, and F.J. Muehlbauer. 1984. The biological species of the genus *Lens* L. Bot. Gaz. 145:253-261.

Lawyer, A.S. 1984. Diseases caued by *Ascochyta* ssp. p. 11-15. In D.J. Hagedorn (ed.) Compendium of pea diseases. Phytopathol. Soc., St. Paul.

Linford, M.B. 1928. A Fusarium wilt of peas in Wisconsin. Wisconsin Agric. Exp. Stn. Res. Bull. 85.

Lockwood, J.L. 1960. Pea introductions with partial resistance to Aphanomyces root rot. Phytopathology 50:621-624.

Makasheva, R. Kh. 1973. The pea. Kolos Publ., Leningrad. (Translated from Russian by B.R. Sharma, 1983. Oxonian Press, New Delhi.)

Marx, G.A., R. Provvidenti, and R. Sandsted. 1979. 'Knight' garden pea. HortScience 14:197.

Marx, G.A., W.T. Schroeder, R. Provvidenti, and W. Mishanec. 1972. A genetic study of tolerance in pea to Aphanomyces root rot. J. Am. Soc. Hortic. Sci. 97:619-621.

Muehlbauer, F.J. 1977. Resistance in lentils to pea seedborne mosaic virus. Lentil Exp. News Serv. 4:31.

Muehlbauer, F.J. 1983. Eight germplasm lines of pea resistant to pea seedborne mosaic virus. Crop Sci. 23:1019.

Muehlbauer, F.J. 1987a. Registration of 'Brewer' and 'Emerald' lentil. Crop Sci. 27:1088-1089.

Muehlbauer, F.J. 1987b. Registration of 'Alaska 81' and 'Umatilla' dry pea. Crop Sci. 27:1089-1090.

Muehlbauer, F.J., and W.J. Kaiser. 1987. Registration of 'Garnet' and 'Tammany' chickpea. Crop Sci. 27:1087-1088.

Muehlbauer, F.J., and W.J. Kaiser. 1991. Registration of 'Sarah' chickpea. Crop Sci. 31:1094.

Muehlbauer, F.J., and A.E. Slinkard. 1985. Lentil improvement in the Americas. p. 351-366. *In* M.C. Saxena and S. Varma (ed.) Proc. Int. Workshop. Faba beans, kabuli chickpeas and lentils for the 1980s. Int. Ctr. Agric. Res. in the Dry Areas, Aleppo, Syria.

Muehlbauer, F.J., V.E. Wilson, J.M. Kraft, and R.E. Witters. 1977. Registration of Garfield and Tracer dry peas. Crop Sci. 17:485.

Nene, Y.L., S.B. Hanounik, S.H. Qureshi, and B. Sen. 1988. Fungal and bacterial foliar diseases of pea, lentil, faba bean and chickpea. p. 577-590. *In* R.J. Summerfield (ed.) World crops: Cool season food legumes. Kluwer Acad. Publ., Dordrecht, Netherlands.

Pandya, B.P., M.P. Pandey, and J.P. Singh. 1980. Development of Pant-L-406 lentil, resistant to rust and wilt. Lentil Exp. News Serv. 7:34-37.

Pesho, G.R., F.J. Muehlbauer, and W.H. Harberts. 1977. Resistance of pea introductions to the pea weevil. J. Econ. Entomol. 70:30-33.

Pickersgill, B., J.K. Jones, G. Ramsay, and H. Stewart. 1985. Problems and prospects of wide crossing in the genus *Vicia* for improvement of faba bean. p. 57-70. *In* M.C. Saxena and S. Verma (ed.) Proc. Int. Workshop. Faba beans, kabuli chickpeas and lentils in the 1980s. Int. Ctr. Agric. Res. in the Dry Areas, Aleppo, Syria.

Polhill, R.M., and L.J.G. van der Maesen. 1985. Taxonomy of grain legumes. p. 3-36. *In* R.J. Summerfield and E.H. Roberts (ed.) Grain legume crops. Collins Professional and Tech. Books, London.

Provvidenti, R. 1987a. List of genes in *Pisum sativum* for resistance to viruses. Pisum Newsl. 19:48-49.

Provvidenti, R. 1987b. Inheritance of resistance to clover yellow vein virus in *Pisum sativum*. J. Hered. 78:126-128.

Provvidenti, R., and R. Alconero. 1988a. Inheritance of resistance to a lentil strain of pea seed-borne mosaic virus in *Pisum sativum*. J. Hered. 79:45-47.

Provvidenti, R., and R. Alconero. 1988b. Inheritance of resistance to a third pathotype of pea seed-borne mosaic virus. J. Hered. 79:76-77.

Provvidenti, R., and R. Alconero. 1988c. Sources of resistance to pathotypes of pea seed-borne mosaic virus in the U.S. plant introductions of *Pisum sativum*. Pisum Newsl. 20:30-31.

Sakar, D. 1980. Techniques for screening pea (*Pisum sativum* L.) genotypes for resistance to root rot and foliar infections caused by *Phoma medicaginis* var. *pinodella*. M.S. thesis. Washington State Univ., Pullman.

Sakar, D., F.J. Muehlbauer, and J.M. Kraft. 1982. Techniques of screening peas for resistance to *Phoma medicaginis* var. *pinodella*. Crop Sci. 22:988-992.

Sakr, B. 1989. Powdery mildew of peas: Chemical and genetic control, genetic resistance and linkage relationships. M.S. thesis. Washington State Univ., Pullman.

Schroeder, W.T., and D.W. Barton. 1958. The nature and inheritance of resistance to the pea enation mosaic virus in garden pea, *Pisum sativum* L. Phytopathology 48:628-632.

Slinkard, A.E. 1978. Laird lentil lincensed in Canada. Lentil Exp. News Serv. 5:24.

Slinkard, A.E. 1980. Resistance to MCPA in P.I.179310 TR. Lentil Exp. News Serv. 7:65.

Slinkard, A.E. 1981. Eston, a new small-seeded lentil cultivar. Lentil Exp. News Serv. 8:30.

Smartt, J. 1990. Pulses of a classical world. p. 176-244. *In* Grain legumes. Cambridge Univ. Press, Cambridge, UK.

Smartt, J., and T. Hymowitz. 1985. Domestication and evolution of grain legumes. p. 37-72. *In* R.J. Summerfield and E.H. Roberts (ed.) Grain legume crops. Collins Professional and Tech. Books, London.

Smith, J.H., L.E. O'Keeffe, D.L. Auld, F.J. Muehlbauer, G.A. Murray, G. Noure-Ghanbalani, and M. Johnson. 1980. Insect resistance in dry peas: Progress report, 1976-1979. Univ. of Idaho, Agric. Exp. Stn. Prog. Rep. 212.

Snyder, W.C., and J.C. Walker. 1935. Fusarium near wilt of peas. Zentralbl. Bakteriol. Parasitenkd. 91:355-378.

Stevenson, W.R., and D.J. Hagedorn. 1971. Reaction of *Pisum sativum* to the pea seedborne mosaic virus. Plant Dis. Rep. 55:408-410.

Tay, J., M. Parades, and V. Kramm. 1981. Araucana-INIA. A new large-seeded lentil cultivar. Lentil Exp. News Serv. 8:30.

Vandenberg, A. 1987. Inheritance and linkage of several qualitative traits in lentil. Ph.D. thesis. Univ. of Saskatchewan, Saskatoon, Canada.

van Emden, H.F., S.L. Ball, and M.R. Rao. 1988. Pest, disease and weed problems in pea, lentil, faba bean and chickpea. p. 519-534. *In* R.J. Summerfield (ed.) World crops: Cool-season food legumes. Kluwer Acad. Publ., Dordrecht, Netherlands.

Wade, B.L., W.J. Zaumeyer, and L.L. Harter. 1938. Variety studies in relation to Fusarium wilt of peas. U.S. Gov. Print. Office, Washington, DC.

Williams, J.T., A.M.C., Sanchez, and M.T. Jackson. 1974. Studies on lentils and their variation. I. The taxonomy of the species. SABRAO J. 6:133-145.

Wilson, V.E., and A.G. Law. 1972. Registration of Tekoa lentil. Crop Sci. 12:255.

Wilson, V.E., and F.J. Muehlbauer. 1983. 'Redchief' lentil. Crop Sci. 23:802-803.

Zohary, D. 1972. The wild progenitor and place of origin of the cultivated lentil, *Lens culinaris*. Econ. Bot. 26:236-332.

Zohary, D. 1973. The origin of cultivated cereals and pulses in the near East. Chromosomes Today 4:307-320.

4 Use of Plant Introductions in Peanut Improvement

T. G. Isleib and J. C. Wynne

North Carolina State University
Raleigh, North Carolina

Commercial production of peanut (*Arachis hypogaea* L.) in the USA is composed of four market types that correspond in large part to three of the four botanical varieties making up the species. The subspecies *A. hypogaea* ssp. *fastigiata* Waldron comprises two botanical varieties: var. *fastigiata*, corresponding to the Valencia market class, and var. *vulgaris* Harz corresponding to the Spanish market class. The second subspecies, *A. hypogaea* ssp. *hypogaea* includes the Virginia and runner market classes that are differentiated primarily by seed size. The runner market type predominates with 70% of national production (Fig. 4-1) while the Virginia, Spanish, and Valencia types constitute 20, 10, and <1%, respectively (Knauft et al., 1987).

Production of peanut in the USA is concentrated in three major geographical areas (Fig. 4-2). The runner is the principal market type grown in the Southeast (Georgia, Alabama, and Florida) and Southwest (Texas and Oklahoma). The Virginia-Carolina production area (North Carolina, South Carolina, and Virginia) produce Virginia types almost exclusively. There is some production of Virginia types in the Southeast and Southwest. The Spanish type is grown primarily as a dryland crop in the Southwest while the Valencia type is grown in New Mexico.

ORIGIN

The variability that led to the four market types originated in South America where the peanut is thought to have been domesticated (Hammons, 1973). Krapovickas (1968, 1973) related variability in cultivared peanut to five geographic areas of South America. Each area was described as a center of diversity. Gregory and Gregory (1976) extended the number of centers to six. Gregory et al. (1980) related the subspecific variation to the six geographical regions (Table 4-1). The Bolivian region was identified as the

---

Copyright © 1992 Crop Science Society of America, 677 S. Segoe Rd., Madison, WI 53711, USA. *Use of Plant Introductions in Cultivar Development, Part 2,* CSSA Special Publication no. 20.

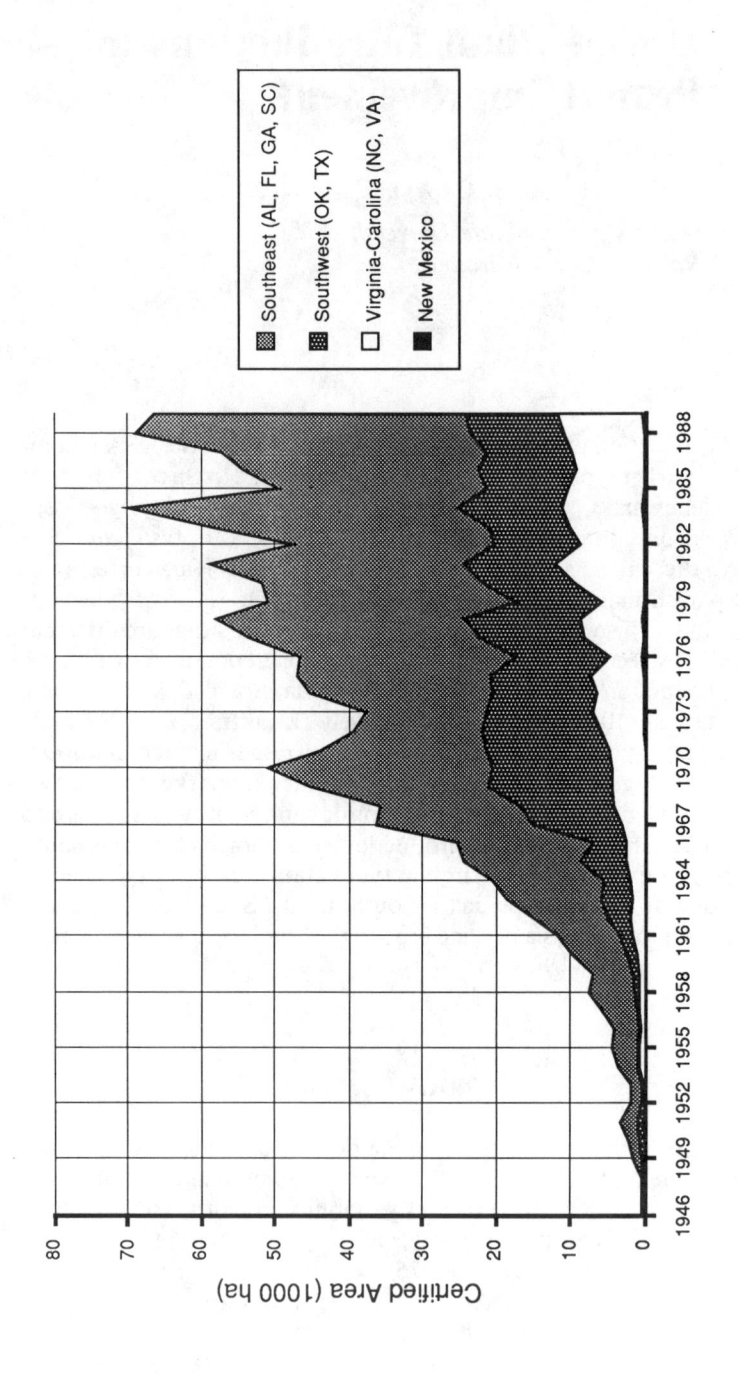

Fig. 4–.1 Distribution of certified peanut seed production by geographic region in the USA, 1946 to 1989. Data from the American Organization of Seed Certifying Agencies, Raleigh, NC.

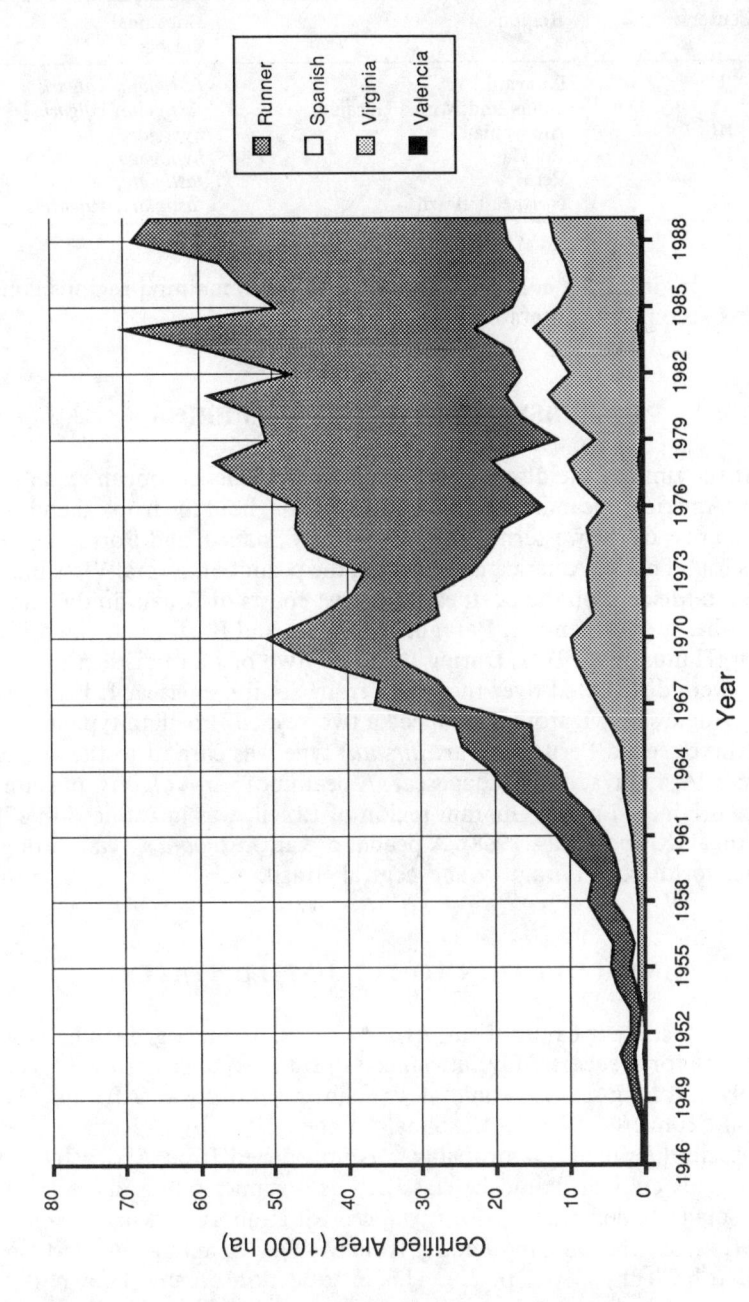

Fig. 4–2. Distribution of certified peanut seed production by market class in the USA, 1946 to 1989. Data from the American Organization of Seed Certifying Agencies, Raleigh, NC.

Table 4-1. Relationship of botanical varieties to centers of diversity in South America.

Center	Region	Botanical variety
I	Guaraní	*fastigiata, vulgaris*
II	Goiás and Minas Gerais	*fastigiata, vulgaris*
III	Amazonian	*hypogaea*
IV	Bolivia	*hypogaea*
V	Peru	*fastigiata, hirsuta*
VI	Northeast Brazil	*fastigiata, vulgaris*

center of origin of the cultivated peanut with the remaining regions considered as secondary centers of diversity.

DISPERSION FROM SOUTH AMERICA

At the time of the discovery of America and the European expansion into the Americas, peanut was grown widely throughout the tropical and subtropical areas of the western hemisphere. Early Spanish and Portuguese explorers found native Americans cultivating the peanut on several West Indian islands, in Mexico, on the northeast and east coasts of Brazil, in the Rio de la Plata basin of Argentina, Paraguay, Bolivia, and Brazil, and extensively in Peru (Hammons, 1973). During this time, two or more distinct types of peanut were distributed over the world from South America. It is thought that Portuguese navigators introduced a two-seeded Brazilian type to Africa. A three-seeded Peruvian (var. *hirsuta*) type was carried to the western Pacific, China, Java, and Madagascar. A peanut of var. *vulgaris*, presumed to have originated in the Guaraní region of Brazil, was introduced in 1784 to Portugal (Krapovickas, 1968). A peanut of var. *fastigiata* spread throughout the world from Paraguay and central Brazil.

INTRODUCTION TO THE UNITED STATES

A small-seeded peanut of var. *hypogaea* with a runner growth habit was the earliest form successfully introduced into the southeastern USA (Higgins, 1951). A long-season peanut, it was known variously as 'African', 'Wilmington Runner', 'North Carolina Runner', 'Georgia Runner', and 'Southeastern Runner'. It probably was introduced from Africa by slave traders. This cultivar would be classified as a runner type today.

A small-podded peanut of var. *vulgaris* with a short growing season was introduced into the USA in quantity from Malaga, Spain in 1868 and again in 1871 (McClenny, 1935, p. 22). This introduction became known as the cv. Spanish which gave rise to the Spanish market type. Peanut of var. *fastigiata* was also introduced to the USA from Valencia, Spain and were known as the cv. Valencia (Beattie, 1911). In his publication, Beattie referred to a promising new cultivar recently introduced from Spain. This name was then applied to a group of introductions with similar traits and is now applied to the Valencia market type.

The origin of the large-seeded Virginia type (var. *hypogaea*) in the USA is uncertain. McClenny (1935) believed that this type was cultivated in Virginia as early as 1844. Chevalier (1933) states, but does not document, that the large-seeded Virginia originated in Bahia, Brazil. Although the cultivation of peanut spread rapidly after 1865, Virginia, North Carolina, and Tennessee still produced the major portion of the crop in 1894 (Handy, 1896). Handy (1896) reported that there were only seven cultivars grown in the USA in 1894. Those seven included two Virginia market types ('Virginia Bunch' and 'Virginia Runner'), one runner market type (North Carolina Runner or African), three Valencia types ('Tennessee White', 'Tennessee Red', and 'Georgia Red'), and one Spanish market type (Spanish). Note that the Georgia Red mentioned here is not the same as the registered cultivar of the same name released by the University of Georgia. Beattie (1911) added Valencia to the cultivar list, indicating that it was similar to Tennessee Red. Beattie (1924) reported that 'Jumbo', a selection from Virginia Bunch, and 'Improved Spanish', a selection from Spanish ("true white Spanish"), had been released to growers. No additional cultivars were listed by Beattie and Beattie (1943).

EARLY BREEDING EFFORTS

The first attempt at improving the peanut by breeding was begun by the USDA in the early 1900s. Mass selection within farmer's seed stocks produced 'Holland Jumbo', 'Spanish 18-38', and 'Improved Spanish 2-B' (Beattie & Batten, 1933; Gregory et al., 1951). State-supported breeding programs began in Florida in 1928, North Carolina in 1929, and Georgia in 1931 (Gregory et al., 1951).

Numerous cultivars were developed by individual plant or mass selection within the germplasm introduced prior to 1911 and grown by U.S. farmers (Table 4-2). Seventeen named cultivars beginning with the release of 'G.F.A. Spanish' in 1941 were developed by selection within farmers' stock. The most recent such release was 'New Mexico Valencia A', a selection derived from Tennessee Red released in 1971. Seven cultivars were developed by selection following hybridization among or mutagenesis of germplasm introduced prior to 1911 (Table 4-3). These began with 'Dixie Runner' released in 1943 and ended in 1977 with the releaase of 'Tifrum'.

The first peanut listed in the USDA Bureau of Plant Industry's inventories was PI 4253, acquired in 1899 by Barbour Lathrop and David G. Fairchild during a visit to Cairo (USDA, 1900). Acquisition of peanut germplasm was sporadic until the mid-1930s when W.A. Archer made an expedition to South America where he collected substantial numbers of accessions. Through 1930, a total of 137 peanut lines were inventoried by the USDA. Between 1930 and 1940, an additional 289 accessions were added to the collection. There was a considerable lag between the acquisition of new peanut germplasm and its release in improved cultivars.

Table 4-2. Peanut cultivars developed by selection within germplasm introduced prior to 1911.

Cultivar	Market class	Other designation	Year of release	Releasing agency	Origin	Reference
Improved Spanish 2B	Spanish			Georgia AES	Selection from local Spanish made ca. 1918 at Florence, SC	Beattie et al., 1954
Spanish 18-38	Spanish			Georgia AES	Selection from farmers' Spanish stocks	Gregory et al., 1951
Tennessee Red	Valencia				Selection from farmers' Valencia stocks	Handy, 1896
GFA Spanish	Spanish		1941	Georgia AES	Selection from 'Small Spanish' obtained from a grower in 1930	Higgins & Bailey, 1955
NC 4	Virginia		1944		Selection from 100 plant isolations made in 1929 from North Carolina farmers' cultivars by P.H. Kime, NCSU agronomist, Selection no. 4 deemed typical Virginia Bunch	W.C. Gregory, no date, personal communication
Holland Jumbo	Virginia		1945	Virginia AES	Selection from farmers' Virginia stocks	Batten, 1945
Holland Virginia Runner	Virginia		1945	Virginia AES	Selection from farmers' Virginia stocks	Batten, 1945

Virginia Bunch 67	Runner	1945	Georgia AES	Selection from 'Virginia Bunch' obtained in 1941 from East Georgia Peanut Co., Bulloch Co., Georgia	Hammons, 1970d
Southeastern Runner 56-15	Runner	1947	Georgia AES	Selection from 'Southeastern Runner'	Hammons, 1970a
Spantex	Spanish	1948	Texas AES	Selection from farmers Spanish stocks	Simpson, 1972a
Virginia Bunch 46-2	Virginia	1952	Virginia AES & USDA	Selection from 'Virginia Bunch Large'	Beattie & Batten, 1953
Virginia Bunch G2	Virginia	1952	Georgia AES	Selection from 'Virginia Bunch' obtained in 1941 from East Georgia Peanut Co., Bulloch Co., Georgia	Higgins & Bailey, 1955
Virginia Bunch G26	Virginia	1952	Georgia AES	Selection from 'Virginia Bunch' obtained in 1941 from W.A. Groover, Bulloch Co., Georgia	Higgins & Bailey, 1955
Virginia 56R	Virginia	1956	Virginia AES	VA A12-2 Selection from 'Atkins Runner'	Alexander & Allison, 1970a
Spanette	Spanish	1959	Georgia AES	Spanish 18-38-42 Selection from Spanish 18-38	Natl. Acad. Sci., 1972
Virginia 61R	Virginia	1962	Virginia AES	VA B22-15 Selection from 'Atkins Runner'	Alexander & Allison, 1970b
New Mexico Valencia A	Valencia	1971	New Mexico AS	Selection from 'New Mexico Valencia'	Hsi & Finkner, 1972

Table 4-3. Peanut cultivars developed by hybridization of germplasm introduced prior to 1911.

Cultivar	Market class	Other designation	Year of release	Releasing agency	Pedigree	Reference
Dixie Runner	Runner	F231-51	1943	Florida AES	Small White Spanish 3x-1 / Dixie Giant	Carver (Hull, 1950; Natl. Acad. Sci. 1972
Early Runner	Runner	F230-118-9-5-1	1952	Florida AES	Small White Spanish 3x-2 / Dixie Giant	Carver et al., 1952; Natl. Acad. Sci. 1972
NC 1	Virginia	A18	1952	NC AES	NC 4 / Improved Spanish 2B	W.C. Gregory, no date, personal communication
Georgia 119-20	Runner	GA 119-20	1954	Georgia AES & USDA-ARS	Southeastern Runner / Dixie Giant, 210-4 // Virginia Runner	Hammons, 1971
NC 4X	Virginia		1959	NC AES	Selection from irradiated 'NC 4'	Gregory and Emery.
Virginia 72R	Virginia	VA 61-24-7	1971	Virginia AES	VA 61R / VA A89-15 (selection from farmers' stocks, perhaps Atkins Runner)	Alexander & Mozingo, 1972
Tifrun	Runner		1977	Georgia AES & USDA-ARS	Florida Small Spanish / Dixie Giant, F231-51 /4/ F385-1-7-2, Pearl (F228) // F68-74 S_3-1-2, McSpan (F13, Small White Spanish) / Virginia Jumbo Runner (F14), F249-42-3-1 /3/ Jenkins Jumbo, T1645 (selection from F416) / T1861, selection made in 1966 from local virginia stock in Georgia, thought to have arisen from a Virginia × spanish hybrid)	R.O. Hammons, 1977, personal communication; D.A. Knauft, 1990, personal communication

The genetic base of peanut was broadened beyond the group of landraces introduced prior to 1911 with the release of two Spanish cultivars: 'Dixie Spanish' in 1950 and 'Argentine' in 1951. Both cultivars were selected directly from plant introductions (Table 4-4), Dixie Spanish from a line collected privately by the Tom Huston Peanut Company of Georgia and Argentine from PI 121070. These releases were followed by that of 'NC 2' in 1952, the first cultivar developed by hybridization with an introduction. One quarter of the ancestry of NC 2 is 'Basse', a small-seeded peanut with spreading growth habit from the Gambia in West Africa. This germplasm was either not documented with a plant inventory number or the number was not subsequently maintained for the accession. There are two inventoried plant introductions from the Gambia that might correspond to Basse. One plant introduction is PI 24114, collected in 1908 at the behest of W.R. Beattie and C.S. Scofield and described by Beattie as "exceptionally valuable for use in the manufacture of candy and other products where shelled nuts are required" (USDA, 1909). The other plant introduction is PI 73968, collected by D.G. Fairchild in 1927 and described as "a white-seeded selection from the red-seeded Philippine variety which was introduced from the Philippine Islands several years ago. This white-seeded selection is the biggest yielder in Gambia" (USDA, 1929).

MODERN BREEDING EFFORTS

Forty-five cultivars with plant introductions in their pedigrees have now been released. Twenty-eight of the 45 lines have ancestral contributions from GA 207 or its siblings derived from a cross (F334) between Basse and Spanish 18-38 (Branch & Hammons, 1984). Twelve inventoried plant introductions appear in the pedigrees of the 45 cultivars (Table 4-5). Following the devastation of the U.S. maize (*Zea mays* L.) crop by race T of southern corn leaf blight [*Bipolaris maydis* (Nisikado & Miyake) Shoemaker] in 1970, there was a surge of interest in the degree of genetic vulnerability of crop species. Peanut was identified as a vulnerable species (Hammons, 1972, 1976) largely due to virtual monoculture within each market class. In 1970, 'Early Runner' dominated the runner class (Fig. 4-3), 'Florigiant' the Virginia (Fig. 4-4), and 'Starr' the Spanish (Fig. 4-5). By 1974, 'Florunner' dominated the runner class to the virtual exclusion of all other cultivars while the dominance of Florigiant and Star had been slightly reduced. The Valencia class has been dominated at various times by 'McRan', 'New Mexico Valencia A', and 'New Mexico Valencia C' (Fig. 4-6). Following the disclosure of the vulnerability of the crop, efforts were initiated to broaden its genetic base. Thirty-two of the 45 cultivars with introduced germplasm in their ancestry have been released since 1970. Computing coefficients of coancestry among cultivars, Knauft and Gorbet (1989) concluded that the genetic base of the crop had broadened considerably since Hammons' 1976 report. These authors did not calculate average coancestries within market classes because of the difficulties in assigning frequencies to the different cultivars.

Table 4-4. Peanut cultivars developed by selection within germplasm introduced prior to 1911.

Cultivar	Market class	Other designation	Year of release	Releasing agency	Origin	Reference
Spanish No. 146	Spanish	Huston Col. No. 146			Spanish introduction (Coll. No. 146) obtained from India by Tom Huston Peanut Co.	Higgins & Bailey, 1955
Dixie Spanish†	Spanish	Huston Co. no. 146, Spanish No. 146	1950	Georgia AES	Selection from Spanish introduction (Coll. No. 146) obtained from India by Tom Huston Peanut Co.	Higgins & Bailey, 1955
Argentine†	Spanish	PI 121070-1, OK P-2	1951	Oklahoma AES	Selection from PI 121070 (var. *vulgaris*)	McGill, 1963
NC 2	Virginia	NC Ac 323	1952	NC AES	Basse4-4 / Spanish 18-38, GA 207-2 // White's Runner	Gregory, 1970
Florispan Runner	Spanish	334A-B	1953	Georgia AES	Basse / Spanish 18-38, GA 207-3 // F230-118-2-2, Small White Spanish 3x-2 / Dixie Grant	Carver, 1953
Florigiant	Virginia	F392-12-5	1961	Florida AES	Basse / Spanish 18-38, GA 207-3 // F230-118-2-2 (same as F230), F334A-5-5-1 /3/ F359-1-3-14, Jenkins Jumbo // F230-118-5-1, Dixie Giant / Small White Spanish 3x-2	Carver, 1969; Natl. Acad. Sci, 1972
Starr	Spanish		1961	Texas AES	Spantex / PI 161317 (var. *vulgaris* obtained in 1947 from Salto, Uruguay)	Simpson, 1972b
NC 5	Virginia	NC Ac 333	1964	NC AES	NC 1 // C12, PI 121067 / NC Bunch	Emery & Gregory, 1972
Shulamith	Virginia	PI 372572, Israel X-30	1968	Israel MinAg-ARO, Georgia AES	Florigiant / F334A-B-17-1 (Florispan derivative)	Goldin, 1970; Natl. Acad. Sci. 1972

PEANUT IMPROVEMENT

Florunner	Runner	F439-16-10, F439R	1969	Florida AES	F334A-3-14 (Florispan sib) / F230-118-B-8-1 (Early Runner sib)	Norden et al., 1969; Natl. Acad. Sci., 1972
NC 17	Virginia	NC Ac 15717, F393-9-5-1-2-2,4	1969	NC AES	F334A-3-5-5-1 (Florispan derivative) / Jenkins Jumbo	Emery, 1970
Spanhoma†	Spanish	Gat-1271, OK P-112	1969	Oklahoma AES & Georgia AES	Selection from 'Argentine'	Natl. Acad. Sci., 1972
Comet†	Spanish		1970	Oklahoma AES & Georgia AES	Selection from 'Starr'	J.S. Kirby, 1990, personal communication
Spancross	Spanish	GA C 32S	1970	Georgia AES, USDA-ARS, & Oklahoma AES	Argentine (PI 121070-1) / PI 405933 (*Arachis monticola*)	Hammons, 1970b
Tifspan	Spanish	GA C 1-27	1970	Georgia AES, USDA-ARS, & Oklahoma AES	Argentine (PI 121070-1) / Spanette	Hammons, 1970c
Altika	Runner	F427B, F427BV	1972	Guyana MinAg, Florida AES	F393-7-1 (NC-FLA 14 sib) /3/ GA 119-20, Southeastern Runner / Dixie Giant, 210-14 // Virginia Runner	Norden & Gorbet, 1974
GK 19	Runner		1973	Gold Kist Peanut Co.	F334-3-5-5-1 (Florispan derivative) / Jenkins Jumbo, F393-6 // F334-9 (Florispan sib)	E. Harvey, 1990, personal communication
McRan†	Valencia		1973	Borden Peanut Seed Co.	Selection from African plant introduction	R.O. Hammons, no date, personal communication
NC-Fla 14	Virginia	NC Ac 15714, F393-1-2-4-3	1973	NC AES & Florida AES	Jenkins Jumbo / F334A-3-5-5-1 (Florispan derivative)	Emery et al., 1974
Keel 29†	Virginia		1974	Keel Peanut Seed Co.	Selection from 'Florigiant'	Mozingo et al., 1987
Tamnut 74	Spanish	TP-716-2-1	1974	Texas AES, Oklahoma AES, & Georgia AES	Starr // TPL 647-2-5, Spantex / *Arachis monticola*	Simpson & Smith, 1975

(continued on next page)

Table 4-4. Continued.

Cultivar	Market class	Other designation	Year of release	Releasing agency	Origin	Reference
Avoca 11†	Virginia		1976	R.J. Reynolds Co.	Selection from 'NC 2'	Mozingo et al., 1987
GK 3	Virginia		1976	Gold Kist Peanut Co.	Florida Small Spanish / Dixie Giant, F231-51 /4/ F385-1-7-2, Pearl (F228) // F68-74 S_3-1-2, McSpan (F13, Small White Spanish) / Virginia Jumbo Runner (F14), F249-42-3-1 /3/ Jenkins Jumbo, F416-2 /5/ F392 (Florigiant sib)	E. Harvey, 1990, personal communication; D.A. Knauft, 1990, personal communication
Goldin I	Spanish		1976	Wilson County Peanut Co., TX	Obtained from E. Goldin, Faculty of Agriculture, Hebrew Univ. of Jerusalem, Rehovot, Israel by the Wilson Co. Peanut Co., Pleasanton, TX	R.O. Hammons, no date, personal communication
NC 6	Virginia	NC Ac 17167	1976	NC AES	NC Bunch / PI 121067, C12 // C37 (same as C12), GP-NC 343 (selection from NC Ac 4508) // VA 61R; Resistant to SCR	Campbell et al., 1977
Early Bunch	Virginia	UF70115, F459B, VA 7324	1977	Florida AES, Georgia AES, USDA-ARS	Virginia Station Jumbo /4/ F385-1-7-4, Pearl (F228) // F68-74 S_3-1-2, McSpan (F13, Small White Spanish) / Virginia Jumbo Runner (F14), F249-42-3-1 /3/ Jenkins Jumbo, F406A /5/ F420, F231-51 (Dixie Runner sib) / F392-12-1-7 (Florigiant sib)	Norden et al., 1978
Florigraze	Rhizoma	GS-1, Gainesville Selection 1	1978	Florida AES, USDA-SCS	Selection from PI 118457 (*Arachis glabrata* Benth. cv. 'Arb', collected by W.A. Archer near Campo Grande, Brazil in 1936)	Prine et al., 1986

Cultivar	Type	Parentage/PI	Year	Origin	Pedigree	Reference
NC 7	Virginia	NC Ac 17209	1978	NC ARS	NC 5 / F393, F334-3-5-5-1 (Florispan derivative) / Jenkins Jumbo	Wynne et al., 1979
New Mexico Valencia C†	Valencia	PI 355987	1979	New Mexico AES	Selection from PI 335987, irradiated 'Colorado Manfredi' obtained from the research station at Manfredi, Argentina	Hsi, 1980
Toalson	Spanish	TP-1025	1979	Texas AES	PI 221057 (var. *vulgaris*) / Selection 26 (Spantex sib), TPL 673-A // Starr	Simpson et al., 1979
Pronto	Spanish		1980	USDA-ARS, Oklahoma AES & Georgia AES	Chico / Comet	Banks & Kirby, 1983
Spanco	Spanish	EC-5, O-20	1981	Oklahoma AES & USDA-ARS	Chico / Comet	Kirby et al, 1989
Virginia 81 Bunch	Virginia	VA 71-347	1981	Virginia AES & USDA-ARS	F392-8 (Florigiant sib) /3/ GA 119-20, Southeastern Runner / Dixie Giant, 210-14 // Virginia Runner	Coffelt et al., 1982
GK 7	Runner		1982	Gold Kist Peanut Co.	F334-3-5-5-1 (Florispan derivative) / Jenkins Jumbo, F393-2 // GK 19	E. Harvey, 1990, personal communication
NC 8C	Virginia	NC Ac 17941	1982	NC ARS	NC 2 // A48, NC 4 / Spanish 2B, NC Ac 3139 /3/ Florigiant	Wynne & Beute, 1983
Sunbelt Runner	Runner	A7109	1982	USDA-ARS & Georgia AES	F393-12-B-28 (Florigiant sib) / VA Bunch 67, A4-4 // Florunner	Mixon, 1982
Sunrunner	Runner	UF75102, F519	1982	Florida AES	F439-16-10-1-1 (Florunner component) // UF393-7-1 (NC-Fla 14 sib), UF334A-3-5-5-1 (Florispan derivative) / Jenkins Jumbo	Norden et al., 1985
Southern Runner	Runner	UF80202, 72 × 93-6-1-1-b3-B, PI 506419	1984	Florida AES	PI 203396 (resistant to *Cercospora arachidicola* and *Phaeoisariopsis personata*) / Florunner	Gorbet et al., 1987

(continued on next page)

Table 4–4. Continued.

Cultivar	Market class	Other designation	Year of release	Releasing agency	Origin	Reference
Arbrook	Rhizoma	PI 262817	1985	Florida IFAS & USDA-SCS	PI 262817 (*Arachis glabrata* Benth. collected by W.C. Gregory (Col. No. 9569) near Trinidad, Itapua Dep., Paraguay, in 1959)	Prine et al., 1990
NC 9	Virginia	NC Ac 17404	1985	NC ARS	NC 2 / Florigiant	Wynne et al., 1986
Georgia Red	Valencia	GA T2461-13	1986	Georgia AES & USDA-ARS	UF439-16-10-3 (Florunner component) / New Mexico Valencia A	Branch & Hammons, 1987
Langley	Runner	TP-107-8, PI 506237	1986	Texas AES	Florunner / PI 109839	Simpson et al., 1987
Okrun	Runner	OK-FH 14	1986	USDA-ARS & Oklahoma AES	Florunner / Spanhoma	Banks et al., 1989
NC 10C	Virginia	NC Ac 18417	1988	NC ARS, Virginia AES, & USDA-ARS	NC 8C / Florigiant	Wynne et al., 1990a
Tamrun 88	Runner	B771174, Tx77174	1988	Texas AES	Goldin I (Wilson County Peanut Co., Pleasanton, TX) / Florunner	Smith & Smith, 1989
NC-V 11	Virginia	NC Ac 18411	1989	NC ARS	Florigiant / NC 5 // Florigiant / PI 337396 (var. *fastigiata*)	Wynne et al., 1990b
Georgia Runner	Runner		1990	Georgia AES	Krinkle-leaf (var. *vulgaris*) / PI 331334 ('Criollo', var. *hypogaea* from Bolivia)	W.D. Branch, 1990, personal communication; Hammons, 1964
MARC I	Runner	UF 79308-1	1990	Florida AES	Early Runner / Florispan, F439-17-2-1-1 (Florunner sib) // F459B-3-2-4-6-2-2-1 (Early Bunch component)	D.W. Gorbet, 1990, personal communication

† Developed by selection within a plant introduction or existing cultivar.

Table 4-5. Introduced germplasm occurring in the pedigrees of cultivars.

Introduction	Year	Other designations	Botanical type	Origin	Description
Arachis monticola			*A. monticola* Krap. et Rig.	From Gambia	Contributes 25% of the ancestry of 'Tamnut 74'.
Basse Huston Col. No. 146		Spanish No. 146	*Vulgaris*	Obtained from India by the Tom Huston Peanut Co.	Parent of GA 207-2 and GA 207-3. Source of 'Dixie Spanish'
McRan			*fastigiata hypogaea*	Introduced from Africa	Source of 'McRan' Parent of 'Langley'
PI 109839	1931	Archer Col. No. 2971, 'Mani'		Seeds collected by W.A. Archer (Agric. Explorer, Bureau of Plant Industry, Soils, and Agric. Eng., Beltsville, MD) at a market in Caracas, Venezuela.	
PI 118457	1936	Archer Col. No. 3990, *Arachis glabrata* Benth. cv. 'Arb'	*A. clabrata* Benth.	Seed collected by W.A. Archer (Agric. Explorer, Bureau of Plant Industry, Soils, and Agric. Eng., Beltsville, MD) near Campo Grande, Brazil.	Source of 'Florigraze'
PI 121067	1937	Archer Col. No. 4998, 'Indio'	*hypogaea*	Seed obtained by W.A. Archer (Agric. Explorer, Bureau of Plant Industry, Soils, and Agric. Eng., Beltsville, MD) from Sr. Clos of the Ministerio de Agricultura, Buenos Aires, Argentina. Originally from Misiones, Argentina.	Parent of C12 and C37. Source of insect resistance in GP-NC 343, NC 10247, NC 10272, NC 15729, NC 15745, and 'NC 6'.
PI 121070	1937	Archer Col. No. 5001, Strain A.H. 1131-1	*vulgaris*	Seed obtained by W.A. Archer (Agric. Explorer, Bureau of Plant Industry, Soils, and Agric. Eng., Beltsville, MD) from Sr. Clos of the Ministerio de Agric., Buenos Aires, Argentina. Originally from Chajarf, Entre Rios, Argentina.	Source of 'Argentine'
PI 161317	1947	No. 31-A	*vulgaris*	Seeds collected by J.H. Stephens (Agric. Explorer, Bureau of Plant Industry, Soils, and Agric. Eng., Beltsville, MD) and Dr. W. Hartley (Australian Counc. for Sci. and Ind. Res., Canberra, Australia) from Salto, Uruguay.	Parent of 'Starr'

(continued on next page)

Table 4-5. Continued.

Introduction	Year	Other designations	Botanical type	Origin	Description
PI 203396	1952	Beetle Col. No. 2201	*hypogaea*	Seeds collected by A.A. Beetle (Agric. Explorer, Bur. of Plant Industry and Agric. Eng., Beltsville, MD) from a market in Pôrto Alegre, Brazil.	Parent of 'Southern Runner'. Source of resistance to *Cercospora arachidicola* and *Phaeoisariopsis personata*.
PI 221057	1954	J.B.M 19/3	*vulgaris*	Inst. Agron., Campinas, São Paulo, Brazil.	"Fruit large, testa violet-colored." Contributes 25% of the ancestry of 'Toalson'.
PI 262817	1960	Gregory Col. No. 9569	*A. glabrata* Benth.	Plants collected by W.C. Gregory (Crop Sci. Dep., NC State Univ.) 1.5 km from Trinidad, Itapua Dep., Paraguay	"Rhizomatous perennial." Released as 'Arbrook' rhizoma peanut.
PI 268661	1960	SB52, Apaxuc 370, 'Chico'	*vulgaris*	Seeds presented by the Mount Makulu Res. Stn., Chilanga, Rhodesia.	"Sequential branching, bunch growth habit." Parent of 'Pronto' and 'Spanco'.
PI 331334	1968	'Criollo', Hammons & Langford Col. No. 169, Plot 590	*hypogaea*	Seed obtained by R.O. Hammons and W.R. Langford (Crops Res. Div., Agric. Res. Serv., Tifton and Exp., GA) from the Inst. Nacional de Tecnologia Agropecuaria, Manfredi, Argentina. Originally from Bolivia.	"Prostrate; pods small; branches alternate; stem purple." Parent of 'Georgia Runner'.
PI 335987	1971	Mf. 66 XM 69	*fastigiata*	Seed presented by J. Pietrarelli, Estacion Exp., Agropecuaria, Manfredi, Argentina.	Mutant selected from X-irradiated 'Colorado Manfredi'. Source of 'New Mexico Valencia C'.
PI 337396	1968	Hammons & Langford Col. No. 250, FAV 78, 1968 Plot 389	*hypogaea*	Collected by R.O. Hammons and W.R. Langford from A. Krapovickas, Faculty of Agronomy and Veterinary, Natl. Univ. of the Northeast, Corrientes, Argentina. Originally from the Corrientes City Market.	Contributes 25% of the ancestry of 'NC-V 11'.
PI 405933	1955	T-1119, *Arachis monticola*		Seed presented by V.A. Rigoni (Agric. Exp. Stn., Manfredi, Argentina.	"An annual decumbent, tetraploid ($2n = 40$) species with biarticulated pods. Widely used in interspecific hybridization since 1958. One parent of cv. 'Spancross'."

PEANUT IMPROVEMENT

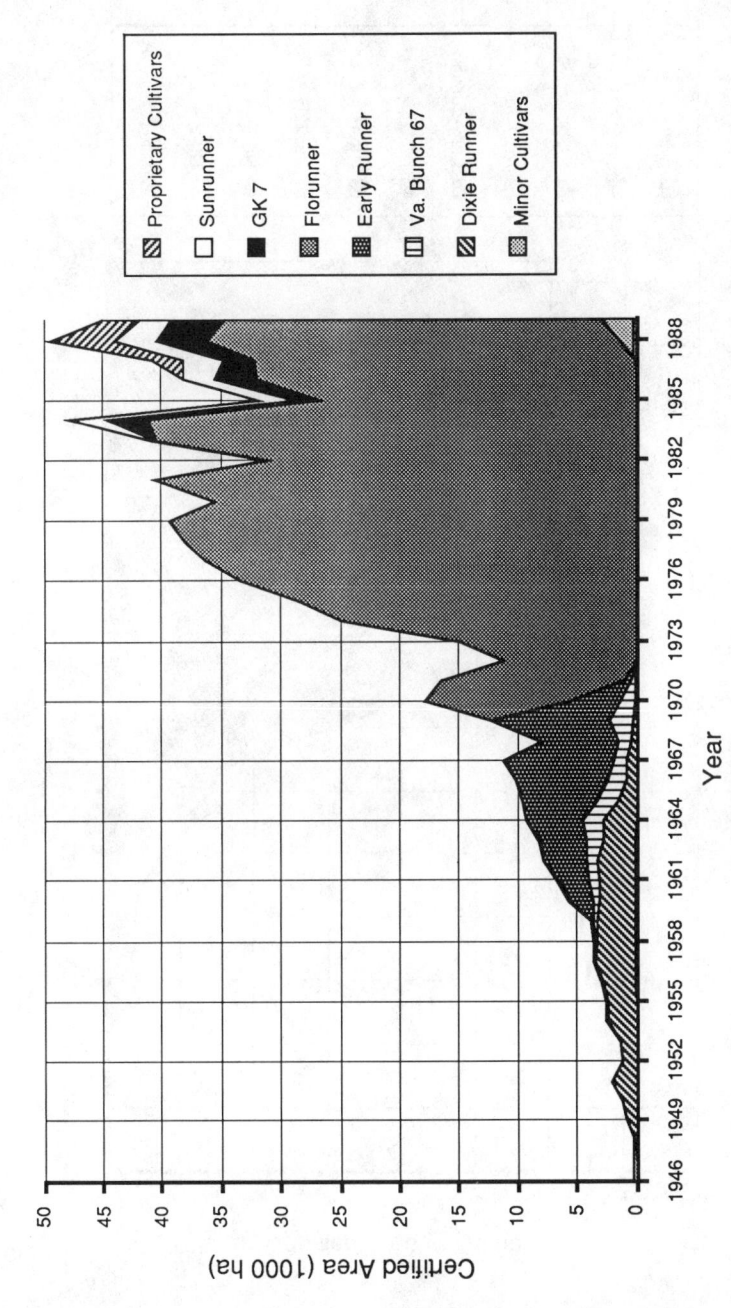

Fig. 4-3. Distribution of certified peanut seed production by cultivar in the runner market class in the USA, 1946 to 1989. Data from the American Organization of Seed Certifying Agencies, Raleigh, NC.

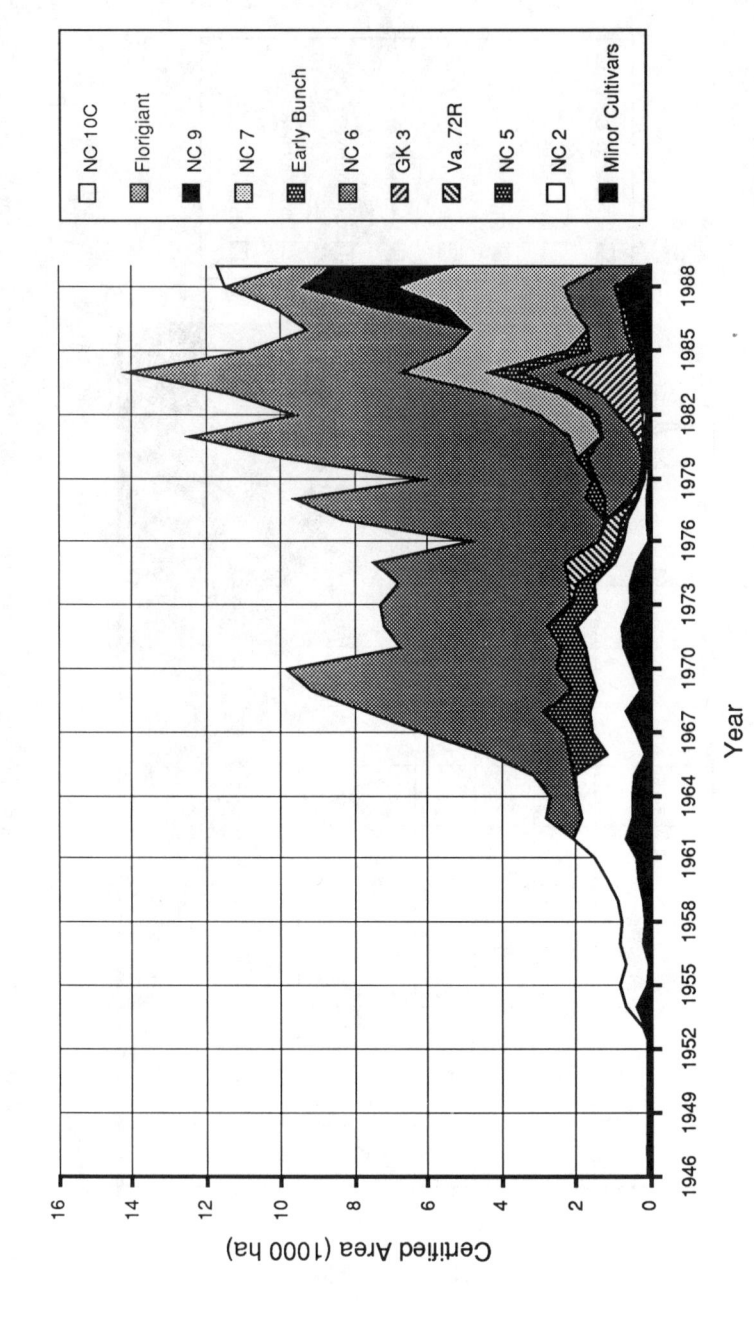

Fig. 4–4. Distribution of certified peanut seed production by cultivar in the Virginia market class in the USA, 1946 to 1989. Data from the American Organization of Seed Certifying Agencies, Raleigh, NC.

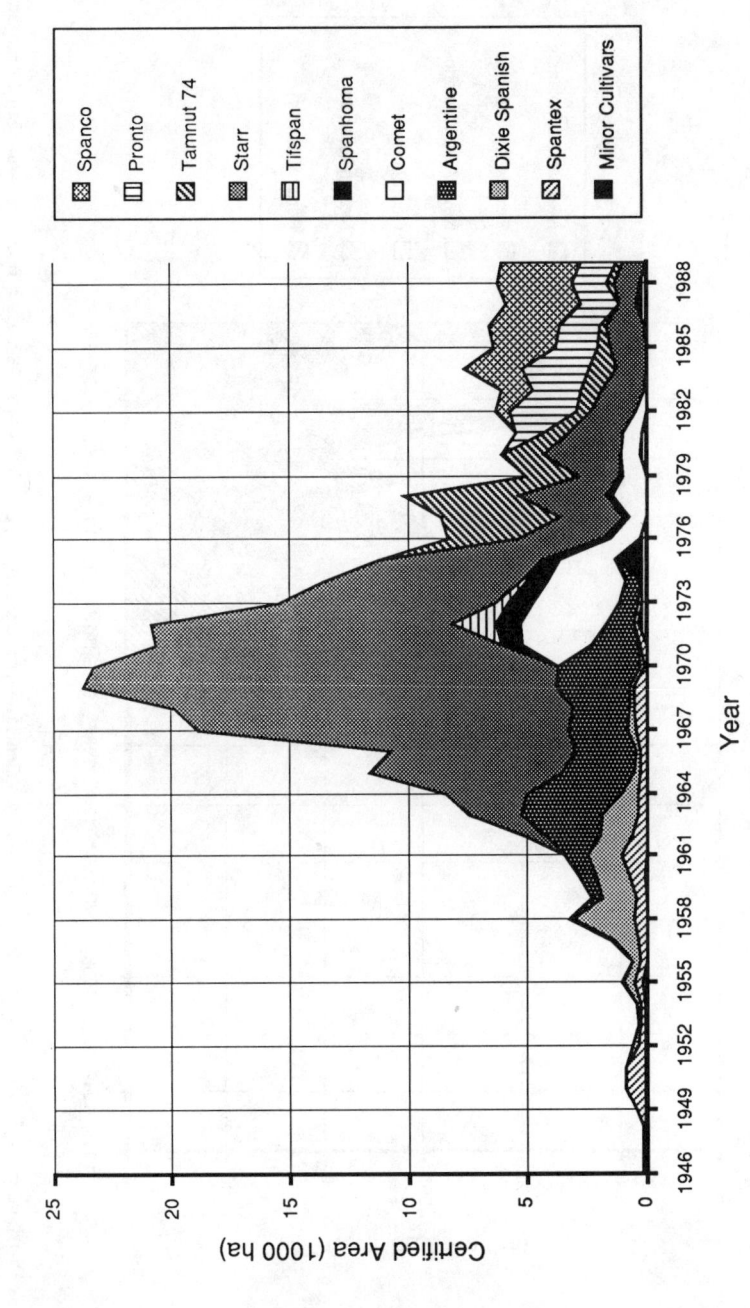

Fig. 4-5. Distribution of certified peanut seed production by cultivar in the Spanish market class in the USA, 1946 to 1989. Data from the American Organization of Seed Certifying Agencies, Raleigh, NC.

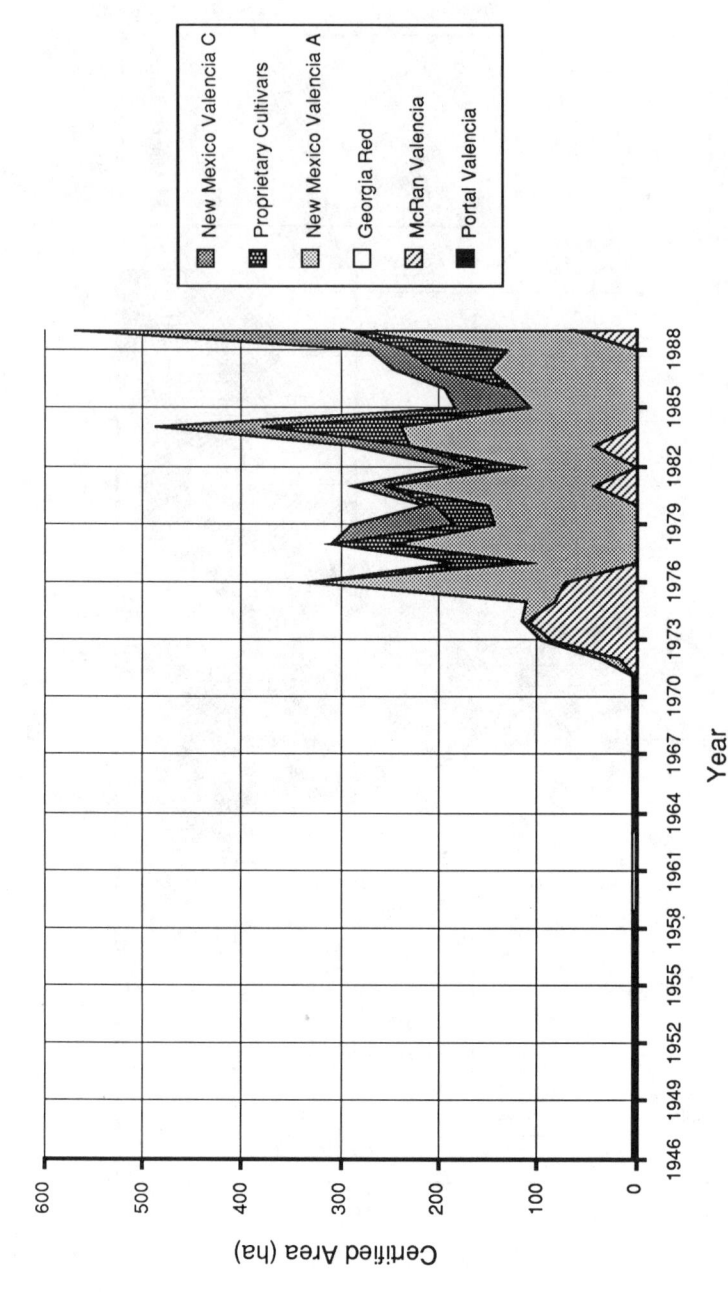

Fig. 4-6. Distribution of certified peanut seed production by Valencia market class in the USA, 1946 to 1989. Data from the American Organization of Seed Certifying Agencies, Raleigh, NC.

To examine the genetic contributions of ancestral lines to the peanut crop in a given year, one must know the pedigrees of the cultivars grown as well as the hectarage of each. Pedigree information was obtained from release notices and breeders' records, and ancestral contributions to individual cultivars were calculated assuming that each parent made a 50% genetic contribution to its progeny. Because little information is available regarding the area planted to different cultivars in commercial production, data reflecting areas certified for seed production were obtained from the American Organization of Seed Certifying Agencies. Certified hectarage cannot be a completely accurate basis for assigning weights to cultivars for several reasons. Due to regional variation in yields, certified acreage does not necessarily reflect seed production. Some farmers do not plant certified seed; the proportion of the crop planted with certified seed varies from state to state. Nevertheless, the certified hectarage values are the best available for use in weighting the relative areas planted to different cultivars.

Examination of the ancestral contributions to the three largest market classes shows that the same germplasm has predominated within each over long periods. In the runner class, 'Small White Spanish' and 'Dixie Giant' have been the largest contributors of germplasm since the late 1940s (Fig. 4–7). Spanish 18–38 and Basse became major contributors with the advent of Florunner in 1969. Only in the 1980s have other ancestral lines made significant contributions: 'Jenkins Jumbo' is now a contributor through 'GK7' and 'Sunrunner'. PI 203396 made a small but observable contribution to the ancestry of runner acreage in 1988 and 1989. The Virginia class has the greatest diversity of ancestral contributions with approximately equal contributions from Jenkins Jumbo, Dixie Giant, Small White Spanish, Spanish 18–38, and Basse (Fig. 4–8). These lines together accounted for approximately two-thirds of the Virginia germplasm grown in 1989. 'White's Runner', PI 121067, 'N.C. Bunch', 'Atkins Runner', 'Improved Spanish 2B', and 'NC 4' accounted for roughly equal shares of the remaining one-third. In the Spanish class, there are currently three major contributors to the class' ancestry' PI 268661 ('Chico'), 'Spantex', and PI 161317 (Fig. 4–9). Approximately two-thirds of the current Spanish germplasm is, therefore, derived from plant introductions. This amount represents an erosion of genetic diversity in the class due to the loss of contribution from PI 121070 ('Argentine') and *A. monticola* Krap. et Rig. The array of ancestors for the entire U.S. crop is the weighted average of the four market classes (Fig. 4–10). Dixie Giant and Small White Spanish, major contributors of genes to the runner and Virginia classes, are the source of nearly one-half the germplasm in the U.S. crop. Spanish 18–38, Basse, and Jenkins Jumbo are the next largest contributors followed by Chico, Spantex, and PI 161317.

In addition to the germplasm releases, peanut breeders are also introducing or using germplasm identified as being useful by scientists at the International Crops Research Institute for the Semi-Arid Tropics (ICRISAT) and national breeding programs in peanut-growing countries. Peanut germplasm from ICRISAT with resistance to early leaf spot, late leaf spot, rust, and *Aspergillus* spp. and with early maturity is currently being incorporated into

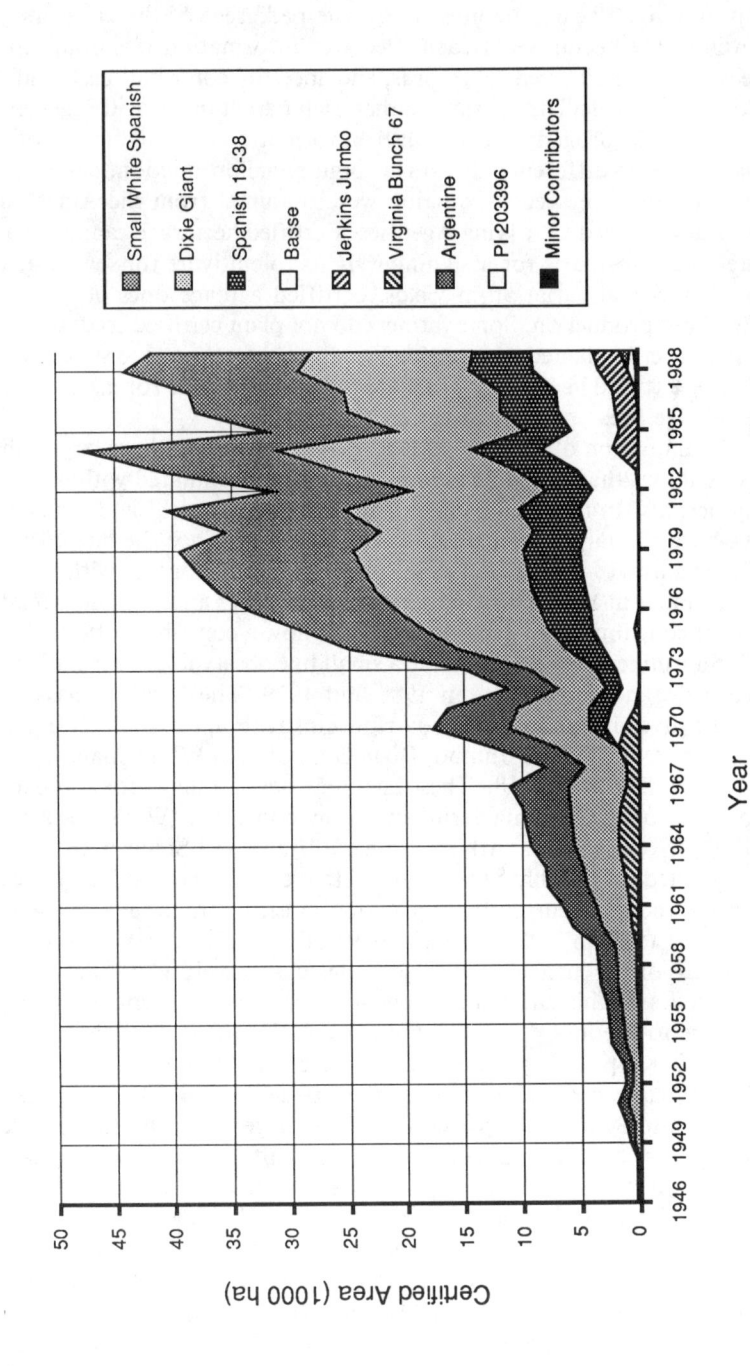

Fig. 4-7. Contributions of ancestral lines to the genetic composition of peanut cultivars in the runner market class, 1946 to 1989, weighted by certified hectareage.

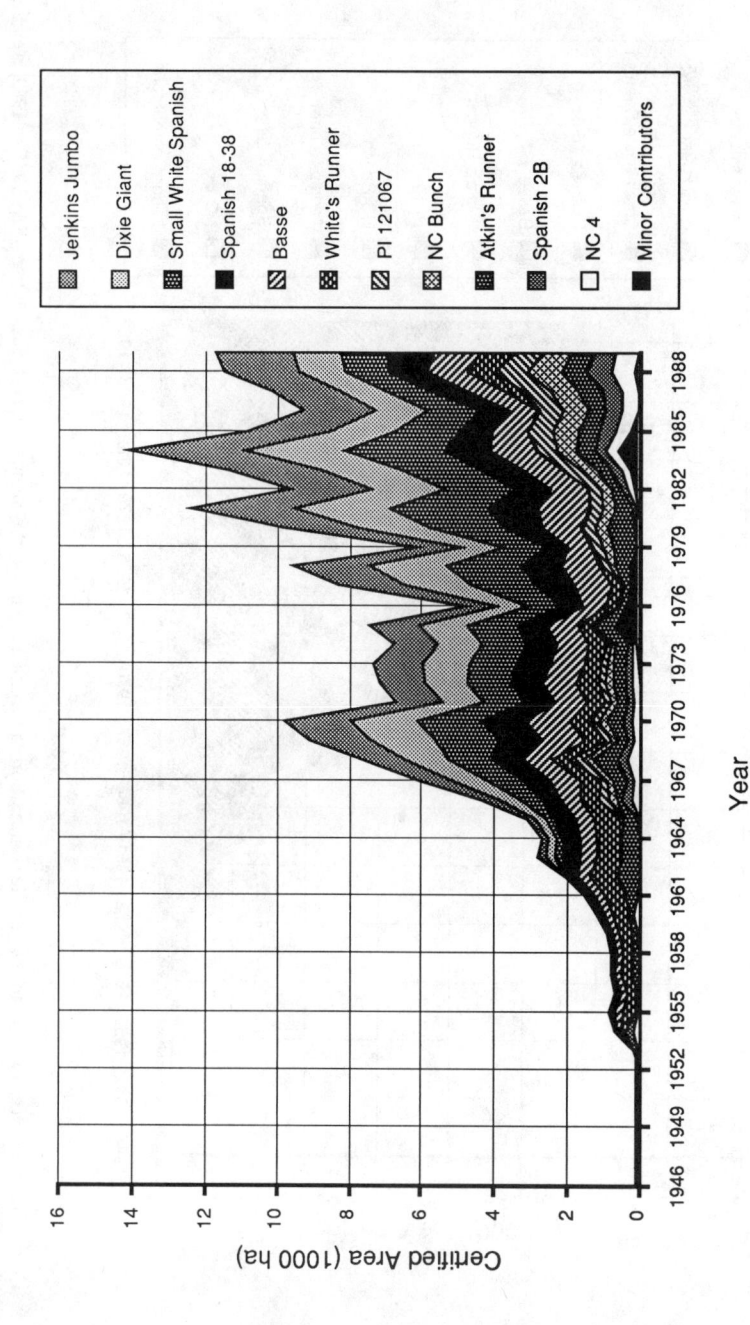

Fig. 4-8. Contributions of ancestral lines to the genetic composition of peanut cultivars in the Virginia market class in the USA, 1946 to 1989, weighted by certified hectareage.

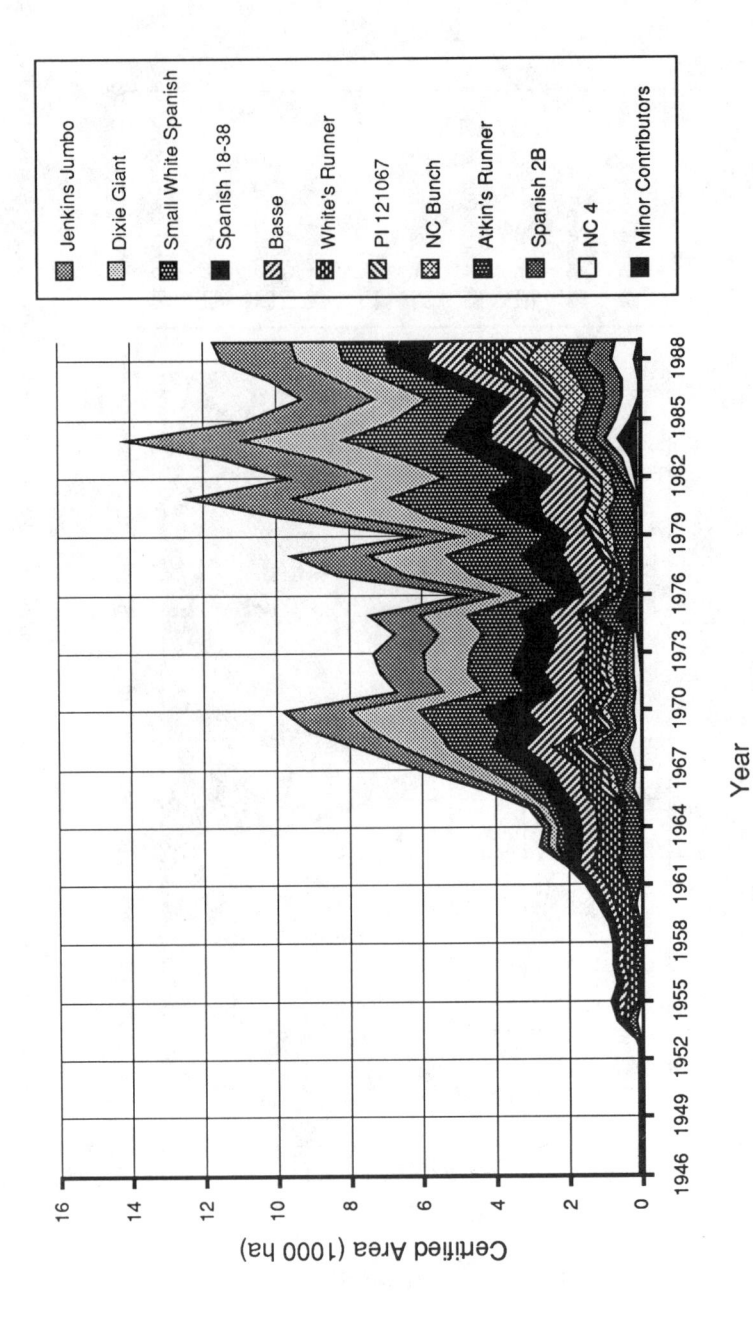

Fig. 4-9. Contribution of ancestral lines to the genetic composition of peanut cultivars in the Spanish market class in the USA, 1946 to 1989, weighted by certified hectareage.

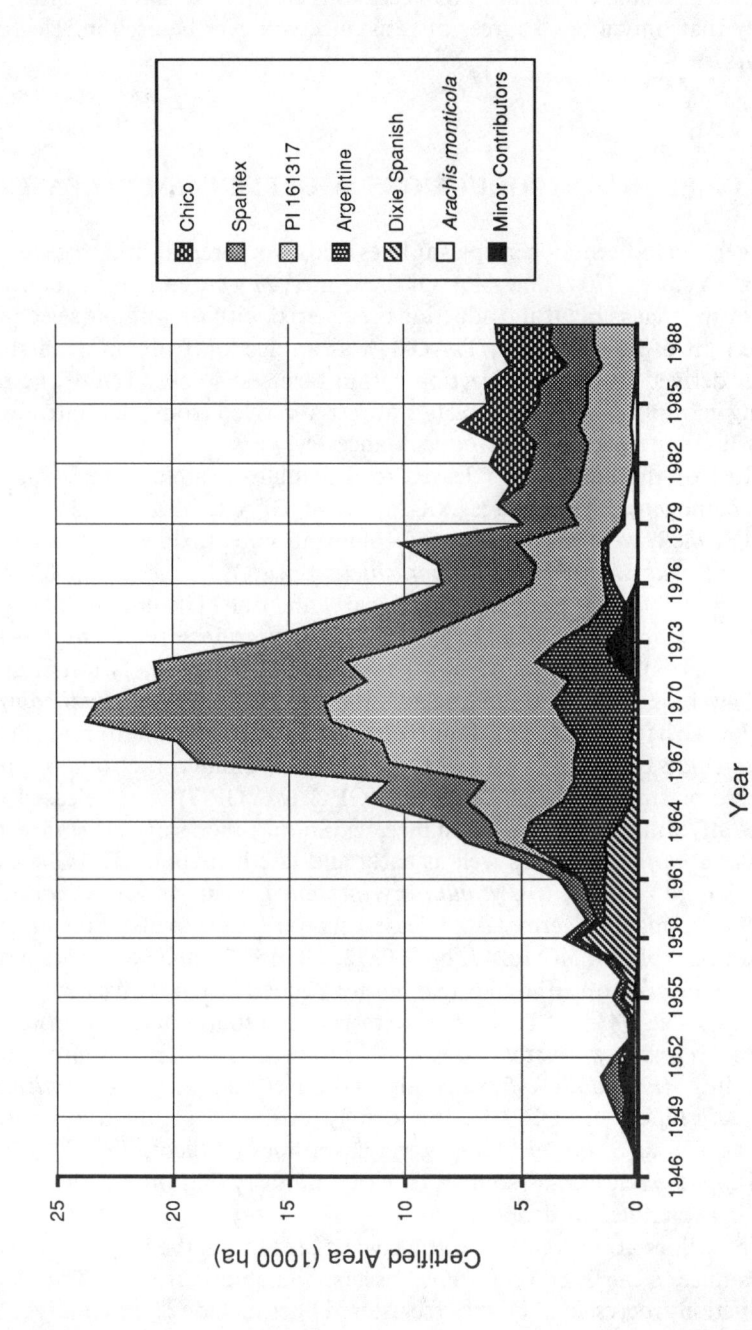

Fig. 4-10. Contributions of ancestral lines to the genetic composition of peanut cultivars in the USA, 1946 to 1989, weighted by certified hectareage.

U.S. breeding programs. Although many genotypes are identified as having resistance to a single pest (e.g., 83 accessions resistant to late leaf spot), it is likely that only a few sources of resistance will ever be used in released cultivars.

USE OF PLANT INTRODUCTIONS IN GERMPLASM RELEASES

There have been 49 germplasm lines and two parental lines registered in the USA since 1970 (Table 4-6). Of these lines, 27 were entirely introduced germplasm, that is plant introductions registered with or without selection for the trait of interest. One, TxAG-1, was a selection from an irradiated cultivar derived from mass selection within farmers' stocks. Ten of the remaining germplasm releases had 50% ancestry derived from plant introductions while nine had 25% introduced ancestry.

Most of the lines were released to distribute germplasm resistant to peanut pathogens. Eight releases (AR-1 to AR-4, GFA-1, GFA-2, PI 337394F, and PI 337409) were resistant to seed colonization by toxigenic *Aspergillus* spp. (*A. flavus* Link:Fr and *A. parasiticus* Speare). Three (NC 3033, PI 109839, and Tifton-8) were resistant to early and one (Tifton-8) to late leaf spot [*Cercospora arachidicola* S. Hori and *Phaeoisariopsis personata*.(Berk. & M.A. Curtis) Arx]. Nine (CBR-R1 to CBR-R6, NC 3033, Tifton-8, and VGP-1) were resistant to Cylindrocladium black rot [*Lasiodiplodia theobromae* (Pat) Griffon & Maubl.]. Fourteen releases were resistant to rust (*Puccinia arachidis* Speg.). NC 3033 was resistant to Pythium rot (*Pythium* spp). Five germplasm lines from Virginia (VGP-2 to VGP-7) were released as sources of multiple disease resistance, exhibiting moderate resistance to *Sclerotinia minor* Jagger as well as early and late leaf spots. TxAG-4 and TxAG-5 were resistant to *Pythium myriotylum* Drechl. and *S. minor*.

Of the remaining germplasm releases, six were made to distribute insect-resistant germplasm. NC 10247, NC 10272, NC 15729, and NC 15745 have resistance to potato leafhopper (*Empoasca fabae* Harris) derived from PI 121067. GP-NC 343 and Tifton-8 were resistant to southern corn rootworm (*Diabrotica undecimpunctata howardi* Barber) and the latter was also resistant to thrips (*Frankliniella fusca* Hinds) and velvetbean caterpillar (*Anticaria gemmatalis* Hübner). VGP-7 was moderately resistant to southern corn rootworm as well as *S. minor*. Three germplasm lines ('Chico', TxAG-1, and TxAG-2) were released as sources of early maturity. Tifton-8 is described as having tolerance to drought.

These lines are currently used by peanut breeders in the USA as sources of resistance to the listed pathogens, insects, and abiotic stresses. The plant introductions represented by these registered lines include representatives of three of the four botanical varieties and were mostly collected since World War II (Table 4-7).

Table 4-6. Peanut germplasm and parental lines registered with the Crop Science Society of America.

Identity	Market class	PI ancestry	Other designations	Year of release	Releasing agency	Origin or pedigree	Reference
TxAG-1	Spanish		GP40, R-22	1985	Texas AES	Selection from irradiated 'Spantex': Early maturing.	Simpson & Smith, 1986.
TxAG-4	Spanish		GP48, PI 535816	1990	Texas AES, USDA-ARS, & Oklahoma AES	F_4-derived selection from Toalson // UF73-4022. Resistant to *Pythium myriotylum* and *Sclerotinia minor*.	Smith et al., 1990
TxAG-5	Spanish		GP49, PI 535817	1990	Texas AES, USDA-ARS, & Oklahoma AES	F_4-derived selection from Toalson // UF73-4022. Resistant to *Pythium myriotylum* and *Sclerotinia minor*.	Smith et al., 1990
Jenkins Jumbo	Virginia		PL1	1978	Georgia AES, Florida AES, & USDA-AES	Selection from stocks obtained from R.B. Jenkins of Sumner, GA.	Hammons & Norden, 1979.
NC 3033	Virginia	Basse, 25%	GP 9, NC Ac 3033	1976	NC AES	Basse / Spanish 18-38, GA 207-7 // A48, NC 4 / Spanish 2B: Resistant to *Cylindrocladium crotalariae, Cercospora arachidicola, Pythium spp.,* & *Sclerotium rolfsii*.	Beute et al., 1976
F334A-B-14	Virginia	Basse, 25%	GP32	1983	Georgia AES	Basse / Spanish 18-38, GA 207-3 // F230-118-2-2, Dixie Giant / Small White Spanish: Resistant to *Diplodia* collar rot.	Hammons et al., 1983
GA 207-3-4	Virginia	Basse, 50%	PL2	1984	Georgia AES & USDA-ARS	Basse / Spanish 18-38	Branch & Hammons, 1984
PI 109839	Virginia	PI 109839	GP10	1979	Georgia AES & USDA-ARS	PI 109839 (Archer Col. No. 2971) obtained in 1931 from a market in Caracas, Venezuela: Resistant to *Cercospora arachidicola*.	Hammons et al., 1980

(continued on next page)

Table 4-6. Continued.

Identity	Market class	PI ancestry	Other designations	Year of release	Releasing agency	Origin or pedigree	Reference
NC 10247	Virginia	PI 121067, 25%	GP 5	1975	NC AES	NC Bunch / PI 121067, F$_7$ #13 // Recurved (irradiated micromutant from NC 4): Resistant to *Empoasca fabae*.	Campbell et al., 1975
NC 10272	Virginia	PI 121067, 25%	GP 6	1975	NC AES	NC Bunch / PI 121067, NC Ac 4508 // Recurved (irradiated macromutant from NC 4): Resistant to *Empoasca fabae*.	Campbell et al., 1975
NC 15729	Virginia	PI 121067, 25%	GP 7	1975	NC AES	NC Bunch / PI 121067, C12 // A18, NC 4 / Spanish 2B: Re-irradiated progeny resistant to *Empoasca fabae*.	Campbell et al., 1975
NC 15745	Virginia	PI 121067, 25%	GP 8	1975	NC AES	NC Bunch / PI 121067, C12 // A18, NC 4 / Spanish 2B: Re-irradiated progeny resistant to *Empoasca fabae*.	Campbell et al., 1975
GP-NC 343	Virginia	PI 121067, 50%	GP 1, NC Ac 343	1970	NC AES	NC Bunch / PI 121067: Resistant to *Diabrotica undecimpunctata howardi*.	Campbell et al., 1971
TxAG-2	Spanish	PI 152125, 25%	GP41, TP-922	1985	Texas AES	R-25 (selection from irradiated 'Spantex') // TPL-206-2-1,26 Selection 1 (selection from Common Spanish) / PI 152125 (Spanish 2B): Early maturing.	Simpson & Smith, 1986
Tifrust-1	Valencia	PI 215696	GP18, ICG 7881, PI 215696	1981	USDA-ARS & Georgia AES	Selection from PI 215696 from Peru: Resistant to *Puccinia arachidis*.	Hammons et al., 1982d

GFA-1	Virginia	PI 246388, 25%	GP33, A72118	1983	USDA-ARS & Georgia AES	F439-16-10 (Florunner sib) / PI 246388 ('Koboka Tjina' from South Africa, *Aspergillus flavus* resistant), A137 // A5-5, 392-12-B-28 (Florigiant sib) / Dixie Spanish: Resistant to *A. flavus*.	Mixon, 1983a
GFA-2	Virginia	PI 246388, 25%	GP34, A72120	1983	USDA-ARS & Georgia AES	F439-16-10 (Florunner sib) / PI 246388 ('Koboka Tjina' from South Africa, *Aspergillus flavus* resistant), A137 // Florunner: Resistant to *A. flavus*.	Mixon, 1983b
Tifton-8	Virginia	PI 261976	GP39	1985	USDA-ARS, Virginia AES, Georgia AES	Virginia-type selection from PI 261976, var. *vulgaris* from Paraguay, resistant to *Cylindrocladium crotalariae*, *Cercospora arachidicola*, *Phaeoisariopsis personata*, *Diabrotica undecimpunctata howardi*, *Frankliniella fusca*, *Anticaria gemmatalis*, and drought.	Coffelt et al., 1985
CBR-R1	Spanish	PI 268573	GP12, PI 268573	1981	Georgia AES & USDA-ARS	Selection from PI 268573, 'Rabat No. 27' from Morocco, obtained in 1960 from Rhodesia: Resistant to *Cylindrocladium crotalariae*.	Hammons, 1981
Chico	Spanish	PI 268661	GP 2, PI 268661, Apaxuc 370	1973	USDA-ARS, Georgia AES, Virginia AES, Oklahoma AES	PI 268661, *Arachis* line No. 370 from Krasnodar Territory, USSR, obtained in 1960 from Rhodesia: Early maturing.	Bailey & Hammons, 1975
VGP 2	Virginia	PI 268661, 50%	GP42, PI 509536, VA 732813	1983	USDA-ARS & Virginia AES	F$_3$-derived selection from Chico / Florigiant, moderately resistant to *Sclerotinia minor*, *Cercospora arachidicola*, and *Phaeoisariopsis personata*.	Coffelt et al., 1987

(continued on next page)

Table 4-6. Continued.

Identity	Market class	PI ancestry	Other designations	Year of release	Releasing agency	Origin or pedigree	Reference
VGP-3	Virginia	PI 268661, 50%	GP43, PI 509537, VA 732815	1986	USDA-ARS & Virginia AES	F_3-derived selection from Chico / Florigiant, moderately resistant to *Sclerotinia minor*, *Cercospora arachidicola*, and *Phaeoisariopsis personata*.	Coffelt et al., 1987
VGP-4	Virginia	PI 268661, 50%	GP44, PI 509538, VA 732816	1986	USDA-ARS & Virginia AES	F_3-derived selection from Chico / Florigiant, moderately resistant to *Sclerotinia minor*, *Cercospora arachidicola*, and *Phaeoisariopsis personata*.	Coffelt et al., 1987
VGP-5	Virginia	PI 268661, 50%	GP45, PI 509539, VA 732817	1986	UDA-ARS & Virginia AES	F_3-derived selection from Chico / Florigiant, moderately resistant to *Sclerotinia minor*, *Cercospora arachidicola*, and *Phaeoisariopsis personata*.	Coffelt et al., 1987
VGP-6	Virginia	PI 268661, 50%	GP46, PI 509540, VA 732818	1986	USDA-ARS & Virginia AES	F_3-derived selection from Chico / Florigiant, moderately resistant to *Sclerotinia minor*, *Cercospora arachidicola*, and *Phaeoisariopsis personata*.	Coffelt et al., 1987
Tifrust-14	Valencia	PI 314817	GP31, PI 314817, ICG 7882	1981	USDA-ARS, Georgia AES, & ICRISAT	PI 314817 obtained by D.H. Timothy from Peru: Resistant to *Puccinia arachidis*.	Hammons et al., 1982a
Tifrust-13	Virginia	PI 315608	GP30, PI 315608, ICG 7883	1981	Georgia AES, USDA-ARS, ICRISAT, & Israel MinAg-ARO	Selection from PI 315608 obtained from Israel: Resistant to *Puccinia arachidis*.	Hammons et al., 1982b

VGP-7	Virginia	PI 319178, 50%	GP47, PI 509541, VA 751014	1986	USDA-ARS & Virginia AES	F$_3$-derived selection from GP-NC 343 / PI 319178, moderately resistant to *Sclerotinia minor* and *Diabrotica undecimpunctata howardii*.	Coffelt et al., 1987
CBR-R2	Virginia	PI 331326	GP13, PI 331326	1981	Georgia AES & USDA-ARS	Selection from PI 331326 (HL Col. 161) from Entre Rios, Argentina: Resistant to *Cylindrocladium crotalariae*.	Hammons, 1981
CBR-R3	Spanish	PI 336931	GP14, PI 336931	1981	Georgia AES & USDA-ARS	PI 336931 (HL Col. 635), 'Correntino Blanco Commun' from Argentina, obtained from Brazil: Resistant to *Cylindrocladium crotalariae*.	Hammons, 1981
PI 337394F	Valencia	PI 337394	GP 3, PI 337394	1974	USDA-ARS, Alabama AES, & Georgia AES	Selection from PI 337394, a mixed lot obtained in 1968 from the Universidad Nacional del Nordeste, Corrientes, Argentina: Resistant to seed colonization by *Aspergillus* spp.	Mixon & Rogers, 1975
AR-4		PI 337349F, 50%	GP 38, Exp. line 7405	1983	UDA-ARS & Georgia AES	PI 337394F (GP 3, *Aspergillus flavus* resistant var. *fastigiata*) / Florunner: Resistant to *A. flavus*	Mixon, 1983a
PI 337409	Valencia	PI 337409	GP 4, PI 337409	1974	USDA-ARS, Alabama AES, & Georgia AES	PI 337409 obtained in 1968 from the Universidad Nacional del Nordeste, Corrientes, Argentina: Resistant to seed colonization by *Aspergillus* spp.	Mixon and Rogers, 1975
AR-1		PI 337409, 50%	GP35, Exp. line 7293	1983	USDA-ARS & Georgia AES	Florunner / PI 337409 (GP 4, *Aspergillus flavus* resistant var. *fastigiata*): Resistant to *A. flavus*.	Mixon, 1983a

(continued on next page)

Table 4-6. Continued.

Identity	Market class	PI ancestry	Other designations	Year of release	Releasing agency	Origin or pedigree	Reference
AR-2		PI 337409, 50%	GP36, Exp. line 7309	1983	USDA-ARS & Georgia AES	F392-12-B-28 (Florigiant sib) / Dixie Spanish, A5-5 // PI 337409 (GP4, *Aspergillus flavus* resistant var. *fastigiata*): Resistant to *A. flavus*.	Mixon, 1983a
AR-3		PI 337432, 50%	GP37, Exp. line 7404	1983	USDA-ARS & Georgia AES	PI 337432 (*Aspergillus flavus* resistant var. *fastigiata*) / Tifspan: Resistant to *A. flavus*	Mixon, 1983a
CBR-R4	Valencia	PI 339974	GP15, PI 339974	1981	Georgia AES & USDA-ARS	Selection from PI 339974 obtained in 1969 from Jujuy Province, Argentina: Resistant to *Cylindrocladium crotalariae*.	Hammons, 1981
VGP-1	Virginia	PI 343381	GP11, VA 751607, PI 343381	1979	USDA-ARS & Virginia AES	Selection from PI 343381, a segregating line from the cross Virginia Sihit Meshubahat / Schwarz 21 obtained from Israel: Resistant to *Cylindrocladium crotalariae*.	Coffelt, 1980
CBR-R5	Spanish	PI 362137	GP16, PI 362137	1981	Georgia AES & USDA-ARS	Selection from PI 362137, 'K3' obtained in 1971 from Punjab Agric. Univ. in India: Resistant to *Cylindrocladium crotalariae*.	Hammons, 1981
CBR-R6	Spanish	PI 362142	GP17, PI 362142	1981	Georgia AES & USDA-ARS	Selection from PI 362142, 'U/4/4/24' from Tozi, Sudan, obtained as EC 21074 from India: Resistant to *Cylindrocladium crotalariae*.	Hammons, 1981
Tifrust-2	Valencia	PI 390593	GP19, ICG 7886, PI 390593	1981	USDA-ARS & Georgia AES	Selection from PI 390593 from Peru: Resistant to *Puccinia arachidis*.	Hammons et al., 1982d
Tifrust-3	Valencia	PI 390595	GP20, ICG 7887, PI 390595	1981	USDA-ARS & Georgia AES	Selection from PI 390595 from Peru: Resistant to *Puccinia arachidis*.	Hammons et al., 1982d

Tifrust-8	Valencia PI 393516	GP25, PI 393516, ICG 7888	1981	USDA-ARS, Georgia AES, & ICRISAT	Selection from PI 393516: Resistant to *Puccinia arachidis*.	Hammons et al. 1982c
Tifrust-9	Valencia PI 393517	GP26, PI 393517, ICG 7889	1981	USDA-ARS, Georgia AES, & ICRISAT	Selection from PI 393517: Resistant to *Puccinia arachidis*.	Hammons et al. 1982c
Tifrust-10	Valencia PI 393526	GP27, PI 393526, ICG 7890	1981	USDA-ARS, Georgia AES, & ICRISAT	Selection from PI 393526: Resistant to *Puccinia arachidis*.	Hammons et al. 1982c
Tifrust-12	Virginia PI 393527	GP29, PI 393527, ICG 7891	1981	USDA-ARS, Georgia AES, & ICRISAT	Selection from PI 393527: Resistant to *Puccinia arachidis*.	Hammons et al. 1982c
Tifrust-11	Valencia PI 393531	GP28, PI 393531, ICG 7893	1981	USDA-ARS, Georgia AES, & ICRISAT	Selection from PI 393531: Resistant to *Puccinia arachidis*.	Hammons et al. 1982c
Tifrust-5	Valencia PI 393641	GP22, PI 393641, ICG 7894	1981	USDA-ARS, Georgia AES, & ICRISAT	Selection from PI 393641: Resistant to *Puccinia arachidis*, moderately resistant to *Cercospora arachidicola* and *Phaeoisariopsis personata*.	Hammons et al. 1982c
Tifrust-6	Valencia PI 393643	GP23, PI 393643, ICG 7895	1981	USDA-ARS, Georgia AES, & ICRISAT	Selection from PI 393643: Resistant to *Puccinia arachidis*.	Hammons et al. 1982c
Tifrust-7	Valencia PI 393646	GP24, PI 393646, ICG 7896	1981	USDA-ARS, Georgia AES, & ICRISAT	Selection from PI 393646: Resistant to *Puccinia arachidis*.	Hammons et al. 1982c
Tifrust-4	Valencia PI 407454	GP21, ICG 7898, PI 407454	1981	USDA-ARS & Georgia AES	Selection from PI 407454 from Ecuador: Resistant to *Puccinia arachidis*.	Hammons et al. 1982d

Table 4-7. Introduced germplasm occurring in the pedigrees of cultivars.

Introduction	Year	Other designations	Botanical type	Origin	Description
Basse PI 109839	1931	Archer Col. No. 2971, 'Mani'	hypogaea	Seeds collected by W.A. Archer (Agricultural Explorer, Bureau of Plant Industry, Soils, and Agric. Eng., Beltsville, MD) at a market in Caracas, Venezuela.	Parent of GA 207-2 and GA 207-3. Resistant to Cercospora arachidicola
PI 121067	1937	Archer Col. No. 4998, 'Indio'	hypogaea	Seed obtained from W.A. Archer (Agricultural Explorer, Bureau of Plant Industry, Soils, and Agric. Eng., Beltsville, MD) from Sr. Clos of the Ministerio de Agricultura, Buenos Aires, Argentina. Originally from Misiones, Argentina.	Parent of C12 and C37. Source of insect resistance in GP-NC 343, NC 10247, NC 10272, NC 15729, NC 15745, and 'NC 6'.
PI 152125	1945	No. 30, Spanish 2B	vulgaris	Seeds obtained through the American Consultate (Porto Allegre, Rio Grande do Sul) from the Inst. Agronômico, Campinas, São Paulo, Brazil.	'Spanish 2B' re-introduced from a Brazilian germplasm collection. Contributes 25% to the ancestry of TxAG-2.
PI 215696	1954	Smith Col. No. 198	fastigiata	Collected by E.E. Smith (Agricultural Explorer, Plant Introduction Section, Horticultural Crops Research Branch, Beltsville, MD) from a market in Lima, Peru.	Source of 'Tifrust-1'. Resistant to Puccinia arachidis.
PI 246388	1958	'Koboka Tjina'	vulgaris	Seeds presented by the Oilseed Control Board, Pretoria, Transvaal, Union of South Africa.	Contributes 25% of the ancestry of 'GFA-1' and 'GFA-2'. Source of resistance to Aspergillus flavus.
PI 261976	1959	RCM 484	vulgaris	Collected by W.C. Gregory (Crop Science Dep., North Carolina State Univ.) on the road to Caaguazu, Salida de Coronel Oviedo, Paraguay.	"Fruit large, testa violet-colored." Source of 'Tifton-8'. Resistant to Cylindrocladium crotalariae, Cercospora arachidicola, Phaeoisariopsis personata, Diabrotica undecimpunctata howardii, Frankliniella fusca, Gemmatalis anticaria, and drought.

PI	Year	Identifier	Subspecies	Source	Notes
PI 268573	1960	SB39, 'Rabat No. 27'	vulgaris	Seeds presented by the Mount Makulu Research Station, Chilanga, Rhodesia. Originally from Morocco.	"Sequential branching, bunch growth habit." Source of 'CBR-R1'. Resistant to *Cylindrocladium crotalariae*.
PI 268661	1960	SB52, Apaxuc 370, 'Chico'	vulgaris	Seeds presented by the Mount Makulu Research Station, Chilanga, Rhodesia.	"Sequential branching, bunch growth habit." Parent of 'Pronto', 'Spanco', and VGP-2, -3, -4, -5, and -6. Source of early maturity.
PI 314817	1966	Timothy Col. No. 200, 'Mani'	fastigiata	Seeds collected by D.H. Timothy (Crop Science Dep., NC State Univ.) at a store in Juanjuí, Province of Mariscal Caceres, San Martin, Peru.	Source of 'Tifrust-14'. Resistant to *Puccinia arachidis*.
PI 315608	1966	Line 136	hypogaea	Seed presented by A. Ashri, Faculty of Agriculture, Hebrew Univ. of Jerusalem, Rehovot, Israel.	"Selection from U.S. introductions." Source of 'Tifrust-13'. Resistant to *Puccinia arachidis*.
PI 319178	1967	X-30 L-33		Seed presented by E. Goldin, Volcani Inst. of Agric. Research, Rehobot, Israel.	Parent of VGP-7.
PI 331326	1968	Hammons & Langford Col. No. 161, Plot 563	hypogaea	Seed obtained by R.O. Hammons and W.R. Langford (Crops Res. Div., Agric. Res. Serv., Tifton and Experiment, GA) from the Inst. Nacional de Tecnologia Agropecuaria, Manfredi, Argentina.	"Runner. Testa white, seed white." Source of 'CBR-R2'. Resistant to *Cylindrocladium crotalariae*.
PI 336931	1968	Hammons & Langford Col. No. 635, Correntino Blanco Commun, CIA 459, RCM 47	vulgaris	Seed obtained by R.O. Hammons and W.R. Langford (Crops Research Div., Agric. Res. Serv., Tifton and Experiment, GA) from the Oilseeds Section, Inst. Agronômico, Campinas, São Paulo, Brazil. Originally from Tucuman, Argentina.	Source of 'CBR-R3'. Resistant to *Cylindrocladium crotalariae*.
PI 337394	1968	Hammons & Langford Col. No. 248, FAV 78, 1968 Plot 389	fastigiata	Seed obtained by R.O. Hammons and W.R. Langford (Crops Research Division, Agricultural Research Service, Tifton and Experiment, GA) from A. Krapovickas, Universidad Nacional del Nordeste, Corrientes, Argentina. Originally from the Corrientes City Market.	"Mixed lot." Source of PI 337394F. Parent of 'AR-4'. Resistant to seed colonization by *Aspergillus flavus*.

(continued on next page)

Table 4-7. Continued.

Introduction	Year	Other designations	Botanical type	Origin	Description
PI 337409	1968	Hammons & Langford Col. No. 263, 'Rosado', FAV 155, 1968 Plot 419	*fastigiata*	Seed obtained by R.O. Hammons and W.R. Langford (Crops Research Division, Agricultural Research Service, Tifton and Experiment, GA) from A. Krapovickas, Universidad Nacional del Nordeste, Corrientes, Argentina. Collected in Yaguaron, Paraguay.	Parent of 'AR-1' and 'AR-2'. Resistant to seed colonization by *Aspergillus flavus*.
PI 337432	1968	Hammons & Langford Col. No. 286, 'Blanco Palmar Grande', FAV 129	*fastigiata*	Seed obtained by R.O. Hammons and W.R. Langford (Crops Research Division, Agricultural Research Service, Tifton and Experiment, GA) from A. Krapovickas, Universidad Nacional del Nordeste, Corrientes, Argentina. Originally from Palmar Grande, Department of Gral Pas, Corrientes.	Parent of 'AR-3'. Resistant to seed colonization by *Aspergillus flavus*.
PI 339974	1969	11.	*fastigiata*	Seed presented by V. Hemsey (Faculdad de Agronomia y Zootecnia, San Miguel de Tucuman) through the Office of Agricultural Attache, American Embassy, Buenos Aires, Argentina. Originally from Yuto, Jujuy Province, Bolivia.	Source of 'CBR-R4'. Resistant to *Cylindrocladium crotalariae*.
PI 343381	1969	1251-10	*hypogaea*	Seed from single plant selections made in 1968, presented by A. Ashri, Faculty of Agriculture, Hebrew Univ. of Jerusalem, Rehovot, Israel.	Segregating F_4-derived population from the cross Virginia Sihit Meshubahat (VSM) / Schwartz No. 21, "resistant to pod rot." Source of 'VGP-1'. Resistant to *Cylindrocladium crotalariae*.

PI	Year	Name	Subspecies	Source	Notes
PI 362137	1971	K3	*vulgaris*	Seed presented by the Punjab Agric. Univ., Ludhiana, India, through the Division of Plant Introduction, Indian Agric. Res. Inst., New Delhi.	Source of 'CBR-R5'. Resistant to *Cylindrocladium crotalariae*.
PI 362142	1971	U4/4/24 (E.C. 21074)	*vulgaris*	Seed presented by the Punjab Agric. Univ., Ludhiana, India, through the Division of Plant Introduction, Indian Agric. Res. Institute, New Delhi.	Source of 'CBR-R6'. Resistant to *Cylindrocladium crotalariae*.
PI 390593	1974	W-C Col. No. 1178	*fastigiata*	Seed collected by H.F. Winters (Germplasm Resources Laboratory, Agric. Res. Ctr., Beltsville, MD) and R.L. Clark (Regional Plant Introduction Station, Ames, IA) at a public market in Tingo Maria, Peru.	"Small to medium size seed. White seed coat. Cultivated." Source of 'Tifrust-2'. Resistant to *Puccinia arachidis*.
PI 390595	1974	W-C Col. No. 1206, 'Yungas'	*fastigiata*	Seed collected by H.F. Winters (Germplasm Resources Laboratory, Agricultural Research Center, Beltsville, MD) and R.L. Clark (Regional Plant Introduction Station, Ames, IA) from the Experiment Station at Tulamayo, Peru.	"Medium to large, very dark kernels. Cultivated." Source of 'Tifrust-3'. Resistant to *Puccinia arachidis*.
PI 393516	1974	'Blanco Huayabamba'	*fastigiata*	Seed collected by L.D. Tripp (Agronomy Dept., Oklahoma State Univ., Stillwater, OK) in Peru.	Source of 'Tifrust-8'. Resistant to *Puccinia arachidis*.
PI 393517	1974	'Blanco Marfil'	*fastigiata*	Seed collected by L.D. Tripp (Agronomy Dep., Oklahoma State Univ., Stillwater, OK) in Peru.	Source of 'Tifrust-9'. Resistant to *Puccinia arachidis*.
PI 393526	1974	'Morado Huayabamba'	*fastigiata*	Seed collected by L.D. Tripp (Agronomy Dep., Oklahoma State Univ., Stillwater, OK) in Peru.	Source of 'Tifrust-10'. Resistant to *Puccinia arachidis*.
PI 393527	1974	'Rojo Gigante'	*hypogaea*	Seed collected by L.D. Tripp (Agronomy Dep., Oklahoma State Univ., Stillwater, OK) in Peru.	Source of 'Tifrust-11'. Resistant to *Puccinia arachidis*.
PI 393531	1974	'Tingo Maria'	*fastigiata*	Seed collected by L.D. Tripp (Agronomy Dep., Oklahoma State Univ., Stillwater, OK) in Peru.	Source of 'Tifrust-12'. Resistant to *Puccinia arachidis*.

(continued on next page)

Table 4-7. Continued.

Introduction	Year	Other designations	Botanical type	Origin	Description
PI 393641	1974		fastigiata	Seed collected by L.D. Tripp (Agronomy Dep., Oklahoma State Univ., Stillwater, OK) from a grower near Cosma, Peru.	"Mixed sample. Some seed with purple testa, others mostly tan with purplish streaks." Source of 'Tifrust-5'. Resistant to *Puccinia arachidis*.
PI 393643	1974		fastigiata	Seed collected by L.D. Tripp (Agronomy Dep., Oklahoma State Univ., Stillwater, OK) from a grower near Iquitos, Peru.	"Tan testa." Source of 'Tifrust-6'. Resistant to *Puccinia arachidis*.
PI 393646	1974		fastigiata	Seed collected by L.D. Tripp (Agronomy Dep., Oklahoma State Univ., Stillwater, OK) at a market in Iquitos, Peru.	"Puplish testa." Source of 'Tifrust-7'. Resistant to *Puccinia arachidis*.
PI 407454	1976	No. 4	fastigiata	Collected by J. Blakeslee (agriculturist, Summer Institute of Linguistics, Quito) from an Indian grower near Limoncocha, near the junction of the Jivino and Napo Rivers in Ecuador.	"Representative sample includes testa colors of 49% purple and flesh, 43% flesh or tan, and 8% purple red." Source of 'Tifrust-4'. Resistant to *Puccinia arachidis*.

USE OF RELATED WILD SPECIES OF THE GENUS *ARACHIS*

In addition to the cultivated peanut in the USDA germplasm collection, there are accessions representing wild species of the genus *Arachis*. Most wild species are diploid ($2x = 20$) but many can be used as genetic donors to the tetraploid cultigen (Stalker & Moss, 1987). To date there have not been significant contributions of the diploid wild species to improved cultivars of *A. hypogaea* in the USA. 'Florigraze' and 'Arbrook', cultivars of diploid perennial rhizoma peanut (*A. glabrata* Benth.), were released for use as a forage crop in 1978 and 1989, respectively. There has been some introgression of germplasm from the tetraploid species, *A. monticola*, into Spanish-breeding populations. Because the wild species exhibit high levels of resistance to pathogens and insect pests, there is a great deal of interest in exploiting wild germplasm by the construction of interspecific hybrids at the tetraploid level.

CONCLUSION

Forty-eight peanut cultivars with plant introductions in their pedigrees have now been released. This number is misleading because 28 of the 48 cultivars have ancestral contributions from GA 207 or its siblings derived from a cross between Basse and Spanish 18-38. Eleven documented plant introductions appear in the pedigrees of the 45 cultivars.

Because of the narrow definitions of the peanut market classes and intense demand by the processing industry for uniformity in pod and seed characteristics, there is substantial inducement for the plant breeder to use as parents only those lines that conform to market and industry standards. The result has been a narrowing of the germplasm base in peanut. Dixie Giant and Small White Spanish, major contributors of genes to the runner and Virginia classes, are the sources of nearly one-half the germplasm in the present U.S. commercial crop. Spanish 18-38, Basse, and Jenkins Jumbo are also large contributors followed by Chico, Spantex, and PI 161317. Numerous plant introductions are now being used in the U.S. peanut breeding programs, usually as sources of specific disease resistances or physiological traits. Most of the introductions do not conform to standards for the U.S. market classes. It is likely that the genetic contributions of these introductions to individual cultivars will be minimized through backcrossing to a commercially acceptable parent. The historical trend of the same superior germplasm predominating over a long period will probably continue.

REFERENCES

Alexander, M.W., and A.H. Allison. 1970a. Registration fo Virginia 56R peanuts (Reg. No. 10). Crop Sci. 10:727.

Alexander, M.W., and A.H. Allison. 1970b. Registration of Virginia 61R peanuts (Reg. No. 11). Crop Sci. 10:728.

Alexander, M.W., and R.W. Mozingo. 1972. Registration of Virginia 72R peanuts (Reg. No. 13). Crop Sci. 12:127.

Bailey, W.K., and R.O. Hammons. 1975. Registration of Chico peanut germplasm (Reg. No. GP 2). Crop Sci. 15:105-106.

Banks, D.J., and J.S. Kirby. 1983. Registration of Pronto peanut (Reg. No. 28). Crop Sci. 23:184.

Banks, D.J., J.S. Kirby, and J.R. Sholar. 1989. Registration of 'Okrun' peanut. Crop Sci. 29:1574.

Batten, E.T. 1945. Two new strains of Virginia type peanuts. Virginia Agric. Exp. Stn. Bull. 370.

Beattie, J.H., and E.T. Batten. 1953. Virginia Bunch 46-2, a new variety of peanut. Virginia Agric. Exp. Stn. Leafl. 1.

Beattie, W.R. 1911. The peanut. USDA Farmers' Bull. 431. U.S. Gov. Print Office, Washington, DC.

Beattie, W.R. 1924. Peanut growing for profit. USDA Farmers' Bull. 1127. U.S. Gov. Print. Office, Washington, DC.

Beattie, W.R., and J.H. Batten. 1933. Tests of varieties and strains of large-seeded Virginia-type peanuts. USDA Circ. 272. U.S. Gov. Print. Office, Washington, DC.

Beattie, W.R., and J.H. Beattie. 1943. Peanut growing. USDA Farmers' Bull. 1656. U.S. Gov. Print. Office, Washington, DC.

Beattie, W.R., F.W. Poos, and B.B. Higgins. 1954. Growing peanuts. USDA Farmers' Bull. 2063. U.S. Gov. Print. Office, Washington, DC.

Beute, M.K., J.C. Wynne, and D.A. Emery. 1976. Registration of NC 3033 peanut germplasm (Reg. No. GP 9). Crop Sci. 16:887.

Branch, W.D., and R.O. Hammons. 1984. Registration of GA 207-3-4 peanut parental line. Crop Sci. 24:1224.

Branch, W.D., and R.O. Hammons. 1987. Registration of 'Georgia Red' peanut. Crop Sci. 27:1090.

Campbell, W.V., D.A. Emery, and W.C. Gregory. 1971. Registration of GP-NC343 peanut germplasms (Reg. No. GP 1). Crop Sci. 11:605.

Campbell, W.V., D.A. Emery, and J.C. Wynne. 1975. Registration of four germplasm lines of peanuts (Reg. Nos. GP 5 to GP 8). Crop Sci. 15:738-739.

Campbell, W.V., J.C. Wynne, D.A. Emery, and R.W. Mozingo. 1977. Registration of NC 6 peanuts (Reg. No. 20). Crop Sci. 17:346.

Carver, W.A. 1953. The Florispan Runner peanut variety. Florida Agric. Exp. Stn. Circ. S-62.

Carver, W.A. 1969. Registration of Florigiant peanuts (Reg. No. 1). Crop Sci. 9:849-850.

Carver, W.A., and F.H. Hull. 1950. Dixie Runner peanuts. Florida Agric. Exp. Stn. Circ. S-16.

Carver, W.A., F.H. Hull, and F. Clark. 1952. The Early Runner peanut variety. Florida Agric. Exp. Stn. Circ. S-52.

Chevalier, A. 1933. Histoire de l'arachide. Rev. Bot. Appl. Agric. Trop. 13:722-752.

Coffelt, T.A. 1980. Registration of VGP 1 peanut germplasm (Reg. No. GP 11). Crop Sci. 20:419.

Coffelt, T.A., D.M. Porter, and R.W. Mozingo. 1982. Registration of Virginia 81 Bunch peanut (Reg. No. 25). Crop Sci. 22:1085-1086.

Coffelt, T.A., D.M. Porter, J.C. Smith, and R.W. Mozingo. 1987. Registration of six peanut germplasm lines with multiple resistance. Crop Sci. 27:1319.

Coffelt, T.A., R.O. Hammons, W.D. Branch, R.W. Mozingo, P.M. Phipps, J.C. Smith, R.E. Lunch, C.S. Kvien, D.L. Ketring, D.M. Porter, and A.C. Mixon. 1985. Registration of Tifton-8 peanut germplasm. Crop Sci. 25:203.

Emery, D.A. 1970. Registration of NC17 peanuts (Reg. No. 7). Crop Sci. 10:460.

Emergy, D.A., A.J. Norden, J.C. Wyne, and R.W. Mozingo. 1974. Registration of NC-Fla 14 peanuts (Reg. No. 17). Crop Sci. 14:494.

Emery, D.A., and W.C. Gregory. 1970. Registration of NC5 peanuts (Reg. No. 6). Crop Sci. 10:460.

Goldin, E. 1970. New early-maturing Virginia-type groundnuts. World Crops 22:241-243.

Gorbet, D.W., A.J. Norden, F.M. Shokes, and D.A. Knauft. 1987. Registration of 'Southern Runner' peanut. Crop Sci. 27:817.

Gregory, W.C. 1970. Registration of NC2 peanuts (Reg. No. 5). Crop Sci. 10:459-460.

Gregory, W.C., and M.P. Gregory. 1976. Groundnut, *Arachis hypogaea* (Leguminosae-Papilionatae). p. 151-154. *In* N.W. Simmonds (ed.) Evolution of crop plants. Longman, New York.

Gregory, W.C., A. Krapovickas, and M.P. Gregory. 1980. Structure, variation, evolution, and classification in *Arachis*. p. 469-481. *In* R.J. Summerfield and A.H. Bunting (ed.) Advances in legume science. Royal Botanic Gardens, Kew, England.

Gregory, W.C., B.W. Smith, and J.A. Yarbrough. 1951. Morphology, genetics, and breeding. p. 28-88. *In* The peanut—The unpredictable legume. Natl. Fert. Assoc., Washington, DC.

Hammons, R.O. 1964. Krinkle, a dominant leaf marker in the peanut, *Arachis hypogaea* L. Crop Sci. 4:22-24.

Hammons, R.O. 1970a. Registration of Southeastern Runner 56-15 peanuts (Reg. No. 9). Crop Sci. 10:727.

Hammons, R.O. 1970b. Registration of Spancross peanuts (Reg. No. 3). Crop Sci. 10:459-460.

Hammons, R.O. 1970c. Registration of Tifspan peanuts (Reg. No. 4). Crop Sci. 10:459.

Hammons, R.O. 1970d. Registration of Virginia Bunch 67 peanuts (Reg. No. 8). Crop Sci. 10:460.

Hammons, R.O. 1971. Registratino of Georgia 119-20 peanuts (Reg. No. 12). Crop Sci. 11:313.

Hammons, R.O. 1972. Peanuts. p. 217-223, 252. *In* Genetic vulnerability of major crop plants. NAS-NRC Agric. Board, Washington, DC.

Hammons, R.O. 1973. Early history and origin of the peanut. p. 17-46. *In* C.T. Wilson (ed.) Peanuts—Culture and uses. Am. Peanut Res. Educ. Assoc., Stillwater, OK.

Hammons, R.O. 1976. Peanuts: Genetic vulnerability and breeding strategy. Crop Sci. 16:527-530.

Hammons, R.O. 1981. Registration of six peanut germplasm lines (Reg. Nos. GP12 to GP17). Crop Sci. 21:992-993.

Hammons, R.O., W.D. Branch, K.R. Bromfield, P. Subrahmanyam, V.R. Rao, S.N. Nigam, and R.W. Gibbons. 1982a. Registration of Tifrust-14 peanut germplasm (Reg. No. GP 31). Crop Sci. 22:697-698.

Hammons, R.O., W.D. Branch, K.R. Bromfield, P. Subrahmanyam, V.R. Rao, S.N. Nigam, R.W. Gibbons, and E. Goldin. 1982b. Registration of Tifrust-13 peanut germplasm (Reg. No. GP 30). Crop Sci. 22:697.

Hammons, R.O., and A.J. Norden. 1979. Registration of Jenkins Jumbo peanut (Reg. No. PL-1). Crop Sci. 19:132.

Hammons, R.O., D.M. Porter, A.J. Norden, and W.A. Carver. 1983. F334A-B-14 peanut germplasm. Crop Sci. 23:1019-1020.

Hammons, R.O., G. Sowell, Jr., and D.H. Smith. 1980. Registration of *Cercospora arachidicola*-resistant peanut germplasm (Reg. No. GP 10). Crop Sci. 20:292.

Hammons, R.O., P. Subrahmanyam, V.R. Rao, S.N. Nigam, and R.W. Gibbons. 1982c. Registration of eight peanut germplasm lines resistant to rust (Reg. Nos. GP 22 to GP 29). Crop Sci. 22:452-453.

Hammons, R.O., P. Subrahmanyam, V.R. Rao, S.N. Nigam, and R.W. Gibbons. 1982d. Registration of peanut germplasms Tifrust-1 to Tifrust-4 (Reg. Nos. GP 18 to GP 21). Crop Sci. 22:453.

Handy, R.B. 1896. Peanuts: Culture and uses. USDA Farmers' Bull. 25. U.S. Gov. Print. Office, Washington, DC.

Higgins, B.B. 1951. Origin and early history of the peanut. p. 18-27. *In* The peanut—The unpredictable legume. Natl. Fert. Assoc., Washington, DC.

Higgins, B.B., and W.K. Bailey. 1955. New varieties and selected strains of peanuts. Georgia Agric. Exp. Stn. Bull. N.S. 11.

Hsi, D.C. 1980. Registration of New Mexico Valencia C peanut (Reg. No. 24). Crop Sci. 20:113-114.

Hsi, D.C., and R.E. Finkner. 1972. Registration of New Mexico Valencia A peanut (Reg. No. 14). Crop Sci. 12:256.

Kirby, J.S., D.J. Banks, and J.R. Sholar. 1989. Registration of 'Spanco' peanut. Crop Sci. 29:1573-1574.

Knauft, D.A., and D.W. Gorbet. 1989. Genetic diversity among peanut cultivars. Crop Sci. 29:1417-1422.

Knauft, D.A., A.J. Norden, and D.W. Gorbet. 1987. Peanut breeding, p. 346-384. *In* W.R. Fehr (ed.) Principles of Cultivar Development, Vol. 2. MacMillan Publ. Co., New York.

Krapovickas, A. 1968. Origin, variabilidad y difusion del mani (*Arachis hypogaea*). Actas Mem. 37th Congr. Int. Am., 2:517-534.

Krapovickas, A. 1973. Evaluation of the genus *Arachis*. p. 135-151. *In* Agricultural genetics. Natl. Counc. Res. and Develop., Jerusalem.

McClenny, W.E. 1935. History of the peanut. Commercial Press, Suffolk, VA.

McGill, J.F. 1963. Peanut varieties. Georgia Coop. Ext. Circ. 518.

Mixon, A.C. 1982. Registration of Sunbelt Runner peanut (Reg. No. 26). Crop Sci. 22:1086.

Mixon, A.C. 1983a. Peanut germplasm lines, AR-1, -2, -3, and -4. Crop Sci. 23:1021.

Mixon, A.C. 1983b. Two peanut germplasm lines, GFA-1 and GFA-2. Crop Sci. 23:1020-1021.

Mixon, A.C., and K.M. Rogers. 1975. Registration of *Aspergillus flavus*-resistant peanut germplasms (Reg. Nos. GP 3 and GP 4). Crop Sci. 15:106.

Mozingo, R.W., T.A. Coffelt, and J.C. Wynne. 1987. Characteristics of Virginia-type peanuts released from 1944-1985. Virginia Agric. Exp. Stn., South. Coop. Ser. Bull. 326.

National Academy of Sciences. 1972. Soybeans and other edible legumes. p. 217-223. *In* Genetic vulnerability of major crops. Natl. Acad. Sci., Washington,, DC.

Norden, A.J., and D.W. Gorbet. 1974. Registration of Altika peanuts (Reg. No. 18). Crop Sci. 14:339.

Norden, A.J., D.W. Gorbet, and D.A. Knauft. 1985. Registration of 'Sunrunner' peanut. Crop Sci. 25:1126.

Norden, A.J., R.O. Hammons, and D.W. Gorbet. 1978. Registration of Early Bunch peanut (Reg. No. 21). Crop Sci. 18:913-914.

Norden, A.J., R.W. Lipscomb, and W.A. Carber. 1969. Registration of Florunner peanuts (Reg. No. 2). Crop Sci. 9:850.

Prine, G.M., L.S. Dunavin, R.J. Glennon, and R.D. Roush. 1990. Registration of 'Arbrook' rhizoma peanut. Crop Sci. 30:743-744.

Prine, G.M., L.S. Dunavin, J.E. Moore, and R.D. Roush. 1986. Registration of 'Florigraze' rhizoma peanut. Crop Sci. 26:1084-1085.

Simpson, C.E. 1972a. Registration of Spantex peanut (Reg. No. 15). Crop Sci. 12:395.

Simpson, C.E. 1972b. Registration of Starr peanut (Reg. No. 16). Crop Sci. 12:395.

Simpson, C.E., and O.D. Smith. 1975. Registration of Tamnut 74 peanut (Reg. No. 19). Crop Sci. 15:603-604.

Simpson, C.E., and O.D. Smith. 1986. Registration of TXAG-1 and TXAG-2 peanut germplasm lines. Crop Sci. 26:391.

Simpson, C.E., O.D. Smith, and T.E. Boswell. 1979. Registration of Toalson peanut (Reg. No. 23). Crop Sci. 19:742-743.

Simpson, C.E., O.D. Smith, and D.H. Smith. 1987. Registration of 'Langley' peanut. Crop Sci. 27:816-817.

Smith, O.D., and C.E. Simpson. 1989. Registration of 'Tamrun 88' peanut. Crop Sci. 29:238.

Smith, O.D., S.M. Aguirre, T.E. Boswell, W.J. Grichar, H.A. Melouk, and C.E. Simpson. 1990. Registration of TxAG-4 and TxAG-5 germplasms. Crop Sci. 30:429.

Stalker, H.T., and J.P. Moss. 1987. Speciation, cytogenetics, and utilization of *Arachis* species. Adv. Agron. 41:1-40.

U.S. Department of Agriculture. 1900. Foreign seeds and plants collected in Austria, Italy, and Egypt by the Honorable Barbour Lathrop and Mr. David G. Fairchild for the Section of Seed and Plant Introduction. USDA Div. of Botany Inventory No. 6. U.S. Gov. Print. Office, Washington, DC.

U.S. Department of Agriculture. 1909. Seeds and plants imported during the period from October 1 to December 31, 1908 (Inventory No. 17; Nos. 23745 to 24429). USDA Bur. Plant Ind. Bull. 153. U.S. Gov. Print. Office, Washington, DC.

U.S. Department of Agriculture. 1929. Seeds and plants imported by the Office of Foreign Seed and Plant Introduction, Bureau of Plant Industry, during the period from January 1 to March 31, 1927 (Nos. 73050 to 74212). USDA Bur. Plant Industry Inventory 91.

Wynne, J.C., and M.K. Beute. 1983. Registration of NC 8C peanut (Reg. No. 27). Crop Sci. 23:184.

Wynne, J.C., M.K. Beute, J. Bailey, and R.W. Mozingo. 1991a. Registration of 'NC 10C' peanut. Crop Sci. 31:484.

Wynne, J.C., T.A. Coffelt, R.W. Mozingo, and W.F. Anderson. 1991b. Registration of 'NC-V11' peanut. Crop Sci. 31:484-485.

Wynne, J.C., R.W. Mozingo, and D.A. Emery. 1979. Registration of NC 7 peanut (Reg. No. 22). Crop Sci. 19:563.

Wynne, J.C., R.W. Mozingo, and D.A. Emery. 1986. Registration of 'NC 9' peanut. Crop Sci. 26:197.

5 Use of Plant Introductions To Improve Populations and Hybrids of Sugarbeet

R. T. Lewellen

USDA-ARS
Salinas, California

Sugarbeet (*Beta vulgaris* L.) is considered the most productive crop under northern temperate conditions (Fischer, 1989). Worldwide, about 40% of sucrose (sugar) is produced from sugarbeet. Yet sugarbeet is one of the youngest major crop plants, with a history of about 200 yr. The history of sugarbeet has been reviewed many times (e.g., Bosemark, 1979; Campbell, 1976; Coons, 1936; Coons et al., 1955; de Bock, 1986; Fischer, 1989; Ford-Lloyd & Williams, 1975; Harris, 1919; Pichat, 1866; Ware, 1880).

It is believed that sugarbeet originated from a relatively limited range of fodder beet types grown in Silesia. Hence, the 'White Silesian' fodder beet is considered the ancestor of present-day sugarbeet (Fischer, 1989). The genetic base is probably narrower than that of most other cross-pollinated crop species (Bosemark, 1979). It has been suggested, however, that the 'Beta Imperialis' sugarbeet developed by the German breeder Knauer in 1858 and known to be the mother of modern sugarbeet may have originated from spontaneous crosses between Silesian beet and North Atlantic forms of wild seabeet [*B. vulgaris* spp. *maritima* (L.) Arcang.] (Bosemark, 1979). Others speculate that sugarbeet originated from crosses between typical fodder beet and chard with three of four major sugar factors coming from fodder beet and the fourth from chard (Zossimovich, 1940; Fischer, 1989; Sativsky, 1936, cited by Coons et al., 1955).

The Silesian fodder beet source and the early development of sugarbeet were thus in a northern temperate climate. This region is still relatively free of diseases, pests, and environmental stresses. There is little pressure to maintain high levels of host-plant resistances. As a consequence, this narrowly based germplasm may never have had or may have lost significant levels of genetic variability for disease resistance or the factors that condition disease resistance occur in the germplasm at low frequencies. The dearth of major dominant genes that condition disease resistance in sugarbeet compared to other major field crops has been observed by most sugarbeet breeders. Lester (1989) suggests that dominant genes including those for resistance to diseases,

---

Copyright © 1992 Crop Science Society of America, 677 S. Segoe Rd., Madison, WI 53711, USA. *Use of Plant Introductions in Cultivar Development, Part 2*, CSSA Special Publication no. 20.

pests, or other adverse environmental conditions are rapidly lost during the development of highly domesticated genotypes. As sugarbeet moved from northern Europe to new environments and particularly to warmer or more humid regions, endemic diseases (e.g., leaf spot caused by *Cercospora beticola* Sacc., curly top virus, black root caused by *Aphanomyces cochlioides* Drechs., root rot caused by *Rhizoctonia solani* Kühn, etc.) were encountered that significantly limited production. In response to these problems, breeding programs in North America were initiated to develop disease-resistant populations and commercial cultivars while concurrently maintaining or increasing levels of productivity. As a dividend from these programs, most of the genetic traits and breeding techniques that permitted the development of monogerm hybrid cultivars and population improvement for heterosis were discovered and put into practice (see Hecker & Helmerick, 1984, for review).

HISTORY OF SUGARBEET IN THE UNITED STATES

Just as the 200-yr history of sugarbeet has been documented, so has its history in the USA (Coons, 1936; Harris, 1919; Hecker & Helmerick, 1984; McFarlane, 1971; Palmer, 1918; Ware, 1880). After numerous efforts to establish a beet sugar industry in the USA between 1830 and 1870, a successful factory was built at Alvarado, CA, in 1870. On a continuing trial-and-error basis, sugarbeet culture and factories were tried in many states. As of 1917, there were 91 factories operating in 18 states (Harris, 1919). By 1989, many small factories had been closed or consolidated and there were 36 operating factories in 13 states processing beets from about 550 000 ha. These factories produced about 3 300 000 t of sugar. Based only upon this beet sugar production, the USA would be one of the top 10 sugar-producing countries in the world.

HISTORY OF SUGARBEET BREEDING IN UNITED STATES

A comprehensive review on the history and methods of sugarbeet breeding in the USA was recently written by Hecker and Helmerick (1984). Other reviews and book chapters have been written by Smith (1980, 1987), McFarlane (1971), and Coons et al. (1955). Earlier, Coons (1936) discussed and summarized breeding activities and the improvement of sugarbeet in the USA up through 1936. The beginning of breeding and seed production in the USA was described by Palmer (1918) and Harris (1919). Up to 1914 practically all sugarbeet seed was imported from Europe with most seed coming from Germany (Palmer, 1918). Even the seed not grown in Germany was primarily from German-produced breeding stocks. By the end of World War I, home-grown seed accounted for most of the domestic needs. After 1920, the USA again imported most of its seed requirements. By 1937, interest in domestic production had been renewed and met about one-third of the USA's seed requirements (Coons, 1936). This renewed domestic production interlocked with the breeding work that had been initiated in the USA by both public and private breeders in the early part of the century. From about 1940 to the mid-1970s, essentially all seed was from domestic production involving breeding stocks that had been developed in the USA by private and public breeders. The origin and breeding development of this important "American" germplasm base will be discussed in this chapter.

In the early 1970s, starting with northern areas that are less disease and pest prone and where conditions were similar to northern Europe, inroads were made by highly bred European and Japanese commercial hybrids and parental lines. This trend has continued into most beet production areas. However, disease resistance needs still are largely met by American germplasm developments in ongoing domestic breeding programs (Table 5-1).

In reality, all sugarbeet and *Beta* germplasm is a result of plant introductions. However, very little if any of the important germplasm used in commercial cultivars and hybrids can be traced through the formal plant introduction stations or the national or international germplasm systems. Instead, the domestic, commercial quality germplasm base appears to be the result of activities by plant breeders, plant pathologists, and seedsmen over the past 80 plus years. Most important has been the germplasm and breeding stocks that resulted from selecting, hybridizing, and resynthesizing within the open-pollinated commercial cultivars that had been imported from Europe. Other important germplasm has been acquired from abroad, directly or in exchange by both public and private breeders. Recently, advanced populations, germplasm lines, parental lines, and commercial hybrids developed in Europe and Japan by international seed companies, often in association with USA cooperators or subsidiaries, have become important in commer-

Table 5-1. History of sugarbeet breeding and cultivars grown in the USA from 1870 to the present.

Period[†]	Type and source of cultivar
1870-1940	European open-pollinated cultivars from imported seed.[‡]
1910-1950	Public and private breeding programs in the USA with European open-pollinated cultivars as the base populations.
1934-1960	Commercial production largely from domestically produced seed of open-pollinated and synthetic cultivars derived from the American germplasm base.
1955-1965	Domestic multigerm hybrids produced from American germplasm. Hybrids mostly diploid, three-way topcrosses.
1960-present	Domestic monogerm hybrids produced from American germplasm. Hybrids mostly three-way diploids but triploids and single and double crosses also grown.
1973-present	Foreign commercial hybrids introduced into Red River Valley and then the Northern Plains area, but not extensively grown elsewhere.
1981-present	Hybrids from mixed domestic and foreign parental lines and elite stocks. Disease-resistant components usually extractions from American germplasm base.

[†] Periods are near approximations. Overlaps occurred as cultivar and germplasm types were phased in and out.
[‡] During World War I, domestic seed production from European stocks occurred.

cial seed developments and sales. This advanced proprietary germplasm is obviously outside of the National Plant Germplasm System and will not be considered in this presentation. Nor will the source and development of this "foreign" commercial germplasm be considered as this information is largely privileged and not freely available.

Because of the needs for a reliable domestic seed source and better regional adaptation and disease resistance not provided by foreign varieties, public and private breeding programs were started early this century (Coons, 1936). In terms of adaptation and disease-resistance needs, sugarbeet production and breeding activities of the American base populations fell into more-or-less distinct regional and disease-resistance types. The major sugarbeet production areas in the USA are:

1. *Great Lakes*: Michigan and Ohio with about 68 000 ha. This area is rain-fed with relatively high humidity and continental climate. Cercospora leaf spot is endemic and black root caused by *Aphanomyces cochlioides* and Rhizoctonia root rot caused by *Rhizoctonia solani* Kühn can be severe.

2. *Red River Valley*: Minnesota and North Dakota with about 220 000 ha. Rain-fed but drier and less humid than the Great Lakes area and with severe winters. Relatively disease free but in the southern parts, Cercospora leaf spot, black root, and Rhizoctonia root rot may be important. Sugarbeet root maggot [*Tetanops myopaeformis* (Röder)] is a severe problem.

3. *Plains*: Colorado, Montana, Nebraska, Texas, and Wyoming with about 110 000 ha. Continental climate where sugarbeet must be irrigated. Disease pressure varies by location and year with Cercospora leaf spot, *Rhizoctonia*, curly top, *Aphanomyces*, and powdery mildew, incited by *Erysiphe polygoni* DC. type ($=E.$ *betae* Weltzier) being important.

4. *Western*: California, Idaho, Oregon, and Washington with about 154 000 ha. Irrigated, arid area with hot summers and mild winters and long growing season. Curly top is endemic. Virus yellows (complex of aphid vectored viruses including beet yellows virus, beet western yellows virus, and beet mosaic virus), powdery mildew, Erwinia root rot incited by *E. carotovora* (Jones) Bergey et al. subsp. *betavasculorum* Thomson et al. can be severe. Rhizomania caused by beet necrotic yellows vein virus vectored by *Polymyxa betae* Keskin and warm-season root rots can be serious. Bolting resistance is necessary for fall- and winter-planted crops in California.

Within this regional framework, the most important traditional American germplasm fit into three fairly definable types or categories. These can be characterized by disease resistance, adaptation, and origin.

1. *Curly top resistant*: Germplasm developed at the Salt Lake City USDA station in cooperation with public and private programs in the western USA. Germplasm is resistant to curly top virus with 'US 1' and ultimately 'US 22' being the base for most subsequent developments. Improvements from these early curly top resistant sources have been made by the USDA at Salinas, CA and Logan, UT and by private breeders. Curly top resistant parental lines from this base are widely used in the Intermountain and Pacific Coast areas where resistance to curly top is a high priority.

2. *Great Western (Colorado)*: Germplasm developed primarily in Colorado by Great Western Sugar Co., American Crystal Sugar Co., Holly Sugar Co. at Sheridan, WY, and the USDA station at Fort Collins, CO. This germplasm is characterized by moderate resistance to Cercospora leaf spot and Fusarium yellows, caused by *F. oxysporum* Schlecht. f. sp. *betae* Snyd. & Hans., and segregation for resistance to root aphid (*Pemphigus populivenae* Fitch) (Wallis & Gaskill, 1963). More recently, breeding lines with resistance to Rhizoctonia root rot have been developed (Hecker & Gaskill, 1972). Open-pollinated cultivar GW359 is the most significant germplasm source and parental line derivatives are still widely grown in commercial hybrids from Texas to Montana.

3. *Eastern*: Germplasm primarily developed at USDA stations in East Lansing, MI; Beltsville, MD; and Waseca, MN. Germplasm combines resistance to Cercospora leaf spot and *A. cochlioides* and has adaptation to the upper Midwest. 'US 401', 'SP5822-0', and their derivatives have been widely used for commercial productions.

SOURCE OF AMERICAN GERMPLASM

From the mid-1930s to the present, the most widely grown germplasm types had become characterized by resistance to specific diseases and adaptation. Within each of the regional germplasm types, one or a few open-pollinated cultivars, populations, or synthetics were pivotal. In each case, these base populations were derived from selections within European open-pollinated cultivars and other accessed breeding stocks. These key synthetic populations were initially used as commercial, open-pollinated cultivars. Then they became the sources from which improved open-pollinated cultivars were developed. Subsequently with the development of hybrid cultivars, they became the populations from which parental lines were derived. To this day, highly selected versions of the original populations are still undergoing population improvement for greater disease resistance and combining ability for yield.

By the time the original synthetic populations became useful as commercial cultivars, they were essentially closed to the infusion of new germplasm. Though breeders continued to work with a wide array of germplasm and produced many populations and breeding lines, some of which have been or are still important or filled specific niches, for example, high sugar L19 (Theurer, 1978), most commercial parental lines and hybrids can still be traced to these early open-pollinated cultivars and synthetics. Examples of some of these pivotal base populations are described below.

Curly Top Resistant (Western) Germplasm

Commercial cultivars grown west of the Continental Divide usually require some degree of resistance to curly top virus. Following the recurrent outbreaks of curly top and partial collapse of the industry early this century

(Bennett, 1971), breeding programs were initiated by the USDA, state agricultural experiment stations, and sugar companies. Principally among these programs were the ones by the USDA at Salt Lake City (later Logan), UT; Riverside and Salinas, CA; and breeding programs by Spreckels Sugar Co.; Amalgamated Sugar Co.; and U & I Sugar Co. The history of these programs has been summarized (Coons, 1936; Bennett, 1971; McFarlane, 1971).

The first curly top resistant cultivar was released as 'US 1'. It had been primarily derived from selections within European cultivars. The most important strains came from the German cv. R & G Old Type, also known as 'Klein E'. Owen et al. (1939, 1946) suggested that inadvertent outcrosses to wild or weed beets growing in California may have been an important source of resistance. Improvements for resistance to curly top led to the subsequent releases of cultivars 'US 11', 'US 33', 'US 34', and others, with highly resistant 'US 22', 'US 22/2', and 'US 22/3', following in the early 1940s (Murphy et al., 1948). Much of the present curly top resistant germplasm, populations, parental lines, and commercial hybrids can be traced directly to US 22/3. The widely used multigerm inbreds CT5, CT7, and CT9 and monogerm inbreds SLC 129, SLC 133, C562, C546, and C718 types were primarily derived from US 22/3 or one of the selections related to US 1. Essentially the only portion of the germplasm in these monogerm lines not from US 22/3 or its ancestors came from SLC 101, the source of the gene for the monogerm trait (Savitsky, 1950).

Commercial hybrids based upon lines selected from US 22/3 were extremely important, not only in publicly released hybrids such as 'US H9' (McFarlane & Skoyen, 1971), 'US H10' (McFarlane et al., 1971a), and 'US H11' (Lewellen et al., 1990, unpublished data), but also for hybrids produced by sugar company breeders in the western USA. These three USDA developments, or similar hybrids from sugar and seed company breeders, were extensively grown from about 1966 to the mid-1980s. They are three-way hybrids with the F_1 seed-bearing parent composed of two partially inbred lines (C562CMS or C563CMS × C546) crossed to a multigerm pollinator, respectively, C13, C17, or C36. C562, C563, and C546 were largely developed from US 22/3 derivatives (75% of their germplasm) and SLC 101 (McFarlane & Skoyen, 1965). From US 22/3, bolting resistant 'US 75' was developed (McFarlane & Price, 1952). In turn, from US 75 virus yellows resistant C13 and C17 were selected (McFarlane et al., 1971b). C36 was selected from C13 for resistance to Erwinia root rot (Whitney & Lewellen, 1978). Based upon these components, the commercial hybrids US H9, US H10, and US H11 were largely bolting and disease resistant, heterotic combinations of extractions from US 22/3.

In the Intermountain area, commercial hybrids from Amalgamated and U & I Sugar companies were equally reliant upon parental lines extracted from US 22/3. Inbred lines CT5, CT7, CT9, SLC 129, and SLC 133 have been highly important (J.C. Theurer, 1990, personal communication).

The other important germplasm source but with lower curly top resistance that has been widely used was 'US 15', derived from the German cultivar type 'R & G Pioneer' (Coons et al., 1950). The open-pollinated cv.

US 15 was crossed to US 22/3 to develop breeding and parental lines C663 and C264 (McFarlane & Skoyen, 1965). More recently, lines with various combinations, resyntheses, and selections tracing from US 22/3 and US 15 were released and have been used commercially, for example, C46 (Lewellen et al., 1985).

In 1965 at Salinas, CA, a new broadly based population was synthesized that combined curly top resistant germplasm with germplasm introductions from Europe. The European introductions were obtained as exchanges between breeders at Salinas and stations in Great Britain, the Netherlands, and Germany. All of the components of this population had been selected for resistance to virus yellows, either in Europe, at Salinas, or both (McFarlane et al., 1969). Following population improvement for resistance to virus yellows and productivity, population C01 was released (Lewellen et al., 1978). After additional cycles of population improvement for resistance to virus yellows, bolting, Erwinia root rot, and powdery mildew and for productivity, population C31 was released (Lewellen et al., 1978). From C01 and C31 germplasm, parental lines were developed by continued line improvement or progeny testing by breeders in private seed companies. Recently, hybrids using these parental lines have been important in commercial production in California. Although the introductions used in the synthesis of C01 were not through the National Plant Germplasm System and more than 20 yr lapsed before these introductions contributed to new commercial hybrids, this population demonstrates that plant introductions are of real value to broaden the diversity and productivity of base breeding material.

Great Western (Plains) Germplasm

Since early this century, there has been a breeding program by Great Western Sugar Co. at Longmont, CO (Brewbaker et al., 1950). Other breeding programs in the Plains area were at Fort Collins, CO (USDA), Rocky Ford, CO (American Crystal Sugar Company), and Sheridan, WY (Holly Sugar Company). The program at Longmont is of particular significance because of its continuity and success. The Great Western cultivar and base germplasm GW359 is noteworthy because of its importance as a cultivar per se and as a germplasm source. The following account is adapted from largely unpublished information provided by R.K. Oldemeyer (1990, personal communication) and gives insights into the breeding activities by one of the private sugar companies in the development of sugarbeet germplasm and use of introductions.

The basic germplasm used in the breeding program by The Great Western Sugar Co., beginning about 1910, was from Europe. Initially, several cultivars were used, mostly from Germany, and in particular from the Rabbethge and Giesecke firm also referred to as Klein Wanzleben. There is no doubt that the cv. R & G Old Type contributed the germplasm that produced the superior productivity and adaptability of the widely grown open-pollinated cultivars introduced initially by Great Western. The cultivars first introduced by Great Western in the mid-1930s were the result of several generations of mass selection for Cercospora resistance and maternal line selection for productivity from R & G Old Type. The first home-grown seed from cultivars developed by Great Western was from these cultivars that were used until the early 1950s, namely 'GW 59' (not to be confused with GW359) and 'GW 85' (Brewbaker et al., 1950).

Two highly productive cultivars with strong Cercospora leaf-spot resistance were released beginning in 1950 to 1952. These varieties, 'GW304' and 'GW359,' were grown for several years. Soon, cultivars bred by selection from GW359 for higher processing quality and higher bolting resistance were introduced. Selfing of many plants from these two cultivars and several closely related ones formed the principal basis of the inbred/hybrid program of Great Western. GW304 and GW359 were synthesized from the best maternal (half-sib) lines from two different maternal line synthetics. GW304 was comprised of 51.1% Cesena, 40.5% Spanish, 3.6% Schmidt, 3.2% Great Western, 0.8% Buszczynski, and 0.8% Eridania germplasm. GW359 proved to be superior to GW304 and differed in composition from GW304 by having a higher proportion of Great Western germplasm. GW359 was comprised of 53.9% Great Western, 23.4% Spanish, 10.3% Cesena, 5.2% Eridania, and 3.6% each of Buszczynski and Mezzano germplasm.

At the beginning of World War II, Rabbethge and Giesecke discontinued their sugarbeet breeding program in the USA. Their Cercospora-resistant breeding material was sold to Great Western, which included material they were breeding for Spain and Italy. At about the same time, Great Western obtained Cercospora-resistant germplasm from the Italian seed companies Eridania, Cesena, and Alba and from Buszczynski in Poland.

Great Western personnel or their agents collected wild beet (*B. maritima*) seed on the shores of the North Sea. Cercospora-resistant races of this material were hybridized with R & G Old Type strains and selection was made among the segregating progeny. Although the synthesized cultivar had high Cercospora resistance, its low productivity and processing quality prevented its use commercially. The Cercospora-resistant material developed by the USDA was used only in a minor way in the synthesis of Great Western cultivars for growing in the irrigated areas of the West. It is known that the Cesena material was derived from the *B. maritima* hybrids of Munerati (1932), sugarbeet breeder and geneticist in Italy, and it is suspected that most other Cercospora-resistant cultivars in Europe had the same origin. GW304 contained a rather high percentage of cytoplasmic male sterile (CMS) plants that very likely arose from the *B. maritima*.

Cultivars for the northern part of the Great Western growing area, the Bighorn Basin of Wyoming and the Yellowstone Valley of Montana, were selected directly from 'Klein Wanzleben E' from Germany and US 22 from the USDA. Maternal line selection was the principal breeding method used. Neither cultivar could be improved substantially by selection. USDA cultivars were used for Great Western's Ohio area until the introduction of monogerm cultivars.

Immediately following the release by the USDA of SLC 101 (Savitsky, 1950), Great Western began a backcross program to introduce that character into the basic cultivars. Thus in the early 1960s, seed of monogerm equivalent cultivars of GW359 (GW 671), the Eastern blackroot and leaf spot-resistant cultivars of the USDA and of the Great Western selections from Klein E (GW 672) and US 22 were introduced to the growers of Great Western. These monogerm cultivars were in every way comparable to the multigerm recurrent parents.

The Great Western Sugar Co. collected samples of cultivars of sugarbeet seed from nearly every country that produces sugarbeet. Most were collected by agents or direct purchase. Very few exchanges were necessary. Great Western always obliged the originator of the seed with trial results. Of the eastern countries, Poland and Hungary were quite free with seed of their cultivars. Seed of a large number of Russian cultivars, including monogerm cultivars, was obtained by one means or another. Czechoslovakian cultivars were offered by an agent in Canada. Seed of cultivars produced by seed companies in the free world was readily available. In the later years, the cv. Klein Wanzleben E was the only foreign cultivar that was good enough to contribute to the germplasm of Great Western. The USDA Ames collection was used for seed samples of cultivars and wild lines. With the advent of "Anisoploid and CMS Hybrid" cultivars, which could not be multiplied directly, genetic techniques were used to isolate pollinator components from seed lots of these cultivars. A massive number of inbred lines was initiated during the period beginning in 1950. Parental material from every sugarbeet cultivar available was used, although few usable lines were ever identified from sources other than those that were adapted to Great Western conditions. The first hybrid cultivars introduced, beginning about 1965, by Great Western were top-cross hybrids that were hybrids of the male-sterile equivalents of the commercial monogerm cultivars crossed to the superior multigerm inbred lines; partial exploitation of hybrid vigor was obtained.

During this developmental period, Great Western indexed a large amount of material for O-type (nonrestorer) and converted the O-type multigerm lines to monogerm, produced selfed lines from O-type selections from monogerm commercial cultivars, and evaluated the considerable number of O-type monogerm inbred lines being developed by the USDA. Three or four excellent ones were identified in the USDA developments and are used to this day. The USDA inbred lines were particularly valuable for increasing disease resistance of commercial hybrids. Considerable specific combining ability also occurred between the USDA inbreds and the lines developed from Great Western commercial open-pollinated cultivars.

In recent years, Great Western's seed division was established as Mono-Hy Seed and is now a subsidiary of Hilleshog Seed Company of Sweden. With this arrangement, the Mono-Hy breeding program has access to all of the germplasm from Hilleshog's worldwide program.

During its breeding and genetic activities, Great Western isolated CMS from GW304 and GW359. CMS was also isolated from Cesena germplasm and 'SP 5822-0'. As far as could be determined, these sources were identical in action to those isolated by Owen (1945). An extensive search of the collection from the Plant Introduction Station at Ames resulted in the isolation of cytoplasmic male-sterility in at least nine annual races; the male-sterility isolated from these sources was never proven better than that which already existed, but several were different and less effective.

Great Western obtained seed of another source of true breeding monogerm from a Western European company before other sources had been released by the USDA. This source was very low in sugar content and was not better for the monogerm character than the one in use from Savitsky (1950). It was never confirmed that this source of monogerm was conditioned by different genes than existed in the one from SLC 101.

Unintentional selection pressure for root aphid resistance and Fusarium yellows resistance in northern Colorado apparently resulted in the cv. GW304 and GW359 being resistant or immune to these two pests. These resistances could not be attributed to any one of the sources used in the breeding program.

Many of these germplasms were deposited in the National Seed Storage Laboratory at Fort Collins, but some were probably lost. GW304 and GW359 have probably entered into the breeding programs of a number of other sugarbeet seed companies and institutes of the world.

As suggested above by R.K. Oldemeyer, GW359 was the likely base for other breeding programs. An example of this is the USDA Rhizoctonia root rot resistant germplasm (Hecker & Gaskill, 1972; Hecker & Ruppel, 1977). As far as is known, this material is currently the sole source for producing commercial hybrids with moderate resistance to *Rhizoctonia*. However, resistant germplasms from other sources have been released.

Eastern Germplasm

The bane of profitable sugarbeet production under humid conditions east of the Rocky Mountains was Cercospora leaf spot. From European sugarbeet cultivars, W.W. Tracy had developed an array of partially inbred lines. In 1925 at Fort Collins and Rocky Ford, CO, 14 of these Tracy inbreds were found to be moderately resistant to leaf spot. They were the initial material for the USDA leaf spot-resistance breeding program (Coons, 1953; Coons et al., 1955). The USDA leaf spot-resistance breeding program evolved into the production of as many distinct inbreds as possible, progeny testing them to identify resistant genotypes, then finding those combinations that produced high yields and retained satisfactory levels of resistance. The first USDA leaf spot-resistant cv. US 217 was introduced in 1937 and was a synthetic of five inbreds (Coons, 1936). US 217 was subsequently replaced by synthetic hybrids 'US 200 × 215' and 'US 215 × 216', which, in the late 1940s, accounted for all of the acreage in the Great Lakes area.

The Munerati (1932) leaf spot-resistant selections derived from *B. maritima* were released to Italian breeding stations and further refined into commercial cultivars by breeders at Cesena and Mezzano. Coons et al. (1955) state that the cv. Cesena contributed leaf spot resistance to GW 304 and GW359, whereas, 'Mezzano 71' was used to breed highly resistant 'US 201'. US 201 is a very well-known germplasm line and continues to be used as a resistant check. However, despite its widespread use by many breeders, to the author's knowledge, it has not contributed to a commercial cultivar.

Currently, the germplasm and most commercial cultivars grown in the Great Lakes area are characterized by moderate resistance to black root and Cercospora leafspot. The black root resistant germplasm base was developed in breeding programs and from selections made under natural epidemics of *Aphanomyces* and *Cercospora* in Michigan, Ohio, and Minnesota. Because all breeding material must pass through a greenhouse or growth chamber screen for Aphanomyces resistance (Schneider, 1954), there appears to have been little introduction of new germplasm into this base in the past 45 or more years.

Resistance to *Aphanomyces* was first observed in inbred line 'US 216' and a cultivar designated as 'Minnesota Synthetic 1' was developed from the USDA leaf spot-resistant inbreds and hybrids (Henderson & Bockstahler, 1946). Currently, most of the germplasm and breeding lines with resistance to black root can be traced to a polycross made in 1946 (Bockstahler & Reese, 1948). This polycross was comprised of several breeding lines and sources that had been selected previously for resistance to leaf spot (Coons, 1953; Coons et al., 1955) and for adaptation to the upper Midwest and included 'US 200', 'US 215', 'US 216', 'American 1', 'American 3', and Minnesota Synthetic 1. Included to a smaller extent were 'US 22' and other curly top resistant lines. In addition, Cesena and other leaf spot-resistant Italian cultivars with *B. maritima* parentage were involved (G.J. Hogaboam, 1990, personal communication). In 1948, selected roots primarily from the 1946 polycross were recombined to produce population 48B3-00. A direct increase was released as 'US 1177'. After an additional cycle of selection from 48B3-00, the open-pollinated cv. US 400 was released and grown commercially. Subsequently, selections from a US 400 polycross (50B3-0) produced 'US 401' which was released in 1955 (G.J. Hogaboam, 1990, personal communication). Based upon the experiences of breeders, this germplasm appears to be unique.

From the 1946 polycross from which US 400 and US 401 were developed by mass selection, population 53AB1 was also developed. Mother line selection (progeny tested polycross generated half sibs) was used in which the best plants from the best progenies were selected, based upon superior sugar yield and combined resistance to leaf spot and black root (G.J. Hogaboam, 1990, personal communication). Population 53AB1 was subsequently important to the leaf spot and black root-resistance breeding programs of the USDA at Beltsville, MD, and East Lansing, MI. Parental lines such as EL 40 (Hogaboam et al., 1982c) and widely used SP 6322-0 (Coe & Hogaboam, 1971a,b) were derived from 53AB1. Population 53AB1 was also the base population for the majority of the monogerm lines released from the East Lansing and Beltsville stations.

The original monogerm line SLC 101 was isolated from a component of the synthetic 'Michigan Hybrid 18' in 1948 (Savitsky, 1950). Thus, some early East Lansing germplasm has been dispersed widely into most breeding programs. Conversely, lines such as EL 44 (reselected SLC 129) (Hogaboam

& Schneider, 1982a) and EL 45 (reselected SLC 133) (Hogaboam & Schneider, 1982b) that showed high combining ability with Aphanomyces resistant lines were derived from curly top resistant US 22 germplasm.

Hybrid Cultivars

By about 1950, sugarbeet production in the USA was dominated by a few major American germplasm sources and the open-pollinated cultivars selected from them. Little additional germplasm was being successfully introgressed into commercial varieties. Plant introductions had become of minor importance in commercial production.

With the change to hybrid cultivars starting about 1960, some of the distinction among cultivar types began to change. This trend has continued and cultivar types are now much more varied. Breeders are targeting hybrids to much more specific areas and disease situations. To capitalize on both combinations of disease resistances and heterotic combinations for yield, recent hybrids may involve parental lines from highly diverse germplasm sources both of domestic and foreign origin. For example, high sugar hybrids improve sucrose extraction by beet processors and have been in demand. Polish germplasm developed by Janasz breeders has extremely high sugar content and has been introduced. Commercial hybrids with parental lines extracted from this Polish germplasm have become important in the past decade. This Polish germplasm appears to be genetically divergent from the majority of the American and Western European germplasm with German ancestry. In areas where relatively low pressure from diseases and stresses permit its use, breeders have designed their programs to take advantage of this diversity and use heterotic combinations between their traditional germplasm lines on one side of the hybrid and Polish extractions on the other.

The demands for improved protection against disease and higher potential productivity have greatly renewed interest in plant introductions and all germplasm resources.

BETA GERMPLASM RESOURCES

Taxonomy

Beta is an Old World genus virtually confined to the Mediterranean Basin and Middle East. Systems of classification have been proposed (Zossimovich, 1940; Coons, 1954; Ford-Lloyd & Williams, 1975; de Bock, 1986). *Beta* has been organized into four sections: *Beta* (formerly *Vulgares*), *Corollinae, Nanae*, and *Procumbentes* (formerly *Patellares*). De Bock (1986) states that the division of *Beta* into four sections fits the results of most investigations and experiences of plant breeders. As four groups, the species relationships agree very well with morphological differences and crossability. Abe et al. (1987) showed that on average the sections of *Beta* were different one from another and that these differences were in agreement with reproductive barriers and differences in morphological and physiological traits.

Sugarbeet and the other cultigens of beet (red beet, beetroot, garden beet, mangold, fodder beet, Swiss chard, spinach beet) are members of highly diverse *B. vulgaris*. Because of the cross affinity among the species of the *Beta* section to the cultigens of beet, it has received the most interest. The evolution and relationships of cultivared *B. vulgaris* have been reviewed (Campbell, 1976; Ford-Lloyd & Williams, 1975).

Ford-Lloyd and Williams (1975) suggested a revision of the section *Beta* (*vulgares*) and provided a comprehensive synonymy. Because of the existence of a continuous variation within the species of this section, they proposed a simplified classification. *Beta vulgaris* would be divided into subspecies *maritima, patula, adanensis, orientalis, lomatogonoides, provulgaris, vulgaris*, and *cicla*. Most of the subspecies were further divided into varieties. For example, the previous species *B. macrocarpa* would become *B. vulgaris* spp. *maritima* var. *macrocarpa*. The International Data Base for *Beta* (IDBB) operating from the Netherlands currently uses a modification of this classification system for the genus *Beta*. The USDA's National Plant Germplasm System data base GRIN uses the revision suggested by Ford-Lloyd and Williams (1975). All accessions in the *Beta* section are classified under the species *B. vulgaris*, and the older, species designations of *vulgaris, maritima*, and *macrocarpa* have been discontinued.

Abe et al. (1986), Abe and Tsuda (1988), and Lange and de Bock (1989) investigated the reproductive barriers within the section *Beta* (*vulgares*). Despite cross affinity and morphological similarity, reproductive isolation has developed among them. *Beta macrocarpa*, based upon distorted segregation ratios and differences in isozymic patterns (Abe et al., 1987), appeared to be the most divergent species in this section.

Germplasm Systems

The National Plant Germplasm System (NPGS) of the USA was recently reviewed (Janick, 1989). This review covered topics that were pertinent to sugarbeet and *Beta* germplasm activities, including: History and operation of the NPGS (White et al., 1989); Information systems (Mowder & Stoner, 1989); Plant exploration (Perdue & Christenson, 1989); Seed maintenance and storage (Clark, 1989); Long-term seed storage (Roos, 1989); and Evaluation and enhancement (Roath, 1989). Details of this system will not be reiterated here.

An international *Beta* network covering world *Beta* genetic resource activities has been organized recently (IBPGR, 1989). In the first report of this network, Frese and van Hintum (1989) reviewed the International Data Base for *Beta* (IDBB) system and the contributing institutes, including gene banks throughout Europe and in the USA, the number of *Beta* accessions held by each gene bank, and the number of accessions in each gene bank by botanical name. Currently, there were more than 7000 *Beta* accessions worldwide, mostly within *B. vulgaris*.

Both nationally and internationally, the domesticated cultigens, wild types, and species of *Beta* are being collected, introduced, maintained, evaluated, catalogued, and distributed. In the USA, these activities fall under the auspices of the NPGS (White et al., 1989; Mowder & Stoner, 1989). Germplasm information for this system is maintained in the Germplasm Resources Information Network (GRIN) and may be accessed through remote computer terminals. New plant introductions are processed through the Plant Introduction Office (PIO) at Beltsville, MD, with the regional Plant Introduction Station at Ames, IA being responsible for *Beta* germplasm. The working collection of *Beta* is maintained at Ames, IA. The base collections for long-term storage are held at the National Seed Storage Laboratory (NSSL) at Ft. Collins, CO. As of 30 Apr., 1989, there was a total of 1905 accessions of *Beta* in the NC-7 Working Collection at Ames and the NSSL.

The Crop Advisory Committee (CAC) for sugarbeet represents the germplasm user community. This committee provides expert guidance on germplasm needs, collection gaps, descriptors, documentation, regeneration, evaluation plans, and research needs (White et al., 1989).

Use of Plant Introductions

D.L. Doney (1990, personal communication), chair of the Sugarbeet CAC, stated that in the past the NC-7 collection of *Beta* at Ames, IA, has been little used. Most breeders have given the collection only cursory attention. This lack of attention in part was due to the method of seed multiplication and high degree of interpollination among accessions. Also, the entries were not well described and have had no useful data base.

In a letter and telephone survey by the author, plant introductions through the NPGS, accessions from the Ames NC-7 Working Collection, or from other formal collections appear to have had little use by USA breeders for the development of commercial varieties. The only exception may be the use of advanced breeding lines and open-pollinated cultivars received in recent exchanges with China through the USDA Plant Introduction Office (PIO). These Chinese introductions were commercial cultivars of sugarbeet and required little reselection or enhancement. They essentially were usable directly as parental lines that contributed resistance to Cercospora leaf spot and high sucrose content.

It is only recently that breeders have taken an active interest in the NC-7 collection. Under the auspices of the CAC, a systematic evaluation of the collection is being made. In recent years, most of the older collection has been evaluated for reaction to various diseases and pests, for agronomic characteristics, and other genetic traits, cultigen type, species relationships, etc. As data are accumulated, they are entered into GRIN.

Prior to about 1980, other than the limited NC-7 collection, most of the *Beta* germplasm in the USA was in the hands of individual breeders and stations. This was particularly true for the wild types and species. The collections of Coons (1975) and other USDA researchers at Beltsville and field stations were assimilated, increased, and partially described by J.S. McFarlane

(Beta Germplasm Preservation, 1982, unpublished data). In the foreword of his report that was distributed to various breeders and stations, Dr. McFarlane writes:

> Preservation of *Beta* germplasm has been a major objective of my research program for the past 6 years. The *Beta* species are not native to the Western Hemisphere so primary emphasis must be placed on collections from Europe, Asia, and North Africa. Beginning in 1925, Dr. G.H. Coons (Coons, 1975) made four collecting trips to Europe and brought back seeds of most of the wild species. Arrangements were made by him with researchers in Europe to make additional collections and send seeds to Beltsville. Seeds of many of these accessions were distributed to breeders throughout the United States. Efforts were also made by Dr. Coons, Mr. Dewey Stewart, and Dr. Gerald Coe to increase this material, but time and facilities were not available to increase all accessions. Good seed storage facilities were lacking at Beltsville and several accessions lost their viability.
>
> Dr. Coe and I went through the Beltsville collection and small packets of most of the accessions were brought to Salinas. These accessions plus material already at Salinas became the basis for my germplasm preservation work. When trips were made to Europe, arrangements were made with various breeding stations to provide additional seed from their collections.
>
> Seed increases were made of most accessions that had viable seed. These increases were produced in greenhouse isolators, in the field, and to a limited extent under paper bags in the greenhouse. From observational field plantings, notes were taken on plant characteristics, outcrossing to sugarbeet, and disease resistance. Collections were also assembled of old European and American sugarbeet germplasm. Much of this material was multigerm and no longer used as cultivars or breeding lines. Arrangements were made through our Plant Introduction Officer to exchange seed of commercial cultivars with the USSR and the People's Republic of China. Seed increases have been made of many of these introductions and of old domestic sugarbeet germplasm.
>
> Seeds of representative accessions of most species and also of sugarbeet germplasm have been placed in the National Seed Storage Laboratory in Fort Collins.

Until recently, much of the wild *Beta* germplasm activities have involved these older collections that were rescued and placed into long-term storage by McFarlane. Accessions were assigned WB (wild beet) numbers. Because of lack of permanent plant introduction (PI) or other accession numbers, items in this collection have been identified in the literature by the WB numbers assigned by Dr. McFarlane (e.g., Lewellen et al., 1987; Whitney, 1989a,b; Doney & Whitney, 1990). Since 1980, renewed emphasis and dedication by both public and private breeders have been shown toward preservation and characterization of *Beta* germplasm resources. Collections of wild *Beta* germplasm particularly within the *Beta* section, have been made (Doney & Whitney, 1990; Doney, 1989; Doney et al., 1990; Ford-Lloyd, 1989). Further collection trips are planned under the auspices of the NPGS and IBPGR (Ford-Lloyd, 1989). Attempts will be made to close gaps in the present collections within the *Beta* section. Coons (1975) made at least two trips to Turkey and the Canary Islands to collect hard-seeded species. His collections, particularly within the *Corollinae*, need to be increased and evaluated. Further collections of the hard-seeded species are needed before the natural populations are destroyed.

In the past 20 yr, breeders in the USA organized germplasm exchanges with the USSR and China through the PIO of the USDA. These exchanges largely involved advanced sugarbeet populations, breeding and parental lines, and commercial cultivars. Much of this germplasm is now in the NSSL and NC-7 collections. The Russian germplasm from these exchanges has proved to be a useful source of resistance to storage rot organisms (Bugbee, 1979; Campbell & Bugbee, 1985).

USEFUL TRAITS FROM GERMPLASM

Variation Within *Beta*

Because of its developmental history, sugarbeet remained largely isolated from much of the genetic diversity within the genus *Beta*. This genetic resource has largely been unexplored and underused. It is likely that important and useful genetic variability could be found in this germplasm for most morphological and physiological characteristics, including yield and sugar content (Bosemark, 1989), and for resistance to diseases and pests. A recent review by Van Geyt et al. (1990) provides a comprehensive review on the known genetic variation within *Beta* and its possible use for breeding sugarbeet.

Germplasm Enhancement

Much of the *Beta* germplasm is exotic, wild, or weedy material. These materials can be difficult to evaluate and use in conventional breeding programs. To be made useful, germplasm enhancement (Jones, 1984) or prebreeding (Rick, 1984) activities have been suggested. Enhancement or prebreeding involve the transfer of useful genes from exotic or wild types into agronomically acceptable backgrounds. Usually, enhancement does not include cultivar development. Enhanced germplasm can then be readily used in breeding programs targeted at cultivar development (Roath, 1989).

Bosemark (1989) suggested methods for introducing new germplasm into elite breeding populations of sugarbeet. Frese (1990) expanded upon these suggestions and outlined a strategy for the introgression of wild and exotic germplasm into the sugarbeet gene pool. They advocated the establishment and improvement of base populations that could be used to feed desirable genetic variability into elite breeding stocks. This scheme is particularly relevant to sugarbeet improvement and the relationships between primitive or wild germplasm and elite stocks and between public and private funding, research, and responsibilities. This linkage between genetic resource and elite breeding stocks was summarized in the following table.

	Genetic resources	Base populations	Elite stock
Objective:	Long term	Medium-long	Short term
Funds:	Public	Both	Private
Data:	Free exchange	Both	Restricted
Seed:	Free exchange	Both	Restricted
Performance:	Very low	Interm.-high	Very high
Traits:	Low frequency	Enriched	Shortage

Once collected and stored, a rational germplasm enhancement program is needed to prevent genetic resources from becoming only museum pieces.

In the future, germplasm resources are likely to be of greater importance to the improvement of sugarbeet populations and commercial cultivars. As the loss of pesticides or their reduced usage is mandated, greater reliance will need to be placed on genes for resistance to insects, diseases, and stresses.

Improvements in physiological and morphological traits may also be necessary to keep sugarbeet a competitive source of food. In addition to the increased interest in germplasm collection and preservation, several breeders and research stations in Europe, Japan, and the USA have initiated programs to search for desirable and unique traits in *Beta* germplasm and to introgress these into sugarbeet.

ACKNOWLEDGMENT

The author extends special thanks to Dr. Robert K. Oldemeyer for his contributions to the manuscript. Thanks are extended also to the plant breeders who contributed information, ideas, and historical perspectives, particularly Drs. G.J. Hogaboam, G.E. Coe, J.S. McFarlane, J.C. Theurer, D.L. Doney, R.J. Hecker, R.H. Helmerick, G.M. Simantel, A.W. Erichsen, J.J. Kern, J.L. Kimmell, J.D. Schulke, J.R. Stander, J.W. Saunders, R.C. Zielke, and L.E. Wiesner. Appreciation is given to Marlene McQueen and Lori Wing for assistance in preparation of the manuscript.

REFERENCES

Abe, J., H. Nakashima, and C. Tsuda. 1987. Isozyme variation and species relationships in the genus *Beta*. Memoirs Fac. Agric. Hokkaido Univ. 15(2):124–132.

Abe, J., and C. Tsuda. 1988. Distorted segregation in the backcrossed progeny between *Beta vulgaris* L. and *B. macrocarpa* Guss. Jpn. J. Breed. 38:309–318.

Abe, J., H. Yoshikawa, and C. Tsuda. 1986. Reproductive barriers in sugarbeet and its wild relatives of the section *Vulgares*, the genus *Beta*. J. Fac. Agric. Hokkaido Univ. 63(1):40–48.

Bennett, C.W. 1971. The curly top disease of sugarbeet and other plants. Monogr. 7. Am. Phytopathol. Soc., St. Paul.

Bockstahler, H.W., and O.E. Reese. 1948. Progress report on breeding of sugarbeets in Minnesota for resistance to black root. Proc. Am. Soc. Sugar Beet Technol. 5:137–141.

Bosemark, N.O. 1979. Genetic poverty of the sugarbeet in Europe. p. 29–35. *In* A.C. Zeven and A.M. Van Harten (ed.) Proc. Conf. Broadening Genet. Base Crops, 1978. PUDOC, Wageningen, Netherlands.

Bosemark, N.O. 1989. Prospects for beet breeding and use of genetic resources. p. 89-97. *In* IBPGR. International crop network series. 3. Report of an international workshop on *Beta* genetic resources. Int. Board for Plant Genet. Resources, Rome.

Brewbaker, H.E., H.L. Bush, and R.R. Wood. 1950. A quarter century of progress in sugar beet improvement by the Great Western Sugar Company. Proc. Am. Soc. Sugar Beet Technol. 6:202-207.

Bugbee, W.M. 1979. The effect of plant age, storage, moisture, and genotype on storage rot evaluation of sugarbeet. Phytopathology 69:414-416.

Campbell, G.K.G. 1976. Sugar beet. p. 25-28. *In* N.W. Simmonds (ed.) Evolution of crop plants. Longman, London.

Campbell, L.G., and W.M. Bugbee. 1985. Registration of storage rot resistant sugarbeet germplasms F1004, F1005, and F1006. Crop Sci. 25:577.

Clark, R.L. 1989. Seed maintenance and storage. p. 95-110. *In* J. Janick (ed.) Plant breeding reviews. Vol. 7. Timber Press, Portland, OR.

Coe, G.E., and G.J. Hogaboam. 1971a. Registration of sugarbeet parental line SP 6322-0. Crop Sci. 11:947.

Coe, G.E., and G.J. Hogaboam. 1971b. Registration of US H20 sugarbeet. Crop Sci. 11:942.

Coons, G.H. 1936. Improvement of the sugar beet. *In* USDA Yearbook Agric. p. 625-656. U.S. Gov. Print. Office, Washington, DC.

Coons, G.H. 1953. Disease resistance breeding of sugar beets—1918-1952. Phytopathology 43:297-303.

Coons, G.H. 1954. The wild species of *Beta*. Proc. Am. Soc. Sugar Beet Technol. 8(2):142-147.

Coons, G.H. 1975. Interspecific hybrids between *Beta vulgaris* L. and the wild species of *Beta*. J. Am. Soc. Sugar Beet Technol. 18:281-306.

Coons, G.H., V.F. Owen, and D. Stewart. 1955. Improvement of the sugar beet in the United States. p. 89-139. *In* Advances in agronomy. Vol. 7. Academic Press, New York.

Coons, G.H., D. Stewart, C. Price, and H.A. Elcock. 1950. The U.S. 15 variety of sugar beet. Proc. Am. Soc. Sugar Beet Technol. 6:208.

de Bock, T.S.M. 1986. The genus *Beta*: Domestication, taxonomy and interspecific hybridization for plant breeding. Acta Hortic. 182:335-343.

Doney, D.L. 1989. Population dynamics of *Beta vulgaris* ssp. *maritima* L. (sea beet) in the British Isles. p. 98-105. *In* IBPGR. International crop network series. 3. Report of an international workshop on *Beta* genetic resources. Int. Board for Plant Genet. Resources, Rome.

Doney, D.L., and E.D. Whitney. 1990. Genetic enhancement in *Beta* for disease resistance using wild relatives: A strong case for the value of genetic conservation. Econ. Bot. 44:445-451.

Doney, D.L., E.D. Whitney, J. Terry, L. Frese, and P. Fitzgerald. 1990. The distribution and dispersal of *Beta vulgaris* L. ssp. *maritima* (L.) Thell. germplasm in England, Wales, and Ireland. J. Sugar Beet Res. 27:29-37.

Fischer, H.E. 1989. Origin of the 'Weisse Schlesische Rübe' (white Silesian beet) and resynthesis of sugar beet. Euphytica 41:75-80.

Ford-Lloyd, B.V. 1989. *Beta* germplasm collection: Current status. p. 106-109. *In* IBPGR. International crop network series. 3. Report of an international workshop on *Beta* genetic resources. Int. Board for Plant Genet. Resources, Rome.

Ford-Lloyd, B.V., and J.T. Williams. 1975. A revision of *Beta* section *Vulgares* (Chenopodiaceae), with new light on the origin of cultivated beets. Bot. J. Linn. Soc. 71:89-102.

Frese, L. 1990. The world *Beta* network cooperation. p. 161-171. *In* Proc. 53 Winter Congress. Int. Inst. for Sugar Beet Res., Brussels.

Frese, L., and T.J.L. van Hintum. 1989. The international data base for *Beta*. p. 17-35. *In* IBPGR. International crop network series. 3. Report of an international workshop on *Beta* genetic resources. Int. Board for Plant Genet. Resources, Rome.

Harris, F.S. 1919. The sugar-beet in America. Macmillan Publ., NY.

Hecker, R.J., and J.O. Gaskill. 1972. Registration of FC 701 and FC 702 sugarbeet germplasm. Crop Sci. 12:400.

Hecker, R.J., and R.H. Helmerick. 1984. Sugar-beet breeding in the United States. p. 37-61. *In* G.E. Russell (ed.) Progress in plant breeding-1. Butterworth, London.

Hecker, R.J., and E.G. Ruppel. 1977. Rhizoctonia root-rot resistance in sugarbeet: Breeding and related research. J. Am. Soc. Sugar Beet Technol. 19:246-256.

Henderson, R.W., and H.W. Bockstahler. 1946. Reaction of sugarbeet strains to *Aphanomyces cochlioides*. Proc. Am. Soc. Sugar Beet Technol. 4:237-245.

Hogaboam, G.J., and C.L. Schneider. 1982a. Registration of EL44 and EL44CMS sugarbeet parental lines. Crop Sci. 22:700.

Hogaboam, G.J., and C.L. Schneider. 1982b. Registration of EL45/2 sugarbeet parental line. Crop Sci. 22:700.

Hogaboam, G.J., R.C. Zielke, and C.L. Schneider. 1982c. Registration of EL40 sugarbeet parental line. Crop Sci. 22:700.

International Board for Plant Genetic Resources. 1989. International crop network series. 3. Report of an international workshop on *Beta* genetic resources. Int. Board for Plant Genet. Resources, Rome.

Janick, J. (ed.) 1989. Plant breeding reviews, the national plant germplasm system of the United States. Vol. 7. Timber Press, Portland, OR.

Jones, Q. 1984. A national plant germplasm system. p. 27–34. *In* W.L. Brown et al. (ed.) Conservation of crop germplasm—An international perspective. CSSA Spec. Publ. 8. CSSA, Madison, WI.

Lange, W., and T.S.M. de Bock. 1989. The diploidised meiosis of tetraploid *Beta macrocarpa* and its possible application in breeding sugar beet. Plant Breed. 103:196–206.

Lester, R.N. 1989. Evolution under domestication involving disturbance of genic balance. Euphytica 44:125–132.

Lewellen, R.T., J.S. McFarlane, and I.O. Skoyen. 1978. Registration of 11 germplasm lines of sugarbeet. Crop Sci. 18:1100–1101.

Lewellen, R.T., I.O. Skoyen, and A.W. Erichsen. 1987. Breeding sugarbeet for resistance to rhizomania: Evaluation of host-plant reactions and selection for and inheritance of resistance. p. 139–156. *In* Proc. 50 Winter Congr. Int. Inst. for Sugar Beet Res., Brussels.

Lewellen, R.T., I.O. Skoyen, and E.D. Whitney. 1985. Registration of C46 sugarbeet parental line. Crop Sci. 25:376.

McFarlane, J.S. 1971. Variety development. p. 401–435. *In* R.T. Johnson et al. (ed.) Advances in sugarbeet production: Principles and practices. Iowa State Univ. Press, Ames.

McFarlane, J.S., and C. Price. 1952. A new non-bolting, curly-top-resistant, sugar beet variety, U.S. 75. Proc. Am. Soc. Sugar Beet Technol. 7:384–386.

McFarlane, J.S., and I.O. Skoyen. 1965. Sugar beet breeding lines combining resistance to bolting and disease. J. Am. Soc. Sugar Beet Technol. 13:555–562.

McFarlane, J.S., and I.O. Skoyen. 1971. Registration of US H9A and US H9B sugarbeet. Crop Sci. 11:942.

McFarlane, J.S., I.O. Skoyen, and R.T. Lewellen. 1969. Development of sugarbeet breeding lines and varieties resistant to yellows. J. Am. Soc. Sugar Beet Technol. 15:347–360.

McFarlane, J.S., I.O. Skoyen, and R.T. Lewellen. 1971a. Registration of US H10A and US H10B sugarbeet. Crop Sci. 11:942.

McFarlane, J.S., I.O. Skoyen, and R.T. Lewellen. 1971b. Registration of sugarbeet parental lines. Crop Sci. 11:946–947.

Mowder, J.D., and A.K. Stoner. 1989. Information systems. p. 57–65. *In* J. Janick (ed.) Plant breeding reviews. Vol. 7. Timber Press, Portland, OR.

Munerati, O. 1932. Sull-incrocio della barbabietola coltivata con la beta selvaggia della costa Adriatica. L'Industria Saccar. Ital. 25:303–304.

Murphy, A.M., F.V. Owen, and G.K. Ryser. 1948. New sugar beet strains from U.S. 22 with higher curly-top resistance. Proc. Am. Soc. Sugar Beet Technol. 5:179–180.

Owen, F.V. 1945. Cytoplasmically inherited male-sterility in sugar beets. J. Agric. Res. 71:423–440.

Owen, F.V., F.A. Abegg, A.M. Murphy, B. Tolman, C. Price, F.G. Larmer, and E. Carsner. 1939. Curly-top-resistant sugar-beet varieties in 1938. USDA Circ. 513, p. 1–3.

Owen, F.V., A.M. Murphy, and G.K. Ryser. 1946. Inbred lines from curly-top-resistant varieties of sugar beets. Proc. Am. Soc. Sugar Beet Technol. 4:246–252.

Palmer, T.G. 1918. Sugar beet seed, history and development. John Wiley and Sons, New York.

Perdue, Jr., R.E., and G.M. Christenson. 1989. Plant exploration. p. 67–94. *In* J. Janick (ed.) Plant breeding reviews. Vol. 7. Timber Press, Portland, OR.

Pichat, C.B. 1866. Della barbabietola. p. 175–200. *In* Agricoltura. Vol. 5. Presso L'Union, Torino, Italy.

Rick, C.W. 1984. Plant germplasm resources. p. 9–37. *In* D.A. Evens et al. (ed.) Handbook of plant cell culture. Macmillan Publ., New York.

Roath, W.W. 1989. Evaluation and enhancement. p. 183–211. *In* J. Janick (ed.) Plant breeding reviews. Vol. 7. Timber Press, Portland, OR.

Roos, E.E. 1989. Long-term seed storage. p. 129–158. *In* J. Janick (ed.) Plant breeding reviews. Vol. 7. Timber Press, Portland, OR.

Savitsky, V.F. 1950. Monogerm sugar beets in the United States. Proc. Am. Soc. Sugar Beet Technol. 6:156–159.

Schneider, C.L. 1954. Methods of inoculating sugar beets with *Aphanomyces cochlioides* Drechs. Proc. Am. Soc. Sugar Beet Technol. 8(1):247–251.

Smith, G.A. 1980. Sugarbeet. p. 601–616. *In* W.R. Fehr and H.H. Hadley (ed.) Hybridization of crop plants. ASA and CSSA, Madison, WI.

Smith, G.A. 1987. Sugar beet. p. 577–625. *In* W.R. Fehr (ed.) Principles of cultivar development. Vol. 2. Macmillan Publ., New York.

Theurer, J.C. 1978. Registration of eight germplasm lines of sugarbeet. Crop Sci. 18:1101.

Van Geyt, J.P.C., W. Lange, M. Oleo, and T.S.M. de Bock. 1990. Natural variation within the genus *Beta* and its possible use for breeding sugar beet: A review. Euphytica 49:57–76.

Wallis, R.L., and J.O. Gaskill. 1963. Sugar-beet root aphid resistance in sugar beet. J. Am. Soc. Sugar Beet Technol. 12:571–572.

Ware, L.S. 1880. The sugar beet. Henry Carey Baird and Co., Philadelphia.

White, G.A., H.L. Shands, and G.R. Lovell. 1989. History and operation of the National Plant Germplasm System. p. 5–56. *In* J. Janick (ed.) Plant breeding reviews. Vol. 7. Timber Press, Portland, OR.

Whitney, E.D. 1989a. Identification, distribution, and testing for resistance to rhizomania in *Beta maritima*. Plant Dis. 73:287–290.

Whitney, E.D. 1989b. *Beta maritima* as a source of powdery mildew resistance in sugar beet. Plant Dis. 73:487–489.

Whitney, E.D., and R.T. Lewellen. 1978. Registration of two sugarbeet parental lines. Crop Sci. 18:920.

Zossimovich, V.P. 1940. Wild species and origin of cultivated beets. Sveklovodstro, Kiev (Sugar Beet Production) 1:17–44. (In Russian.)

6   Use of Plant Introductions in Sugarcane Cultivar Development

J. D. Miller and P. Y. P. Tai

USDA-ARS
Sugarcane Field Station
Canal Point, Florida

Sugarcane belongs to the genus *Saccharum* which consists of six species, *S. officinarum* L. (noble cane), *S. spontaneum* L., *S. barberi*, Jesw., *S. sinense* Roxb., *S. robustum* Brandes and Jeswiet ex. Grassl, and *S. edule* Hassk. Related genera include *Erianthus, Miscanthus, Sclerostachya*, and *Narenga*. These genera together have been called the *Saccharum* complex (Mukherjee, 1954, 1957; Daniels & Roach, 1987). A majority of the species of these genera originated in Asia and the south Pacific islands.

In most places in the world where sugarcane was cultivated prior to 1900, the plant most commonly grown was a selection of noble cane. All cultivar development up to that time had depended upon selection of mutant types (sports) or selection of different original clones from the wild.

An appreciation of the value of germplasm is long established in sugarcane. After the 1858 discovery of true seed in Barbados, work was started in Java by Soltwedel in 1888 to hybridize *S. officinarum* cultivars (Bremer, 1961). Crosses also were made with a wild cane, Kassoer (a natural hybrid between *S. officinarum* and *S. spontaneum*). Kassoer, was resistant to sereh disease, which was causing serious yield losses in the *S. officinarum* cultivars. A clone of *S. barberi*, Chunnee, was also crossed to *S. officinarum* in 1897 by J.D. Kobus (Bremer, 1961). These hybrids were backcrossed to *S. officinarum* to develop the commercial cultivars that were resistant to sereh disease.

Early sugarcane production in the USA (principally in Louisiana, Puerto Rico, and Hawaii) was also based on clones of *S. officinarum*. Sugarcane mosaic virus nearly eliminated sugar production in Louisiana in the mid-1920s. Total sugar production was reduced from 262 730 Mg in 1921 to 38 195 Mg in 1926 (Rosenfeld, 1930). The mainland sugarcane industry imported early generation hybrids from both Java (POJ) in 1919 and India (Co) in 1924. They subsequently became important commercial cultivars in the USA and in most sugarcane-producing countries around the world. The

---

Copyright © 1992 Crop Science Society of America, 677 S. Segoe Rd., Madison, WI 53711, USA. *Use of Plant Introductions in Cultivar Development, Part 2*, CSSA Special Publication no. 20.

early hybrids developed in Java and India involved only 13 original clones of *S. officinarum*, *S. spontaneum*, and *S. barberi* (Tew, 1987). Most sugarcane breeding programs in the world are founded upon these hybrids (Tew, 1987). The germplasm base used for breeding in the mainland USA (Tai & Miller, 1978) was restricted because many of the tropically bred cultivars failed to flower in the subtropical environment at Canal Point, FL. The range of adapted cultivars in Louisiana is limited by cold winters (Irvine & Legendre, 1985). In Florida, high N levels in the muck soils (Forsee, 1952) cause most imported cultivars to produce high cane tonnage but unacceptably low sucrose contents.

Breeders in Hawaii recognized the importance of continued introduction of new germplasm. In 1931, they made crosses with *S. robustum* clones introduced into their melting pots (polycrosses where only the female parent is known) (Heinz, 1967).

Arceneaux (1967) studied the pedigrees of 100 commercial cultivars and found highly disproportionate use of *S. officinarum* as parents when compared to the use of *S. spontaneum, S. barberi, S. sinense*, and *S. robustum*. He concluded that only a few clones of the recognized species were included in the pedigrees of commercial cultivars and that sugarcane breeders had sampled only a few of the genetic combinations possible within *Saccharum*.

WORLD COLLECTION

All sugarcane germplasm in the USA (which include the original clones of *Saccharum*, hybrids among *Saccharum* spp., and related grasses) was introduced. None of the members of the *Saccharum* complex are native to North America except for the six species of American *Erianthus* and these have not been crossed with *Saccharum*.

Sugarcane breeders have recognized the importance of collecting and preserving basic clones of *Saccharum*. The first collections of additional germplasm were made in 1853 from New Caledonia and the New Hebrides islands by workers from Reunion (Artschwager & Brandes, 1958). Other germplasm collections were made by researchers from Australia, and joint collection trips were conducted under the auspices of International Society of Sugar Cane Technologists and private industry (Naidu & Sreenivasan, 1987).

One of the two World Collections of Sugarcane and Related Grasses is maintained by the USDA-ARS at the National Clonal Germplasm Repository at Miami, FL and the other collection is maintained by the Sugarcane Breeding Institute, Coimbatore, India. A summary of sugarcane germplasm maintained in the World Collections of Sugarcane and Related Grasses is presented in Table 6-1 (Schnell, 1991; Naidu & Sreenivasan, 1987). Recent additions to the collections were from India, Indonesia, New Guinea, Philippines, and Thailand. In addition, individual clones are added to the collection as they become available from other countries. *Saccharum officinarum* has the greatest number of clones represented in the collection because this

Table 6-1. Listing of the number of clones of different genera and *Saccharum* spp. in the World Collection of Sugarcane and Related Grasses at the National Clonal Germplasm Repository in Miami, FL and by the Sugarcane Breeding Institute at Coimbatore, India.

Source	Number of clones USA	Number of clones India
Erianthus spp.	196	--
Erianthus, Sclerostachya, and *Narenga*	--	235
Miscanthus spp.	33	--
Miscanthus hybrids	17	--
Saccharum barberi	57	43
S. edule	15	--
S. hybrids	201	--
S. officinarum	568	--
S. officinarum and nathral hybrids	--	754
S. robustum	135	140
S. sinense	38	29
S. spontaneum	308	489
Man-made hybrids	200	1743
Recent collections from India: 1981, 1982, 1983, 1984, 1985	--	484
New accessions	130	83

species has the greatest likelihood of being lost as its habitat becomes more developed.

PROBLEMS RELATED TO GERMPLASM UTILIZATION

Many of the problems of using related genera in crosses are similar to those that occur when trying to intercross clones within *Saccharum*. Members of the *Saccharum* complex flower at different times. For instance, *S. spontaneum* clones flower from August (clones from more northerly latitudes) to January (more tropical types) at Canal Point, FL (Tai, 1990; Panje, 1972). Commercial cultivars generally flower from late November to January. Crosses involving plants with different flowering dates are difficult. Parental clones flower asynchronously so techniques must be used to manipulate the flowering time of at least one of the parental clones. Currently, it is possible to delay the early flowering clones through the use of daylength extension (James, 1968); trimming leaves after induction has occurred (Chu & Serapion, 1980); or the use of the growth regulator, ethophon (Deuber & Irvine, 1987). Time of flowering may also be regulated through the use of photoperiod treatments to induce flowering to coincide with the natural flowering of the other clone (Dunckelman & Legendre, 1982; James & Miller, 1972; Paliatseas, 1972).

The preservation and storage of viable pollen may also overcome the barrier of asynchronous flowering. Furthermore, preservation of viable pollen should greatly enhance the use of sugarcane germplasm for breeding. Brandes (1937) and Sartoris (1942) used stored *S. spontaneum* pollen to cross with a commercial cultivar in an attempt to transfer cold-tolerant genes from *S. spontaneum*. Tai (1988, 1990) was successful in storing *S. spontaneum* pollen for more than 1 yr at low temperatures. Procedures included collecting the pollen in the early morning or night immediately after anthesis and then drying for 3 to 4 h in an air-conditioned (20 °C or lower) dehumidified room to reduce the moisture content of the pollen to 10% or lower. The pollen was put in plastic cryotubes and stored in an ultra-cold freezer (-80 °C) or in liquid N (-196 °C). The viability of pollen stored in liquid N for more than 2 yr is shown in Table 6-2. Results indicated that pollen from some clones maintained viability better than others. Pollen of *S. spontaneum* "Coimbatore" (PI 286650) retained relatively high viability stored at -80 °C for more than 2 yr (Tai, 1988, 1990). These results also indicate that pollen viability was reduced after 2 yr of storage. Whether the loss in pollen viability occurs before, during, or after, storage needs to be examined. This storage technique was used to preserve pollen from other *Saccharum* spp., commercial sugarcane cultivars, *Erianthus*, *Miscanthus*, *Narenga*, and *Sclerostachya* (P.Y.P. Tai, 1991, unpublished data). Their pollen viability was not as consistent as that from *S. spontaneum* clones. Procedures used in the preparation of pollen for storage may need to be varied from that used for the *S. spontaneum* clones. Improvement in pollen storage techniques is needed to effectively preserve viable pollen of other species.

The breeding program at Canal Point produced seed for the sugarcane breeding programs in Florida, Louisiana, and Texas, with little input from foreign commercial cultivars until the present photoperiod house was built in 1982. In this facility, clones of *S. officinarum*, *S. robustum*, *S. sinense*, *S. barberi*, and foreign cultivars were induced to flower and were used to

Table 6-2. Viability of *S. spontaneum* pollen after storage in liquid N (-196 °C) for various periods as measured by seed set (the average number of hybrid seedlings per 5 g of fuzz).

Clone	Storage time	Seed set	Clone	Storage time	Seed set
Coimbatore	83	37	SES 289C	127	344
PI 286650	394	81	PI 440898	488	151
	755	49		854	0
Holes I	199	115	SES 390	94	174
Imp. 3033	476	72	PI 286742	439	125
	836	3		760	6
Karenko	120	2	SES 501	128	48
PI 235883	469	3	PI 286755	476	107
	802	162		843	0
Tainan 2n = 96	128	0	S66-121	128	128
PI 160342	465	16	PI 423575	486	27
	842	0		853	0
SES 196	131	133	Spontaneum #28	128	0
PI 286695	480	4	Imp. 9967	486	15
	847	24		853	0
SES 234	123	0			
	437	301			
Imp. 8547	800	24			

broaden the germplasm base of our present cultivars. Selection of foreign commercial cultivars was based primarily on their resistance to three diseases [smut (caused by *Ustilago scitaminea* Syd.), rust (caused by *Puccinia melanocephala* H. Syd. and P. Syd.), and Fiji disease (caused by a virus)]. Fiji disease is not known to exist in the USA but both rust and smut were recently discovered in Florida. Some of the progenies derived from crosses between Canal Point bred cultivars and foreign commercial cultivars were selected and advanced to regular cultivar yield trials. However, none outyielded the standard cultivars. In most cases, this was due to low sucrose content. However, they are being used extensively as parents for further improvement of cane yield and disease resistance.

The breeding philosophy at Canal Point in recent years has been to try to minimize generation intervals. Results of a recent survey indicate a maximum of 5 to 11 generations between the original crosses and present commercial cultivars (Table 6-3). Thus, there has been a maximum of 11 opportunities for sexual recombination to occur in sugarcane breeding. The minimum number of generations between current commercial cultivars and the basic clones ranges from 2 to 7. The view that sugarcane breeders have exhausted genetic variability and reached yield plateaus should be put in the following perspective. Sugarcane is a complex polyploid that has been bred

Table 6-3. The maximum and minimum number of generations away from basic germplasm within the pedigrees of up to three recently released commercial cultivars per breeding station.

Country	No. of generations[†] Max.	Min.	Citation
Australia			
BSES	7	4	D.M. Hogarth, 1990, personal communication
CSR	6, 8	2, 4	A.W. Wood & W.W. Symington, 1990, personal communication
Barbados	5, 6, 5,	4, 3, 4	Tew, 1987
Brazil	7	3	W.M. daSilva, 1990, personal communication
Colombia	9, 5	3, 2	C. Cassalett, 1990, personal communication
India	9, 5, 5	4, 4, 3	Tew, 1987
Indonesia	8, 8, 5	4, 4, 4	G. Sukarso, 1990, personal communication
Mauritius	8, 7, 8	5, 5, 3	R. Domainque, 1990, personal communication
Mexico	7, 9, 6	4, 5, 5	C.A. Morrill, 1990, personal communication
Puerto Rico	5, 5	4, 3	J.L. Rodriguez, 1990, personal communication
South Africa	8, 6, 5	3, 3, 4	K.J. Nuss, 1990, personal communication
Taiwan	9, 7, 8	7, 5, 4	C.C. Lo, 1990, personal communication
USA			
Canal Point, FL	11, 11, 10	8, 6, 5	Tai & Miller, 1978
Houma, LA	9, 8, 8	6, 7, 5	Tew, 1987
HSPA, HI	11, 7, 7	7, 5, 6	Tew, 1987
Weslaco, TX	8, 9, 10	6, 5, 6	J.E. Irvine, 1991, personal communication

[†] Maximum and minimum number, respectively, of generations between basic crosses and commercial cultivars in the pedigrees of up to three cultivars per breeding station. For example, cultivar 1 from CSR had a maximum of six and a minimum of two generations from basic germplasm in its pedigree whereas cultivar 2 had a maximum of eight and a minimum of four generations away from basic germplasm in its pedigree.

for a small number of generations. By contrast, response to selection for high and low oil and protein content in corn (a $2N = 20$ diploid) was maintained for 76 generations (Dudley, 1977).

USE OF *SACCHARUM SPONTANEUM*

There has been renewed emphasis on the use of basic germplasm in the USA and around the world. A partial listing of basic *Saccharum* germplasm usage around the world is presented in Table 6-4. Data are based on literature and a survey conducted of sugarcane-breeding stations in 1990. It is evident that considerable effort has been expended to try to improve sugarcane cultivars through the use of new germplasm. Usually the first selections to be advanced to final yield trials were not released as commercial cultivars but have been used extensively as parents. Legendre (1989) reported planting an average of 24 698 basic seedlings yr^{-1} over the 15-yr period from 1972 to 1986. From this group, a total of 82 selections were evaluated as potential commercial cultivars. The results obtained in Louisiana were similar to those obtained by Roach (1977) while trying to nobilize clones of *S. spontaneum*. The information in Table 6-4 suggests that many countries should have new breeding lines developed that will start making significant contributions to the development of new cultivars in the near future. Two commercial cultivars (TUCCP 77-42 and LHo 83-153) were released from crosses made at Houma, LA (B.L. Legendre, 1991, personal communication). TUCCP 77-42 was selected in Argentina from progeny of a cross with SES 147B, a clone of *S. spontaneum* (Mariotti et al., 1991). LHo 83-153 was selected at Louisiana State University Agricultural Center, Baton Rouge, from BC$_4$ seed produced from *S. spontaneum* line US 56-15-8 (PI 230855) (Fig. 6-1).

Use of basic germplasm from the sugarcane world collections and new collections increased in the 1960s (Dunckelman, 1974; Dunckelman & Breaux, 1972; Heinz, 1967; Panje, 1972; Roach, 1972). The emphasis in mainland USA, Australia, and India was mostly in using new clones of *S. spontaneum*. Roach (1977) cytologically and agronomically analyzed crosses between clones of *S. officinarum* and *S. spontaneum* as well as crosses of *S. spontaneum* with commercial cultivars. He indicated that care should be taken to select the best possible clones of both parental groups, that inbreeding should be avoided and serious consideration be given to using an elite commercial cultivar for the backcross parent.

Stored pollen of more than 30 clones of *S. spontaneum* has been used successfully to make crosses with commercial cultivars, *S. officinarum* and other *Saccharum* spp. (Table 6-5). The juice quality of F_1 hybrids from commercial cultivars × *S. spontaneum* crosses varied depending upon both the commercial cultivar and clone of *S. spontaneum* used in the cross. These F_1 hybrids exhibited considerable reduction in sucrose content in comparison to commercial reference cultivars. These data agree with that of Symington (1989) and Roach (1986) in that acceptable agronomic segregates with high sucrose content were very difficult to obtain. Some of the superior F_1

SUGARCANE CULTIVAR DEVELOPMENT

Table 6-4. Listing of sugarcane breeding stations conducting basic breeding with *Saccharum* or related genera and stage of development of the germplasm.

Country	Species	Stage of development	Citation
Argentina	*S. spontaneum*	Release of TUCCP 77-42	Mariotti et al., 1991
Australia BSES	*S. spontaneum*	Release of Q 138	D.M. Hogarth, 1990, personal communication
	S. officinarum	Testing	
CSR	*S. spontaneum*	Release of BN 78-8031 & BN 78-8032	A.W. Wood & W.W. Symington, 1990, personal communication
	S. robustum	Testing	Roach, 1989a,b
	S. officinarum	Testing	
Barbados	*S. officinarum*	Testing	Walker, 1987
	S. robustum	Testing	
	S. spontaneum	Testing	
	Erianthus		
Fiji	*S. officinarum*	Testing	Krishnamurthi, 1985
	S. robustum	Testing	
	S. spontaneum	Testing	
	Erianthus	Testing	
	Narenga	Testing	
India	*S. officinarum*	Testing	Sreenivasan, 1989
	S. robustum	Testing†	
	S. sinense/barberi	Testing†	
Mauritius	*S. officinarum*	Early generation	R. Domaingue, 1990, personal communication
	S. robustum	Early generation	
	S. spontaneum	Early generation	
Puerto Rico	*S. spontaneum*	Testing	Chu & Rodriguez, 1982
South Africa	*S. spontaneum*	Release of J 59/3	K.J. Nuss, 1990, personal communication
Taiwan	*Miscanthus*	Final testing	Lo & Chen, 1989
	S. spontaneum	Final testing	Hsu & Shih, 1989
USA Canal Point, FL	*Miscanthus*	Early generations	Tai & Miller, 1988
	Erianthus	Early generations	
	S. officinarum	Early generations	
	S. robustum	Early generations	
	S. spontaneum	Final testing	
Houma, LA	*Erianthus*	Early generation	Legendre, 1989
	S. spontaneum	Final testing	
	Sclerostachya	Early generation	
HSPA, HI	*S. spontaneum*	Release of H 69-9103 and H 69-9092	Heinz, 1980
	S. robustum	Release of H 73-8505	

† Under cooperative PL 480 project with USA.

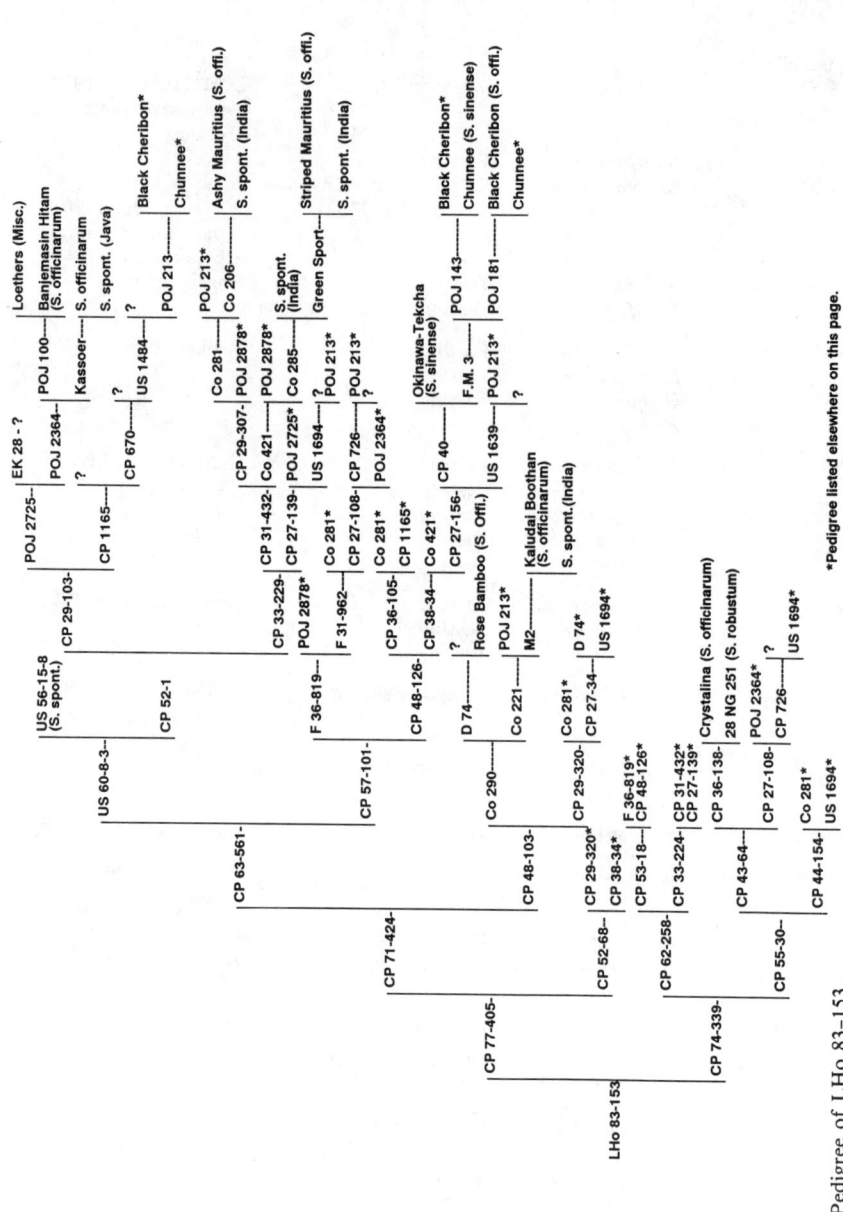

Fig. 6-1. Pedigree of LHo 83-153.

SUGARCANE CULTIVAR DEVELOPMENT

Table 6-5. Juice quality of F_1 hybrids from commercial cultivar × *S. spontaneum* crosses and the commercial check cultivars.

Cross	ID no.	Brix, %	Sucrose, %
CP 80-1902 × Tainan 2n = 96	PI 160342	13.18	8.27
CP 80-1902 × SES 501	PI 286755	13.53	8.29
CP 80-1902 × SES 196	PI 286695	11.30	7.61
CP 79-302 × Karenko	PI 235883	12.00	7.21
CP 80-1902 × Karenko	PI 235883	10.80	5.64
CP 65-357 × Tainan 2n = 96	PI 160342	13.20	7.76
CP 65-357 × SES 184 B	PI 318789	10.14	5.35
CP 65-357 × Karenko	PI 235883	11.28	6.27
CP 65-357 × Holes 1	Imp. 3033	10.63	5.84
CP 72-378 × SES 246	Imp. 8549	12.03	7.29
CP 80-1902 × SES 246	Imp. 8549	10.90	5.59
POJ 2725 × Holes 1	Imp. 3033	8.62	3.64
POJ 2725 × SES 246	Imp. 8549	11.50	7.09
CP 80-1902 × SES 234	Imp. 8547	14.00	9.49
POJ 2725 × SES 234	Imp. 8547	9.28	3.38
CP 65-357 × SES 246	Imp. 8549	11.90	7.86
CP 65-357 × SES 234	Imp. 8547	10.73	5.74
CP 79-302 × Holes 1	Imp. 3033	11.30	6.11
CP 80-1902 × S 1	Imp. 8195	12.32	8.02
CP 65-357 × 28 NG 292	PI 111347	12.10	7.32
POJ 2725 × 28 NG 292	PI 111347	10.10	4.56
CP 65-357 × SES 390	PI 286742	13.10	7.88
CP 79-302 × 28 NG 292	PI 111347	13.60	9.13
CP 80-1902 × Gehra bon	PI 246000	10.65	5.03
CP 80-1902 × 51 NG 28	Imp. 1936	11.04	5.87
CP 72-378 × Gehra bon	PI 246000	11.20	5.30
POJ 2725 × Gehra bon	PI 246000	10.10	4.28
POJ 2725 × SES 519	PI 286759	12.50	8.56
CP 65-357 × Coimbatore	PI 286650	11.50	7.21
POJ 2725 × Coimbatore	PI 286650	9.30	3.38
CP 80-1902 × Coimbatore	PI 286650	14.70	7.18
CP 79-302 × Gehra bon	PI 246000	10.45	4.73
CP 72-378 × Coimbatore	PI 286650	11.88	5.75
POJ 2725 × US 56-15-8	PI 230855	10.00	4.98
CP 80-1902 × US 56-15-8	PI 230855	12.30	7.64
CP 72-378 × US 56-15-8	PI 230855	11.60	7.05
CP 65-357 × US 56-15-8	PI 230855	11.88	7.10
CP 65-357 × Uganda	Imp. 9961	10.71	5.18
CP 65-357		19.70	18.10
CP 80-1902		18.73	16.60
CP 72-1210		19.60	17.00

hybrids are being used as parental clones in the Canal Point nobilization program.

USE OF INTERGENERIC HYBRIDS

Grassl (1962) discussed the possibility of intergeneric hybridization. He indicated that at least one species of *Erianthus, Miscanthidium, Miscanthus,*

Narenga, Sclerostachya, and *Sorghum* genera had been successfully hybridized with *Saccharum*. The potential variation produced by breeding at the intergeneric levels is staggering when one ponders the number of potential species and characteristics they possess. Grassl (1962) defined breeding at the intergeneric level as "essentially experiments in controlled evolution by introgression from the related genus." Characteristics in some of the related genera that would be beneficial to sugarcane breeders are: disease resistance (i.e., resistance to sugarcane smut, rust, and downy mildew); tolerance to extreme environmental conditions (i.e., resistance to freeze damage, drought, floods, and ability to grow at low temperatures); and presence of desirable agronomic characters (i.e., high sucrose content, ratooning ability, high stalk populations, and vigor in ratoon crops).

Sugarcane breeders at the Taiwan Sugar Research Institute made an intensive effort to use *Miscanthus* germplasm in their sugarcane breeding program (Chen et al., 1983; Chen & Lo, 1988; Lo et al., 1986; Lo & Chen, 1989). They obtained selections from crosses between sugarcane and *Miscanthus* that were resistant to downy mildew, top rot, rust, leaf scorch, and mosaic diseases. The *Saccharum* × *Miscanthus* hybrids are also a promising biomass resource. High-fiber cultivars developed through intergeneric hybridization could help sugar industries increase profitability levels by more effective utilization of all plant components. An intergeneric breeding effort was initiated to use *Miscanthus* and *Erianthus* germplasm in the sugarcane cultivar improvement program at Canal Point, FL in 1985 (Tai & Miller, 1988). The species used in this program include *E. arundinaceus, M. sinensis*, and *Miscanthidium sorghum* (this formerly *Miscanthus violaceum* [C.O. Grassl, 1986, personal communication]). Our results verify those from Taiwan that *Saccharum* × *Miscanthus* hybrids contribute agronomically desirable traits to their progenies (P.Y.P. Tai & J.D. Miller, 1988; 1991 unpublished data). Gill and Grassl (1986) proposed exploiting $2n$ unreduced gametes as a mechanism to facilitate genetic transfer between intergeneric hybrids and sugarcane. However, this technique has not yet been tested.

SUMMARY

Roach (1989b) described a program for sampling the genetic diversity in the *Saccharum* complex. He divided this complex into five subprograms: (i) first nobilization of *S. spontaneum*; (ii) increasing genetic diversity at the F_1 *S. spontaneum level; (iii) first nobilization of S. robustum*; (iv) nobilization of bred and selected *S. robustum*; and (v) nobilization of *Erianthus arundinaceum*. Work on each of the five subprograms is being carried on simultaneously. While this work is still in the early stages, subprogram two has thus far shown significant improvement in germination and early growth. Walker (1987) proposed four alternatives to classic nobilization, starting in all cases with collection of the wild species: (i) select wild species for desired trait(s), synchronize flowering and cross with *S. officinarum*, select in F_1 generation and backcross to a different noble; (ii) synchronize flowering and cross with adapted commercial parent, select in F_1 generation, cross with another commercial parent; (iii) synchronize flowering and cross with random nobles, select in F_1 generation, polycross or make biparental crosses among unrelated F_1's; and (iv) synchronize flowering among the wild species and polycross, select improved basic species and go to either (i) or (ii). Utilization of the germplasm pools described by Roach (1989b) and Walker (1987) should provide the genetic diversity needed to keep sugarcane breeding programs going for years.

Our approach to using basic germplasm has been to follow the practice of intermating F_1's as well as using a straight nobilization procedure. The generation interval is also being kept to a minimum with some as low as 2 yr but generally averaging about 3 yr. The real problem with conducting basic breeding programs is the necessity to achieve the proper balance between the basic program and the need to develop commercial cultivars. The Sugarcane World Collection provides us with a great resource of genes. Additionally, the advances of biotechnology should open up new horizons for using these resources. Sugarcane breeders, however, face constant changes in agricultural practices, disease and pest attacks, and environmental stresses. The task of breeding improved sugarcane cultivars continues to be a challenge.

REFERENCES

Arceneaux, G. 1967. Cultivated sugarcanes of the world and their botanical derivation. Proc. Int. Soc. Sugar Cane Technol. 12:844–854.

Artschwager, E., and E.W. Brandes. 1958. Sugarcane (*Saccharum officinarum*)—Origin, characteristics, and descriptions of representative clones. USDA Agric. Handb. 122. U.S. Gov. Print. Office, Washington, DC.

Brandes, E.W. 1937. Possibilities of further progress in breeding sugarcane for cold tolerance. Sugar Bull. 15(4):5-7.

Bremer, G. 1961. Problems in breeding and cytology of sugar cane. I. A short history of sugar cane breeding. Euphytica 10:59–78.

Chen, Y.H., Y.J. Huang, I.S. Shen, and S.C. Shih. 1983. Utilization of *Miscanthus* germplasm in sugarcane breeding in Taiwan. Proc. Int. Soc. Sugar Cane Technol. 18:590–595.

Chen, Y.H., and C.C. Lo. 1988. Disease resistance and sugar content in *Saccharum-Miscanthus* hybrids. p. 1–7. *In* Rep. 120. Taiwan Sugar Res. Inst., Tainan, Taiwan.

Chu, T.L., and J.L. Rodriguez. 1982. Sugarcane breeding in Puerto Rico. p. 124–129. *In* Proc. 3rd Inter-American Sugar Cane Seminar-Varieties Breed. Vol. 3.

Chu, T.L., and J.L. Serapion. 1980. Leaf removal as a means of delaying flowering in sugarcane breeding. Proc. Int. Soc. Sugar Cane Technol. 17:1307–1316.

Daniels, J. and Brian T. Roach. 1987. Taxonomy and evolution. p. 7–84. *In* D.J. Heinz (ed.) Sugarcane improvement through breeding. Elsevier, New York.

Deuber, R., and J.E. Irvine. 1987. Controle de florescimento de cana-de acucar com aplicacao de ethephon. Bol. Tec. COPERSUCAR 36:16–24.

Dudley, J.W. 1977. 76 generations of selection for oil and protein percentage in maize. p. 459–473. *In* Proc. Int. Conf. on Quantitative Genetics. The Iowa Univ. Press, Ames.

Dunckelman, P.H. 1974. Production of true seed from basic lines of *Saccharum* and related genera in new crosses at Houma, Louisiana. Proc. Am. Soc. Sugar Cane Technol. 3(NS):40–41.

Dunckelman, P.H., and R.D. Breaux. 1972. Breeding sugarcane varieties for Louisiana with new germplasm. Proc. Int. Soc. Sugar Cane Technol. 14:233–239.

Dunckelman, P.H., and B.L. Legendre. 1982. Guide to sugarcane breeding in the temperate zone. USDA-ARS, ARM-S-22. U.S. Gov. Print. Office, Washington, DC.

Forsee, W.T., Jr. 1952. Fertilizer requirements of vegetable crops growing on the organic soils of the Florida everglades. Veg. Grow. Assoc. Am. 44:79-82.

Gill, B.S., and C.O. Gasssl. 1986. Pathways of genetic transfer in intergenetic hybrids of sugarcane. Sugar Cane 2:2-7.

Grassl, C.O. 1962. Problems and potentialities of intergeneric hybridization in a sugarcane breeding program. Proc. Int. Soc. Sugar Cane Technol. 11:447-456.

Heinz, D.J. 1967. Wild *Saccharum* species for breeding in Hawaii. Proc. Int. Soc. Sugar Cane Technol. 12:1037-1043.

Heinz, D.J. 1980. Thailand *S. spontaneum* hybrid progeny as a new germplasm source. Proc. Int. Soc. Sugar Cane Technol. 17:1347-1364.

Hsu, S.Y., and S.C. Shih. 1989. Development of prominent breeding stocks through nobilization of *Saccharum spontaneum*. Proc. Int. Soc. Sugar Cane Technol. 20:911-917.

Irvine, J.E., and B.L. Legendre. 1985. Resistance of sugar cane varieties to deterioration following freezing. Sugar Cane 4:1-4.

James, N.I. 1968. Graduated delay of flowering in sugarcane with 11.5-hr. darkperiod. Proc. Int. Soc. Sugar Cane Technol. 13:984-991.

James, N.I., and J.D. Miller. 1972. Photoperiod control in the USDA sugarcane crossing program. Proc. Int. Soc. Sugar Cane Technol. 14:341-353.

Krishnamurthy, M. 1985. Utilization of genetic resources in sugarcane. p. 147-156. *In* A cooperative regional programme in Southeast Asia. Proc. 1st meeting of the working group on sugarcane. December 1969. Int. Board of Plant Genetic Resources, Rome.

Legendre, B.L. 1989. Use of feral germplasm for sugarcane improvement in Louisiana. Proc. Int. Soc. Sugar Cane Technol. 20:883-891.

Lo, C.C., and Y.H. Chen. 1989. Breeding of *Saccharum—Miscanthus* hybrids for fibre resources. Proc. Int. Soc. Sugar Cane Technol. 20:892-899.

Lo, C.C., Y.H. Chen, Y.J. Huang, and S.C. Shih. 1986. Recent progress in *Miscanthus* nobilization program. Proc. Int. Soc. Sugar Cane Technol. 19:514-521.

Mariotti, J.A., C.A. Levi, P.H. Dunckelman, and B.L. Legendre. 1991. Registration of 'TUCCP 77-42' Sugarcane. Crop Sci. 31:492.

Mukherjee, S.K. 1954. Revision of the Genus *Saccharum*. Bull. Bot. Soc. Bengal 8:143-148.

Mukherjee, S.K. 1957. Origin and distribution of *Saccharum*. Bot. Gaz. 119:55-61.

Naidu, K. Mohan, and T.V. Sreenivasan. 1987. Conservation of sugarcane germplasm. p. 33-53. *In* Copersucar International Sugarcane Breeding Workshop. Copersucar Technology Center. Piracicaba, SP Brazil.

Paliatseas, E.D. 1972. Flowering of sugarcane with reference to induction and inhibition. Proc. Int. Soc. Sugar Cane Technol. 14:354-364.

Panje, R.R. 1972. The role of *Saccharum spontaneum* in sugarcane breeding. Proc. Int. Soc. Sugar Cane Technol. 14:217-223.

Roach, B.T. 1972. Nobilisation of sugarcane. Proc. Int. Soc. Sugar Cane Technol. 14:206-216.

Roach, B.T. 1977. Utilisation of *Saccharum-spontaneum* in sugarcane breeding. Proc. Int. Soc. Sugar Cane Technol. 16:43-58.

Roach, B.T. 1986. Evaluation and breeding use of sugarcane germplasm. Proc. Int. Soc. Sugar Cane Technol. 19:492-502.

Roach, B.T. 1989a. Origin and improvement of the genetic base of sugarcane. Proc. Aust. Soc. Sugar Cane Technol. 1989:34-47.

Roach, B.T. 1989b. A programme for sugarcane improvement from genetic diversity: Background and preliminary results. Proc. Int. Soc. Sugar Cane Technol. 20:900-910.

Rosenfeld, A.H. 1930. The decline and renaissance of Louisiana's sugar industry. Proc. Int. Soc. Sugar Cane Technol. 3:317-324.

Sartoris, G.B. 1942. Longevity of sugarcane and corn pollen a method for long distance shipment of sugarcane pollen by airplane. Am. J. Bot. 29:295-400.

Schnell, R.J. 1991. Clones in the World Collection of sugarcane and related grasses. Listing by USDA-ARS of Entries in Germplasm collection.

Sreenivasan, T.V. 1989. Sugarcane genetic resources activities in India and in vitro germplasm conservation. p. 177-193. *In* K.M. Naidu et al. (ed.) Sugarcane varietal improvement. Proc. Int. Symp. Coimbatore, India. 3-7 Sept. 1987. Sugarcane Breed. Inst., Coimbatore, India.

Symington, W.M. 1989. Commercial potential of Macknade nobilisations for yield, sugar content and stress tolerance. Proc. Aust. Sugar Cane Technol. 1989:48-53.

Tai, P.Y.P. 1988. Long-term storage of *Saccharum spontaneum* L. pollen at low temperature. Sugar Cane (Spring 1988 Suppl.) p.12-16.

Tai, P.Y.P. 1990. Low temperature preservation of *Saccharum* pollen. Proc. Int. Soc. Sugar Cane Technol. 20:865-871.

Tai, P.Y.P., and J.D. Miller. 1978. The pedigree of selected Canal Point (CP) varieties of sugarcane. Proc. Am. Soc. Sugar Cane Technol. 8:34-39.

Tai, P.Y.P., and J.D. Miller. 1988. Phenotypic characteristics of the hybrids of sugarcane × related grasses. J. Am. Soc. Sugar Cane Technol. 8:5-11.

Tew, T.L. 1987. New varieties. p. 559-594. *In* D.J. Heinz (ed.) Sugarcane improvement through breeding. Elsevier, New York.

Walker, D.I.T. 1987. Manipulating the genetic base of sugarcane. p. 321-334. *In* Copersucar Tecnology Center (ed.) Copersucar international sugarcane breeding workshop. Proc. Copersucar Int. Sugarcane Breed. Workshop. 17-28 May. Copersucar Tech. Ctr., Piracicabar SP, Brazil.

7 Introduced Germplasm Use in Sunflower Inbred and Hybrid Development

J. F. Miller, G. J. Seiler, and C. C. Jan

USDA-ARS
Fargo, North Dakota

Even though the early European explorers of the Americas were primarily interested in metallic wealth, the plant life in the new world fortunately did not escape their notice. Many new plants were introduced into Europe in the 16th century, including maize (*Zea mays* L.), potato (*Solanum tuberosum* L.), tomato (*Lycopersicon lycopersicum* L.), pepper (*Capsicum annuum* L.), and sunflower (*Helianthus* spp.). Sunflower is one of the few crop species that originated in North America, more specifically in the southwestern USA (Heiser, 1978). The first introduction of sunflower into Europe was by the Spaniards. Other introductions were made by the English and French from sources of sunflower grown on the east coast of the USA (Heiser, 1976).

Early European explorers recorded the use of sunflower as a food by the American Indians. Seeds were pounded and rubbed between smooth stones to make a meal, which when mixed with corn meal, made a nutritious cake or mush. Seeds were also boiled in water, and after cooling, the oil floating on the surface was collected. The oil from sunflower was used in cooking and as a base for pigments that were used in paints for coloring basketry and pottery (Heiser, 1978).

The American Indian should be credited for the first cultivation of sunflower. Several tribes had recognized the value of the single-headed plant type that produced much larger seeds and shattered less. Evidence that the tribes practiced selection is based on the diverse colors of the achenes, with some tribes preferring white, black, striped, or an achene with high amounts of red or purple anthocyanin. Archaeological finds of cultivated sunflowers have been reported from several localities in central and northeastern North America (Fig. 7-1). Achene size from these sites is not much different than that of cultivars grown today (Heiser, 1978).

Seed of sunflower taken to Europe was cultivated by the Indians and produced single-headed and extremely tall plants. Height of these sunflowers often exceeded 4.5 m. The first published record of sunflower appeared

---

Copyright © 1992 Crop Science Society of America, 677 S. Segoe Rd., Madison, WI 53711, USA. *Use of Plant Introductions in Cultivar Development, Part 2*, CSSA Special Publication no. 20.

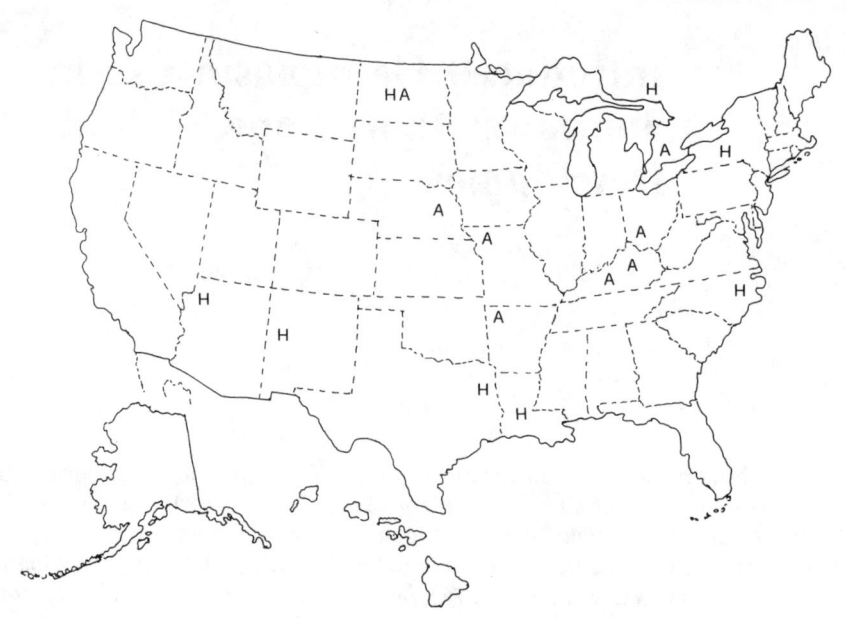

Fig. 7-1. Principal sites where archaeological sunflowers have been found (A), and sites where historical records of sunflower cultivation among the American Indians have been documented (H) (Heiser, 1976).

in 1568 in reports written by the Belgian Rembert Dodonaeus, and by the herbalist Matthiolus in 1586 (Putt, 1978). The plant was grown primarily as a novelty or for ornamental purposes, as the chief interest of early botanists was for plant species with medicinal value. The food value of sunflower was largely ignored until 1716, nearly two centuries later, when an English patent was granted to Arthur Bunyan for a process to expel the oil which was found to be edible. This realization led to the development of a crop that has since become the second leading edible vegetable oilseed crop in the world.

Sunflower spread throughout Europe and eventually reached the USSR where it became extremely successful for two reasons. Sunflower had the genetic diversity to become adaptable to their diverse environments and no other edible oilseed crop was available for northern latitudes. Thus, sunflower was used as a source of protein and oil, and the USSR became the world's largest producer, a position which it maintains today.

Immigrants from the USSR during the 1800s brought sunflower seed with them to the USA. In addition, similar types of sunflower were developed in other countries and introduced into the USA. Many of these open-pollinated cultivars can still be found in seedhouses across America. Some of the first accessions entered into the National Plant Gemrplasm System (NPGS) were the large-seeded, striped type, with oil percentages ranging from 21 to 32% (Table 7-1). The sunflower germplasm collection is maintained at the USDA-ARS North Central Regional Plant Introduction Station located at Iowa State Univ., Ames.

SUNFLOWER INBRED AND HYBRID DEVELOPMENT

Table 7-1. Confectionery sunflower cultivars introduced into the USA.

Cultivar	Plant introduction no.	Source
Russian Graystripe	PI 377529	USSR
Mammoth Russian	PI 476853	USSR
Mennonite	Ames 7574	USSR
Commander	Ames 7575	Canada
Kenya White	PI 377530	Kenya
Hatzor Ayala	PI 386096	Israel
Ruman	PI 354906	Iran

The creation of the oilseed type of sunflower is usually credited to the program of V.S. Pustovoit, located at the All-Union Research Institute for Oil Crops (VNIIMK), Krasnodar, USSR. In 1920, the average oil content of the large-seeded confectionery cultivars commercially grown was 32 to 43%. Through the breeding efforts of Pustovoit, oil contents of new lines reached 40 to 43% by 1960. About two-thirds of the increase in seed oil resulted from a reduction in hull percentage and about one-third from an increase in kernel oil percentage (Gundaev, 1971).

OPEN-POLLINATED CULTIVARS

The open-pollinated cultivar, Peredovik, was licensed in 1964 in Canada. It had a yield similar to the widely grown cultivar Advent, but averaged 43.6% oil compared with 32.8% for Advent (Putt, 1965). The high oil percentage of Peredovik greatly increased efficiency of the processing operation and due to higher commodity prices, interest in sunflower as a crop increased significantly.

Peredovik (PI 287231) was introduced into the USA, and with the support of the U.S. oilseed processing industry, more than 39 000 ha were grown by 1967 (Putt, 1978). This introduction was the start of a new industry and a virtually new crop for the USA. The popularity of the oil, high in polyunsaturated fatty acids with pleasant flavor and excellent color, perpetuates the utilization of this crop. Today, sunflower oil is considered a premium oil due to its quality. Peredovik was the main cultivar grown in the USA from 1965 to 1975. It virtually established the U.S. sunflower industry. The processing industry developed crushing and refinement procedures. Agronomic and cultural recommendations were developed, including optimum plant population, row spacing, fertilization, herbicide and insecticide recommendations.

The potential of Peredovik thus stimulated the number of accessions introduced into the USA with the high oil characteristic. Several lines found in pedigrees of early breeding materials are listed in Table 7-2.

Open-pollinated cultivars such as Peredovik were not without a number of problems. The most evident problem was a lack of uniform height, flower, maturity, and dry-down rate after maturity. Effective insecticide application depends on the florets of different receptacles reaching anthesis at

Table 7-2. Sunflower cultivars with high oil content introduced into the USA from the USSR and used in early breeding efforts.

Cultivar	Plant introduction no.
VNIIMK 1646	PI 257642
VNIIMK 6540	PI 265503
VNIIMK 8931	PI 262517
VNIIMK 8883	PI 265103
Armavirsky 3497	PI 340781
Armavirsky 9345	PI 265101
Jdanovskii 8281	PI 262520

approximately the same time. Also, shattering of seed at harvest occurs when plants mature unevenly and have differential dry-down rates. Differential height of plants can also cause problems with combine harvest. The open-pollinated cultivars also were susceptible to prevalent races of downy mildew and rust, the most important diseases of sunflower. The lack of autogamy in the cultivars was important. If cultivars were grown in areas where pollinators were not prevalent, seed set on the receptacles was decreased and yields were reduced. Pollinators, such as honey bees (*Apis* spp.), placed near fields increased yields dramatically. These problems as well as hybrid heterosis providing increased yields led to a search for a hybrid sunflower.

HYBRID SUNFLOWER

Cytoplasmic Male Sterility

Leclercq in France crossed an accession of *Helianthus petiolaris* Nutt., introduced from the USA with a high oil Russian cv., Armavirsky 9345 (Leclercq, 1969). He observed male sterile plants and subsequently backcrossed these plants with Armavirsky 9345 pollen. He verified that the observed sterility was cytoplasmic in origin and reported that this sterility was stable. However, he did not succeed in finding a male-fertility restorer among accessions in his breeding program.

Male Fertility Restoration

The cytoplasmic male sterile (CMS) source was introduced into the USA as PI 343765 and was sent to Kinman in Texas, Putt in Canada, and several other breeding programs. Kinman had a line derived from the pedigree Texas wild *H. annuus*/Armavirsky 3497, numbered 953-102-1-1, which had been selected for rust resistance by Putt in Canada. The line was crossed to Peredovik to create a breeding line T66006-2-1-31-1-1. Crossing this breeding line to the CMS PI 343765 resulted in male fertility restoration. Other researchers have reported finding sources of restoration (Miller, 1987). The line T66006-2-31-1-1 is present in the pedigree of a majority of male fertility restorer lines used throughout the world and is the primary source of the

Table 7-3. Introductions used in development of maintainer (B-lines) lines for use in producing high-yielding, high oil sunflower hybrids.

Line	Pedigree
HA 89	CM 303, VNIIMK 8931 (PI 262517)
HA 99	CM 303, VNIIMK 8931 (PI 262517)
HA 113	VNIIMK 1646 (PI 257642)
HA 124	VNIIMK 8883 (PI 265103)
HA 224	Armavirsky 9345 (PI 265101)/HA8 (Sunrise/*H. annuus*)
HA 232	Smena *2 (PI 294658)/HA6, HA8
HA 234	Smena *2 (PI 294658)/HA6, HA8
HA 300	Peredovik 301 (PI 372172)
HA 301	Peredovik 301 (PI 372172)
HA 302	Peredovik 304 (PI 372173)
HA 303	Voshod (PI 371936)
HA 821	Peredovik 301 (PI 372173)

Rf^1 male fertility restorer gene. This line is the original source of the rust resistance R^1 gene, contributed the downy mildew Pl^2 resistance gene, and possessed the recessively controlled branching gene, b^1. The branching character is important for male lines in hybrid production as the pollination period is approximately doubled, enabling better nick with the flowering or anthesis of female lines.

Development of Inbred Lines

More than 200 maintainer, CMS, and restorer lines have been developed by USDA-ARS programs or other public researchers. Several of these lines have plant introductions in their pedigrees. The maintainer or B-lines most used by industry are shown in Table 7-3. HA 89, a line still used in several hybrids, was one line which contributed the V^1 gene for *Verticillium* wilt resistance. This line was also found to be high in autogamy, and contributed this characteristic to its hybrids.

The combination of CMS and male fertility restorer lines, many of which are based on introduction germplasm, led to the development of uniform, high yielding, high oil hybrids with resistance to downy mildew, rust, *Verticillium* wilt, and having a high degree of autogamy.

WILD SPECIES ACCESSIONS

The *Helianthus* wild species collection was begun in 1976 at Bushland, TX. In 1985, this collection and other wild species accessions maintained in programs located at Davis, CA, and Fargo, ND, were incorporated into one collection at Ames, IA (National Plant Germplasm System). Of the 3294 accessions presently in the collection, 2245 were wild species. All wild accessions in the collection have now been assigned PI numbers, National Seed Storage (NSSL) numbers, or Ames collection numbers.

The genus *Helianthus* contains 49 species and 19 subspecies, with 13 being annual and 36 being perennial species (Heiser et al., 1969; Schilling & Heiser, 1981) (Table 7-4). There appear to be three primary genomes in *Helianthus*, all of which have the basic chromosome number X = 17. The diploid species are most prevalent, with hexaploid and tetraploid species less prevalent. The species of *Helianthus* are placed in four sections and six series (Schilling & Heiser, 1981).

Methods of using *Helianthus* wild species are being improved. Techniques for the germination of wild species seeds have been developed (Chandler & Jan, 1985). Interspecific hybridization with cultivated lines were made easier with the use of an embryo culture technique (Chandler & Beard, 1983). Chromosome doubling of sterile F_1 interspecific hybrids greatly increases the F_1 fertility for sib-pollination or further backcrossing (Jan, 1988).

Germplasm evaluations, conducted at Fargo, ND, by T. Gulya, revealed high frequencies of resistance to both downy mildew [*Plasmopara halstedii* (Farl.) Berl. & de Toni] and rust (*Puccinia helianthi* Schw.) among wild species accessions. The *Helianthus* wild species collection has provided useful genes for major steps in sunflower improvement such as resistance to *Verticillium* wilt, rust, and downy mildew, cytoplasmic male sterility and fertility restoration, and recessive branching. This collection is likely to provide more genetic diversity when introgressed into cultivated sunflower to reduce genetic vulnerability and maximize stability of sunflower production.

EXAMPLES OF INTRODUCTIONS USED IN PRESENT-DAY BREEDING

Downy mildew resistance. Causal organism: *Plasmopara halstedii* (Farl.) Berl. & de Toni.

Race 1 of downy mildew is the predominant race in Europe whereas race 2, commonly referred to as the Red River race, is prevalent in North America. Race 2 is effectively controlled by the Pl^2 gene identified in most male fertility restorer lines used by industry. However, in 1980, Carson (1981) and Fick and Auwarter (1981) reported a new race of downy mildew, race 3, in the USA. Six hundred ninety-five accessions from the NPGS collection were evaluated for resistance to race 3. Nine accessions (Table 7-5) were found to have resistant plants. Plants homozygous resistant to race 3 were random mated and the germplasm composite of seed was released as DM-1 (NSSL 192207). Four generations of self-pollination and testing for resistance of plants selected from two accessions, 'Novinka' (PI 430538) and 'Progress (PI 430541), were used to stabilize and identify homozygous resistant lines. Two germplasm composites were released in 1984 for reselection and development of downy mildew resistant hybrids, DM-2 (GP-21), originating from Novinka, and DM-3 (GP-22), originating from Progress.

Table 7-4. Intrageneric classification of *Helianthus* spp. by Section and Series.

Section	Series	Species	Ploidy	Annual or perennial	Crossing reported	No. PI acc.
Helianthus	--	*H. annuus* L.	D†	A‡	X	2183
		H. anomalus Blake	D	A	X	11
		H. argophyllus T. & G.	D	A	X	47
		H. bolanderi Gray	D	A	X	18
		H. debilis T. & G.	D	A	X	66
		H. deserticola Heiser	D	A	X	11
		H. neglectus Heiser	D	A	X	28
		H. niveus (Benth) Bran.	D	A	X	19
		H. paradoxus Heiser	D	A	X	10
		H. petiolaris	D	A	X	148
		H. praecox Eng. & Gray	D	A	X	44
Agrestes	--	*H. agrestis* Pollard	D	A		5
Ciliares	Ciliares	*H. arizonensis* Jackson	D	P		2
		H. ciliares DC.	T,H	P		7
		H. laciniatus Gray	D	P		1
Ciliares	Pumili	*H. cusickii* Gray	D	P	X	5
		H. gracilentus Gray	D	P	X	6
		H. pumilus Nutt.	D	P	X	3
Divaricati	Corona-solis	*H. californicus* DC.	H	P	X	2
		H. decapetalus L.	D,T	P	X	20
		H. divaricatus L.	D	P	X	39
		H. eggertii Small	H	P		2
		H. giganteus L.	D	P	X	27
		H. grosseserratus Mar.	D	P	X	41
		H. hirsutus Raf.	D	P	X	21
		H. maximiliani Schr.	D	P	X	50
		H. mollis Lam.	D	P	X	26
		H. nuttallii T. & G.	D	P	X	24
		H. resinosus Small	H	P	X	10
		H. salicifolius Dietr.	D	P	X	4
		H. schweinitzii T. & G.	H	P		2
		H. strumosus L.	T,H	P	X	53
		H. tuberosus L.	H	P	X	113
Divaricati	Microcephali	*H. glaucophyllus* Smith	D	P		2
		H. laevigatus T. & G.	T	P		9
		H. microcephalus T. & G.	D	P		17
		H. porteri (A. Gray) He.	D	A		1
		H. smithii Heiser	T	P		2
Divaricati	Atrorubentes	*H. atrorubens* L.	D	P		16
		H. occidentalis Riddell	D	P	X	17
		H. rigidus (Cass.) Desf.	H	P	X	34
		H. silphioides Nutt.	D	P	X	6
Divaricati	Augustifolii	*H. angustifolius* L.	D	P	X	22
		H. carnosus Small	D	P		1
		H. floridanus G. × Ch.	D	P	X	7
		H. heterophyllus Nutt.	D	P		9
		H. longifolius Pursh	D	P		1
		H. radula (Pursh) T. & G.	D	P		18
		H. simulans Watson	D	P		4

† D = diploid ($n = 17$); T = tetraploid ($n = 34$); H = hexaploid ($n = 51$).
‡ A = annual; P = perennial.

Table 7-5. Sunflower accessions with resistance to race 3 downy mildew, and percentage of plants resistant to race 3 and a race 2-race 3 composite (Miller & Gulya, 1984).

Accession	Plant introduction no.	Race 3, % resistant	Races 2 & 3 composite, % resistant
Kenya White	PI 377530	34	11
Voshod	PI 371936	19	4
Chernyanka W-13	PI 343794	14	11
Sputnik-70	PI 380575	13	0
Austria derived	PI 219651	8	18
Armivirsky 3497	PI 372254	11	6
France derived	PI 376216	12	10
Novinka	PI 430538	10	--
Progress	PI 430541	19	--

In 1985, a new race, race 4 was reported in the USA (Gulya & Urs, 1985). The nine accessions previously reported to be resistant to race 3 were found to be susceptible to race 4 as were DM-1, DM-2, and DM-3. Resistance to race 4 was found in lines derived from interspecific crosses of cultivated sunflower with three species of wild sunflower. The wild species used, *H. annuus* 423 (PI 435434), *H. annuus* 432 (PI 435437), *H. praecox* (PI 435852), and *H. argophyllus* 415 (PI 435629), were collected from the coastal area of Texas. More extensive collections of these species, and other species present in this area should be made and tested for resistance to downy mildew. The Sunflower Crop Advisory Committee of the NPGS designated downy mildew resistance as a priority descriptor and the USDA-ARS funded evaluation. Several additional accessions having resistance to race 4 downy mildew have been identified (Table 7-6).

Table 7-6. Sunflower accessions with resistance to race 4 downy mildew, source, and year introduced into National Plant Germplasm System. (T.J. Gulya, Sunflower CAC Evaluation).

Plant introduction no.	Source	Year introduced
PI 431528	USSR	1979
PI 431529	USSR	1979
PI 431530	USSR	1979
PI 431532	USSR	1979
PI 431544	Yugoslavia	1979
PI 431545	Yugoslavia	1979
PI 431546	Yugoslavia	1979
PI 486367	Odessa, USSR	1984
PI 505836	Odessa, USSR	1986
PI 507923	Hungary	1987
NSSL 192205	HA-R4, Saenz Pena, Argentina	1985
NSSL 192206	HA-R5, Guayacan INTA, Argentina	1985

Powdery mildew resistance. Causal organism: *Erysiphe cichoracearum* **DC.**

The powdery mildew resistant sunflower germplasm pool, PM-1 (PI 518661) was released in 1987 (Jan & Chandler, 1988). PM-1 was derived from interspecific hybridization between *H. debilis* (PI 435667) and cultivated sunflower. Greenhouse evaluation indicated the mean infection percentage measured as the percent of leaf surface covered by mildew was 0 for PI 435667, 15 for PM-1, and 100 for a reselection of Peredovik, P-21. Resistance was controlled by one or more major genes.

Rust resistance. Causal organism: *Puccinia helianthi* **Schw.**

Sunflower rust has potential to cause severe losses in yield and quality. Several new races of rust have been identified in the USA, Australia, and Argentina. To prevent these losses, several accessions were tested for resistance and five were found to be resistant to race 4. These accessions were purified for their resistance and released. The release, source, and germplasm identifications are: HA-R1, Pergamino 71/538 (NSSL 192202); HA-R2, Impira INTA (NSSL 192203); HA-R3, Charata (NSSL 192204); HA-R4, Saenz Pena 74-1-2 (NSSL 192205); and HA-R5, Guayacan INTA (NSSL 192206).

Sunflower moth insect resistance. *Homoeosoma electellum* **(Hulst.)**

The sunflower moth is an economically damaging insect pest of cultivated sunflower in the USA. Wild species of sunflower have been used as sources for increased resistance to achene injury from larvae of the sunflower moth (Rogers et al., 1984). SFM 1 (NSSL 181954) and SFM 3 (NSSL 181956) were developed from interspecific crosses of *H. petiolaris* (PI 423011) and cultivated sunflower. SFM 2 (NSSL 181956) was derived from crosses with the USSR cv. Skorospelka (PI 356301) and a USA inbred line, HA 89. The three germplasms have a phytomelanin layer that becomes extremely dense after its deposition in the pericarp, making the achenes with this characteristic more resistant to mechanical puncture by larvae at an earlier stage of development (Stafford et al., 1984).

High Oleic Fatty Acid

The quality of sunflower oil has generally been associated with the relative content of linoleic acid, a polyunsaturated fatty acid. However, the development of a sunflower with high levels of oleic acid, a monounsaturated fatty acid, was reported by Soldatov (1976). A high oleic cv., Pervenets, was developed and introduced into the USA as PI 483077. Sunflower oil with high oleic acid content is less susceptible to oxidative changes during refining, storage, and frying. The oil can be heated to a higher temperature without smoking, so that food is cooked faster and absorbs less oil. Furthermore, the quality of the oil is retained longer during storage of both the processed oil and seed, which is important to processors of confectionary as well as oilseed sunflower (Yodice, 1990). Reports suggest that diets with a fat content containing a larger percentage of oleic acid could be used to effectively reduce plasma cholesterol. Therefore, considerable interest has been generated in the quality characteristics of PI 483077.

The USDA-ARS program developed adapted inbred lines of oilseed B-lines (PI 509051-PI 509053), oilseed R-lines (PI 509054-PI 509058), confectionary B-lines (PI 509059-PI 509063), and confectionary R-lines (PI 509064-PI 509065), for utilization in crossing to create high oleic oilseed and confectionary hybrids. These hybrids, with high yield and oil characteristics, are adapted to the North Central Region of the USA (Miller et al., 1987).

FUTURE UTILIZATION OF PLANT INTRODUCTIONS IN IMPROVEMENT OF SUNFLOWER

Wild *Helianthus* germplasm, besides constituting the basic genetic stock from which cultivated sunflower originated, continues to contribute specific characteristics for sunflower improvement (Thompson et al., 1981; Seiler, 1988). The use of wild germplasm in breeding programs has the potential for markedly improving commercial hybrid sunflower production (Thompson et al., 1981; Dorrell & Whalen, 1978; Laferriere, 1986).

Since cultivated sunflower lacks genes for acceptable levels of resistance for a majority of the sunflower diseases, genetic variability of cultivated sunflower may be increased by using the numerous wild species introductions to obtain genes for disease resistance. Several potential sources of resistance genes for some of the major diseases have been identified from the wild species (Table 7-7). Potential sources of resistance have been identified for the major disease, *Phomopsis/Diaporthe helianthi* Munt. Cvet et al. There has been less success with finding resistance to *Sclerotinia sclerotiorum* (Lib.) de Bary because it does not appear that a single dominant gene is adequate for resistance to a complex disease which attacks the head, stem, and roots. It may also be possible that not enough populations have been screened to locate genetic resistance.

Since wild sunflowers are native to the USA, their associated herbivorous insects and their entomophages have co-evolved in natural communities. This has resulted in an acute pest problem. Since wild sunflowers are living, evolving populations, they offer the best potential source of resistance for improving cultivated sunflower. Several wild species have been identified as potential sources of insect resistance (Table 7-8). Host resistance in cultivated sunflower via incorporation of germplasm from wild *Helianthus* offers potential for long-lasting economical and environmentally responsible management of several insect pests of cultivated sunflower.

Wild sunflower species plant introductions possess considerable variability for most economic and agronomic characteristics. One of these is seed oil concentration. Most of the wild species have lower seed oil concentration than standard oil seed hybrids (Table 7-9). If wild species are used as a source of pest resistance, oil concentration in interspecific hybrids can be rapidly increased by backcrossing to bring the oil concentration to an acceptable level.

Table 7-7. Potential sources of disease resistance from wild *Helianthus* spp. plant introductions.

Disease	Potential sources
Alternaria helianthi†	*H. resinosus* (P)‡
	H. rigidus ssp. *subrhomboideus* (P)
	H. tuberosus (P)
	H. hirsutus (P)
Phomopsis/Diaporthe helianthi§	*H. annuus* (A)
	H. argophyllus (A)
	H. dibilis (A)
	H. hirsutus (P)
	H. rigidus ssp. *rigidus* (P)
	H. resinosus (P)
	H. salicifolius (P)
	H. tuberosus (P)
Sclerotinia sclerotiorum¶	
Stem	*H. laevigatus* (P)
	H. mollis (P)
	H. resinosus (P)
	H. rigidus (P)
	H. salicifolius (P)
	H. giganteus (P)
Root	*H. mollis* (P)
	H. nuttallii (P)
	H. resinosus (P)
Head	*H. tuberosus* (P)
	H. rigidus ssp. *rigidus* (P)

† Sources: Morris et al. (1983); Skoric (1987).
‡ P = perennial, A = annual.
§ Sources: Stem = Serieys (1987); Skoric (1987). Roots = Skoric (1987). Head = Pustovoit and Gubin (1974).

Fatty acid concentration, especially linoleic acid, is an important quality characteristic of sunflower oil. Wild sunflower species contain considerable variability for this characteristic. Several potential sources have been identified that could be used to increase linoleic acid (Table 7-10). The other important fatty acid is oleic acid (Table 7-11). The fatty acid concentrations found in several wild species are comparable to those found in commercial oil seed hybrids and react similarly to environmental conditions (Seiler, 1983, 1986a). Utilization of wild sunflower species for other characteristics do not appear to be detrimental to the fatty acid concentration of the oil.

Wild sunflower species may have potential for improving the chemical composition of cultivated sunflower seed (Laferriere, 1986). Sufficient variability for seed protein exists in the wild *Helianthus* spp. to be useful in breeding programs with an objective to increase seed protein (Table 7-12).

Several wild species are native to salt-impacted habitats and may possess genes for salt tolerance. Chandler and Jan (1984) evaluated three wild *Helianthus* spp. for salt tolerance: *H. paradoxus*, *H. debilis*, and a *H. annuus* population native to salty desert areas. *Helianthus debilis* tolerated a salt concentration about the same as cultivated sunflower, dying at a NaCl concentration of 250 to 400 mM. The wild ecotype of *H. annuus* had a higher

Table 7-8. Potential sources of insect resistance from wild *Helianthus* spp. plant introductions.

Insect	Potential sources
Homoeosoma electellum†	*H. ciliaris* (P)‡
	H. decapetalus (P)
	H. maximiliani (P)
	H. occidentals ssp. *occidentalis* (P)
	H. pumilus (P)
	H. petiolaris ssp. *petiolaris* (A)
	H. silphioides (P)
	H. strumosus (P)
	H. tuberosus (P)
Cylindrocopturus adsperus§	*H. debilis* ssp. *debilis* (A)
	H. debilis ssp. *vestitus* (A)
	H. divaricatus (P)
	H. giganteus (P)
	H. glaucophyllus (P)
	H. niveus ssp. *canescens* (A)
	H. praecox ssp. *runyonii* (A)
	H. tuberosus (P)
Zygograma exclamationis¶	*H. agrestis* (A)
	H. arizonensis (P)
	H. atrorubens (P)
	H. bolanderi (A)
	H. carnosus (P)
	H. ciliaris (P)
	H. floridanus (P)
	H. grosseserratus (P)
	H. X *laetiflorus* (P)
	H. paradoxus (A)
	H. praecox ssp. *hirtus* (P)
	H. salicifolius (P)
	H. tuberosus (P)

† Sources: Rogers (1981); Rogers et al. (1984); Kinman (1966).
‡ P = perennial, A = annual.
§ Source: Rogers and Seiler (1985).
¶ Source: Rogers and Thompson (1978, 1980).

Table 7-9. Potential sources for increasing oil concentration from wild *Helianthus* spp. plant introductions.†

Source spp.	Oil concentration
	g kg^{-1}
Annual	
H. niveus ssp. *canescens*	402
H. anomalus	379
H. petiolaris ssp. *fallax*	377
H. petiolaris ssp. *petiolaris*	374
H. niveus ssp. *tephrodes*	374
H. deserticola	343
H. annuus	220–300
Perennial	
H. salicifolius	370

† Sources: Thompson et al. (1981); Seiler (1985).

Table 7-10. Potential sources for increasing linoleic acid concentration from wild *Helianthus* spp. plant introductions.†

Source spp.	Linoleic acid concentration
	g kg^{-1}
Annual	
H. porteri	823
H. debilis ssp. tardiflorus	776
H. exilis	778
Perennial	
H. simulans	780
H. laevigatus	775
H. radula	766
H. hetrophyllus	755
H. smithii	752
H. rigidus ssp. subrhomboides	751
H. microcephalus	741
H. strumosus	737
H. cusickii	728

† Sources: Thompson et al. (1981); Seiler (1985).

tolerance, with some plants surviving at 800 mM. *Helianthus paradoxus* was highly salt tolerant with some plants surviving at 1300 mM. Salt tolerance was a dominant trait, with hybrids between *H. paradoxus* and cultivated *H. annuus* having similar tolerance as the wild *H. paradoxus* parent.

The present cultivated sunflower uses a narrow genetic base, particularly the CMS cytoplasm derived from the wild species, *H. petiolaris* (Leclercq, 1969). As a result, the cultivated sunflower is potentially vulnerable to an impending disaster. Several new sources of CMS have been identified from the wild sunflower plant introductions (Table 7-13). Some of these cytoplasms are unstable and lack complementary restoration systems. Other useful cytoplasms may eventually be found in the wild species plant introductions in the future.

Table 7-11. Potential sources for increasing oleic acid concentration from wild *Helianthus* spp. plant introductions.†

Source spp.	Oleic acid concentration
	g kg^{-1}
Annual	
H. agrophyllus	475
H. annuus	463
H. praecox ssp. runyonii	410
H. debilis ssp. cucumerifolius	401
Perennial	
H. atrorubens	538
H. hirsutus	468
H. silphioides	457
H. resinosus	448
H. arizonensis	411

† Sources: Thompson et al. (1981); Seiler (1985).

Table 7-12. Potential sources for increasing seed protein concentration from wild *Helianthus* spp. plant introductions.†

Source spp.	Protein concentration
	g kg^{-1}
Annual	
H. porteri	305
H. paradoxus	227
H. debilis ssp. *debilis*	211
H. bolandri	206
Perennial	
H. nuttallii ssp. *nuttallii*	348
H. silphioides	315
H. maximiliani	284
H. hetrophyllus	282
H. laevigatus	268
H. atrorubens	268
H. salicifolius	264
H. giganteus	260

† Sources: Seiler (1984, 1986b).

Utilization of some wild species for pest resistance or other characteristics will not be an easy task. Several of the potential sources are perennial species and have different ploidy levels than the cultivated annual crop. Early attempts to incorporate some of the identified pest resistance from the wild species into cultivated lines has been unsuccessful. Increased use of wild sunflower species in the future may depend on the practical application of molecular techniques. Many sources of desirable genes for pest resistance exist in the germplasm collection, but associated genes detrimental to yield potential are also present. The challenge will be to identify the desirable genes on a diverse segment of the chromosome dealing with the desired trait using such techniques as restriction fragment length polymorphisms (RFLPs). Once the genes are identified, the cloning and transfer of DNA, or gene segments from the wild species through transformation techniques may offer an op-

Table 7-13. Potential sources of new cytoplasms from wild *Helianthus* spp. plant introductions.

Source spp.	Named cytoplasm	Authority
H. petiolaris	PET1	Leclercq, 1969
H. petiolaris	PET3	Leclercq, 1983
H. petiolaris	PET2	Whalen & Dedio, 1980
H. petiolaris ssp. *fallax*	PEF1	Serieys, 1987
H. annuus ssp. *lenticularis*	ANL1	Anashchenko, 1977
H. annuus ssp. *lenticularis*	ANL2	Heiser, 1982
H. annuus ssp. *texanus*	ANT1	Vranceanu et al., 1986
H. annuus	ANN1	Serieys, 1987
H. giganteus	GIG1	Whalen & Dedio, 1980
H. maximiliani	MAX1	Whalen & Dedio, 1980
H. bolanderi	BOL1	Serieys, 1987
H. niveus ssp. *canescens*	NIV1	Serieys, 1987

portunity for utilization of the wild germplasm. The challenge will be to concentrate on the desirable traits and mask or delete the deleterious ones while still maintaining a satisfactory yield level. Technology and techniques will need to be developed and refined to identify genes, map genomes, and reliably transfer specific genes within and across the wild species and the cultivated crop.

REFERENCES

Anashchenko, A.V. 1977. Some economically useful donors in the sunflower collection. Tr. Prikl. Bot. Genet. Sel. 59(3):130-136.

Carson, M.L. 1981. A new race of *Plasmopara halstedii* virulent on resistant sunflower in South Dakota. Plant Dis. Rep. 65:842-843.

Chandler, J.M., and B.H. Beard. 1983. Embryo culture of *Helianthus* hybrids. Crop Sci. 23:1004-1007.

Chandler, J.M., and C.C. Jan. 1984. Identification of salt-tolerant germplasm sources in the *Helianthus* species. p. 61. *In* Agronomy abstract. ASA, Madison, WI.

Chandler, J.M., and C.C. Jan. 1985. Comparison of germination techniques for wild *Helianthus* seeds. Crop Sci. 25:356-358.

Cuk, L. 1982. The uses of wild species in sunflower breeding. Uljarstvo. 1:23-27. (English summary.)

Dorrell, D.G., and E.D.P. Whalen. 1978. Chemical and morpohological characteristics of seeds of some sunflower species. Crop Sci. 18:969-971.

Dozet, B.M. 1990. Resistance to *Diaporthe/Phomopsis helianthi* Munt. Cvet. et al. in wild sunflower species. p. 86-87. *In* Proc. Sunflower Research Workshop, Fargo, ND. 8-9 Jan. Natl. Sunflower Assoc., Bismarck, ND.

Fick, G.N., and G.W. Auwarter. 1981. A new race of downy mildew affecting sunflower. p. 15-16. *In* Proc. Sunflower Res. Workshop, Fargo, ND. 27-28 Jan. Natl. Sunflower Assoc., Bismarck, ND.

Gulya, T.J., and N.V.R.R. Urs. 1985. A new race of sunflower downy mildew. Phytopathology 75:1339.

Gundaev, A.E. 1971. Basic principles of sunflower selection. p. 417-465. *In* Genetic principles of plant selection. Nauka, Moscow. [Trans. Dep. of the Secretary of State, Ottawa, Canada. 1972].

Heiser, C.B. 1976. The sunflower. Univ. of Oklahoma Press, Norman, OK.

Heiser, C.B. 1978. Taxonomy of *Helianthus* and origin of domesticated sunflower. p. 31-53. *In* J.F. Carter (ed.) Sunflower science and technology. Agron. Monogr. 19. ASA, CSSA, and SSSA, Madison, WI.

Heiser, C.B. 1982. Registration of Indiana-1 CMS sunflower gemrplasm. Crop Sci. 22:1089.

Heiser, C.B., D.M. Smith, S.B. Clevenger, and W.C. Martin. 1969. The North American Sunflowers (*Helianthus*). Mem. Torr. Bot. Club 22(3):1-218.

Jan, C.C. 1988. Chromosome doubling of wild × cultivated sunflower interspecific hybrids and its direct effect on backcross success. Vol. 2. p. 287-292. *In* Proc. 12th Int. Sunflower Conf., Novi Sad, Yugoslavia. 25-29 July. Int. Sunflower Assoc., Toowoomba Queensland, Australia.

Jan, C.C., and J.M. Chandler. 1988. Registration of a powdery mildew resistant sunflower germplasm pool, PM 1. Crop Sci. 28:1040.

Kinman, M.L. 1966. Tentative resistance to the larvae of *Homoeosoma electellum* in *Helianthus*. p. 72-74. *In* Proc. 2nd Int. Sunflower Conf., Morden, Manitoba, Canada. 17-18 Aug. Int. Sunflower Assoc., Toowoomba, Queensland, Australia.

Laferriere, J.E. 1986. Interspecific hybridization in sunflowers: An illustration of the importance of wild genetic resources in plant breeding. Outlook Agric. 15(3):104-129.

Leclercq, P. 1969. Une sterilite male cytoplasmique chez le tournesol. Ann. Amelior Plantes 19:99-106.

Leclercq, P. 1983. Estude de divers cas de sterilite male cytoplasmique chez le tournesol. Agronomie 3:185-187.

Miller, J.F. 1987. Sunflower. p. 626-668. *In* W.R. Fehr (ed.) Principles of cultivar development. Vol. 2. Macmillan Publ. Co., New York.

Miller, J.F., and T.J. Gulya. 1984. Sources and inheritance of resistance to Race 3 downy mildew in sunflower. Helia 7:17-20.

Miller, J.F., D.C. Zimmerman, B.A. Vick, and W.W. Roath. 1987. Registration of sixteen high oleic sunflower germplasm lines and bulk population. Crop Sci. 27:1323.

Morris, J.B., S.M. Yang, and L. Wilson. 1983. Reaction of *Helianthus* species to *Alternaria helianthi*. Plant Dis. 67:539-540.

Pustovoit, G.V., and I.A. Gubin. 1974. Results and prospects in sunflower breeding for group immunity by using the interspecific hybridization method. p. 373-381. *In* Proc. 6th Int. Sunflower Conf., Bucharest, Romania. 22-24 July. Int. Sunflower Assoc., Toowoomba, Queensland, Australia.

Putt, E.D. 1965. Sunflower variety Peredovik. Can. J. Plant Sci. 45:207.

Putt, E.D. 1978. History and present world status. p. 1-29. *In* J.F. Carter (ed.) Sunflower science and technology. Agron. Monogr. 19. ASA, CSSA, and SSSA, Madison, WI.

Rogers, C.E. 1981. Breeding sunflower for resistance to insects and diseases in the United States. p. 175-212. *In* Proc. EUCARPIA, Prague, Czechoslovakia.

Rogers, C.E., and G.J. Seiler. 1985. Sunflower (*Helianthus*) resistance to a stem weevil *Cylindrocopturus adspersus*. Environ. Entomol. 14:624-628.

Rogers, C.E., and T.E. Thompson. 1978. Resistance of wild *Helianthus* to the sunflower beetle. J. Econ. Entomol. 71:622-623.

Rogers, C.E., and T.E. Thompson. 1980. *Helianthus* resistance to the sunflower beetle. J. Kans. Entomol. Soc. 53:727-730.

Rogers, C.E., T.E. Thompson, and G.J. Seiler. 1984. Registration of three *Helianthus* germplasms for resistance to the sunflower moth. Crop Sci. 24:212-213.

Schilling, E.E., and C.B. Heiser. 1981. Infrageneric classification of *Helianthus* (Compositae). Taxonomy 30:393-403.

Seiler, G.J. 1983. Effect of genotype, flowering date, and environment on oil content and oil quality of wild sunflower seed. Crop Sci. 23:1063-1068.

Seiler, G.J. 1984. Protein and mineral concentration of selected wild sunflower species. Agron. J. 76:289-294.

Seiler, G.J. 1985. Evaluation of seeds of sunflower species for several chemical and morphological characteristics. Crop Sci. 25:183-187.

Seiler, G.J. 1986a. Analysis of the relationships of environmental factors with seed oil and fatty acid concentrations of wild annual sunflower. Field Crops Res. 15:57-72.

Seiler, G.J. 1986b. Forage quality of selected wild sunflower species. Agron. J. 78:1059-1064.

Seiler, G.J. 1988. The genus *Helianthus* as a source of genetic variability for cultivated sunflower. Vol. 1. p. 17-58. *In* Proc. 12th Int. Sunflower Conf., Novi Sad, Yugoslavia. 25-29 July. Int. Sunflower Assoc., Toowoomba, Queensland, Australia.

Serieys, H.A. 1987. FAO subnetwork report 1984-1986. p. 1-23. *In* D. Skoric (ed.) Genetic evaluation and use of *Helianthus* wild species and their use in breeding programs. FAO, Rome.

Skoric, D. 1985. Sunflower breeding for resistance to *Diaporthe/Phomopsis helianthii*. Helia 8:21-24.

Skoric, D. 1987. FAO subnetwork report 1984-1985. p. 1-17. *In* D. Skoric (ed.) Genetic evaluation and use of *Helianthus* wild species and their use in breeding programs. FAO, Rome.

Soldatov, K.I. 1976. Chemical mutagenesis in sunflower breeding. p. 352-357. *In* Proc. 7th Int. Sunflower Conf., Krasnodar, USSR. 27 June-3 July. Int. Sunflower Assoc., Toowoomba, Queensland, Australia.

Stafford, R.E., C.E. Rogers, and G.J. Seiler. 1984. Pericarp resistance to mechanical puncture in sunflower achenes. Crop Sci. 24:891-894.

Thompson, T.E., D.C. Zimmerman, and C.E. Rogers. 1981. Wild *Helianthus* as a genetic resistance. Field Crops Res. 4:333-343.

Vranceanu, A.V., M. Iuoras, and F.M. Stoenescu. 1986. A contribution to the diversification of cytoplasmic male sterility sources in sunflower. Helia 6:21-25.

Whalen, E.D.P., and W. Dedio. 1980. Registration of sunflower germplasm composite crosses CMG-1, CMG-2, and CMG-3. Crop Sci. 20:382.

Yodice, R. 1990. Nutritional and stability characteristics of high oleic sunflower seed oil. Fat Sci. Technol. 3:121-126.